READER REVIEWS

"*The Marionettist* is an exciting new creature—a suspenseful thriller with Orthodoxy at its heart. The battle between Andonellis's loveable heroine and an ancient evil as formidable as C.S. Lewis's Screwtape, **will keep you reading to the last page.** Clear your schedule and keep your children close, because you'll be making the sign of the cross over them before you're through!"
--Georgia Briggs, bestselling author of *Icon: A Novel*

"**The work is brilliant, and at times poetic.**
Mind-numbing how good this is, especially as a first novel."
--K. A. De Welf, screenwriter

"**Though not a Christian, I found this novel to be stirring, uplifting and thoughtful.** Throughout the adventure, the author never loses sight of the overarching spiritual themes that are the true engine driving this tale. **I would not hesitate to recommend it to friends of any faith**, as it was recommended to me. I look forward to reading Ari's future adventures. One final warning: Do *not* begin the last 10 chapters late in the evening.
You will not be able to put it down."
--Dr. Avery Jenkins, author of *Dark River*

THE MARIONETTIST

THE MARIONETTIST

A Novel

AVYE ANDONELLIS

Xifos Press

Xifos Press, LLC

This book is a work of fiction. Any references to historical events, real people, or real places are used fictitiously. Other names, characters, places, and events are products of the author's imagination, and any resemblance to actual events or places or persons, living or dead, is entirely coincidental.

Copyright © 2021 by Dawn Yoakam

All rights reserved. No part of this book may be reproduced in any manner whatsoever without written permission except in the case of brief quotations embodied in critical articles and reviews.

For information address: Xifos Press, LLC, 100 Main Street North, PMB 237, Southbury, CT 06488-3840.

Xifos Press can bring authors to your live event. To book an event, visit www.XifosPress.com

Library of Congress Cataloging-in-Publication Data is available upon request.

ISBN: 978-1-7360655-0-1
eBook ISBN: 978-1-7360655-1-8

Printed in the United States of America

12 11 10 9 8 7 6 5 4 3 2 1

First Printing, 2021

For My Beloveds

CONTENTS

1	Areté Apostollis	1
2	Deirdre "Deedee" Morrigan	7
3	Laurie Locke	10
4	The Marionettist	19
5	Trooper	26
6	Deedee	30
7	Bienvenue	31
8	River Water	34
9	Tophet	37
10	Hector Apostollis	43
11	Boogeyman	49
12	Women's Interfaith Fellowship	54
13	The Ashuelot Hollow Inn	69
14	Room 236	72

15	Deedee In Room 236	74
16	Baby's Breath	78
17	Samael	82
18	Friend Potential	86
19	Amy	99
20	Fireball	102
21	The Glory of Love	105
22	Pommes Frites	110
23	Iden	120
24	Sansennoi	127
25	Ace Guns	140
26	The Alphabet of ben Sira	143
27	Metal Chick	151
28	The Onerous Path	158
29	Power Metaller	160
30	Midnight Metal Mania	164
31	Jinx & Jezebel	169
32	CPR	173
33	Iggy	177
34	The Serpent in the Garden	179

35	Room Service	182
36	Snake Kiss	184
37	Ache Enemy	188
38	Tail	192
39	Gethsemane	194
40	Runes	203
41	Laurie Waffles	208
42	The Rhodium Rule	210
43	Four Olives on a Sword	218
44	Anniversary	226
45	Un-Locked	230
46	Deedee the Watcher	236
47	Hair of the Dog	238
48	Hunter College	246
49	The 86th Street Station	248
50	An Element of Grief	255
51	Hell's Kitchen	258
52	The Highway Home	261
53	Home	269
54	Cookie	272

55	Randy—the Philandering, Pringle-Eating Warthog	278
56	randyRandy	286
57	The Damning Thread	291
58	Man Plans, God Laughs	294
59	Father Leonidas	298
60	Do Not Disturb	304
61	Blankie	311
62	Demon Candy	314
63	Jacuzzi	320
64	A Sepulcher for the Soul	333
65	The Exorcism of Deirdre Ethane Morrigan	342
66	Pit Bull	352
67	The Clash	366

Epilogue	379
Acknowledgments	383
About The Authoress	386

CHAPTER 1

Areté Apostollis

Saturday Afternoon 2:07 PM | October 31st | Samhain

They say if you don't like the weather in New Hampshire, wait five minutes. That uncertainty makes the residents resilient and shoveling sixty inches of snow in the winter makes them strong. Areté Apostollis was both. Even so, she wasn't ready for winter and was glad the valley where their small town of Ashuelot Hollow sat was still half-clothed in the remaining vibrant yellows, oranges, and reds of autumn. In Vermont there was already snow in the mountains.

'Ari' looked out the windshield at the fat black-bellied clouds rolling into the valley headed for the hardware store where she was parked. Rain or snow—she couldn't tell. It smelled like rain.

Ari didn't pray much, but she always had her *yiayiá's* * prayer

---

*Yiayiá - Greek for *grandmother*.

rope with her. It had been in her family for generations. She put her hand in her jacket pocket and rolled its smooth hematite beads in her fingers. It soothed her nerves like it always did.

"Those clouds are ominous," she said to Dorothea in the back seat.

"They're creepy, Mamá."

"That's kinda what 'ominous' means, honey."

"I wanna go 'ome to *Babbá*.* " Dorothea was sucking her thumb.

"I know you're tired. The guy's going to load the salt, then we can go home, OK?"

The young man from the hardware store tapped on the passenger side window. "Open your lift gate, Ma'am."

She watched him in the rear view mirror to make sure he loaded all seven bags.

One... two... three. The silver BMW X3 bounced from the weight of the forty-pound bags. Ari took her glasses off and smile-checked her face in the visor mirror. Her eyes crinkled at the corners, the only lines on her smooth face.

Four... five... six. Short heavy bounces and lower still.

Seven. No bounce this time, just a dead weight in the back. She'd have to drive slowly over the frost heaves on the back road home.

The young man shut the lift gate hard. Ari jolted in her seat. She held her ringing ears as he came around to Dorothea's window. "Trick or treat!" He held up a pumpkin-shaped bucket of candy.

---

*Babbá- Greek for *daddy*.

"Can I have one, Mamá?" Dorothea asked.

"May I see that first?" Ari said.

"Sure. You can take one too." The young man handed her the bucket.

She fished out two dum-dums. She popped a cream soda into her mouth and handed Dorothea a root beer one. *You can't hide a needle in these.* "Here *moró mou**. Say thank you to the young man."

"Tank you!" The lollipop was already in her mouth.

The young man smiled at Dorothea. "You goin' trick-or-treatin' with your Gramma tonight?"

Ari's front teeth bit hard into the lollipop stick. *I should be used to this by now.* But she wasn't. Nowhere close. "I'm her *mother*." She finger-combed her long platinum hair into a ponytail so he could see her youthful skin.

"Sorry ma'am." He pulled his phone from his back pocket and turned away punching at it with his thumbs.

Yeah, call me ma'am, too. "Let's get out of here." As Ari shifted into Drive, a gigantic pickup truck barreled into the lot and halted one foot in front of her. The black bull truck towered above the BMW, its diesel nostrils spewing steam from under the hood. Yiayiá's prayer rope felt heavy in her pocket.

Her hand froze on the gear shift. The pickup was fitted with humongous tires and stacked exhaust pipes behind the cab which curved outward like silver horns. She shifted into Park and peered into the truck cab. "How much does this guy have to make up for?"

---

*Moró mou- Greek for *my baby*.

The driver glowered at her.

Her stomach filled with electricity. Ari, never one to look away, stared back.

His black glare was a tangible beam which penetrated her windshield and went through and beyond her.

Ari faced the truck. Its hefty grill guard jutted out in a row of tall chrome teeth. The ominous storm clouds were closing in. A gust of wind blew a muddy piece of shrink-wrap under the truck. *You are in my way.*

She tried to drive around the pickup, but there wasn't enough room in between it and the salt bags stacked on pallets in front of the store. She got stuck catty-corner alongside the behemoth.

"*Sh*—sheez, this is worse!"

"That's the biggest truck, Mamá."

The man jumped out of his truck. Even in work boots his head didn't clear the hood. Ari smirked at being right about him having something to prove.

The man adjusted his jeans with his thumbs. He wore only a dingy undershirt in 39°F weather. He honed in on her, a cigarette jammed in the corner of his mouth, and twirled his finger for her to roll down the window.

Ari's whole body stiffened. She lowered the window a third of the way.

He stopped at the point of the V in between her side mirror and his headlight. He sucked hard on the cigarette and blew the acrid smoke in her face. She coughed and pressed the button to close the window. He grabbed the glass and shoved it back down. "You damn near hit my truck."

Dorothea sneezed. The man's eyes darted to her. He laid his left forearm on the window and leaned in grinning with tobacco-stained teeth. "Sing the good ship lollipop for me, darlin'." His voice was a rotten peach.

Ari wanted to slam him in the gut with the door. "She's not a trick dog."

He directed his cold dark gaze at her.

She blinked to warm her eyes from his stare. "Hey look, I'm sorry I almost hit your truck. Can't you please move back so we can go before the storm hits?" She motioned at the black clouds. Her fingers shook. She dropped her hand back on her lap and fused it with the other.

His eyes moved to her throat to the white gold cross hanging there. He cocked his head to the side, an animal noticing a strange object in its path. "You're not going anywhere now, *sister*."

"Couldn't you back up a little? I need to get—"

"We never back up." He leaned in, his elbow rested on the roof.

We? His use of the plural and his proximity unnerved Ari. She stiffened, unable to move.

The man took another drag on his cigarette. "Better keep an eye on that pretty girlie ya' got there." He pointed his thumb at Dorothea. "Ya' never know who might wanna take 'er off yer hands." He laughed, an awful, mirthless sound, then strode toward the store's office in an old trailer approximately fifteen feet away.

Ari rolled up the window and nervously punched at the door lock. She put both hands on the steering wheel to calm them.

She'd wait for the *vlákas** to finish his business, then they'd burn out of there. She looked at Dorothea. She had her blankie pressed against her cheek and was sucking mightily on her thumb. "Oh, don't be scared, baby. He's gone."

Dorothea pointed her tiny finger at the truck. A pair of pink cowboy boots attached to two twiggy legs balanced themselves on the running board, then a ball of pink tumbled to the ground. A little girl in a pink hoodie stood and brushed herself off. Ari's hand went to her heart. *"Panayia mou**!"*

The girl was not much older than Dorothea. She ran after the man. "Daddy, wait up!" she cried. The man didn't turn around.

How delicate she looked! The wind could pick her up in its gusty palms and blow her away in a pink kiss.

When the man and the little girl went inside the store, Ari grabbed the writer's notebook and pen she always had with her. Now that there was a child involved, she wanted to get his license plate number. "Moró mou, I'll be back in a minute." She got out of the car from the passenger's side and locked it—twice. The moment she did, it poured rain.

---

*Vlákas- Greek for *jerk*.

**Panayia mou! - Greek for *My Virgin Mary!*

CHAPTER 2

Deirdre "Deedee" Morrigan

Saturday Morning 3:00 AM | October 31st | Samhain

Deedee was at a service station this time. There was no moon and no one. Her hands perched on the steering wheel. She was wearing the oxblood gauntlet gloves again.

She stumbled out of her Jaguar gasping for air. She clawed at the gloves, but the soft lambskin gripped her fingers like a Chinese finger trap. She strained to pull them off and threw them to the ground.

Big LED flood lights illuminated the parking lot, but only the dimmed off-hour lights were on inside the store. A low wall of snow surrounded the lot and the trees had an unfamiliar outline. Deedee felt for her glasses on her face. They weren't there. She no longer needed them to see far away. She got back in the car shivering.

She grabbled inside her purse for her antidepressants. She twisted the bottle open into her cupped palm and without counting, slapped the pills into her mouth. There was a paper cup in the holder—she had no idea what was inside. She raised it to her lips. Coffee. Espresso, cold but not congealed. She swallowed the bitter liquid down her throat and coughed.

Deedee slumped into the seat pulling at the ends of her long red hair while her brain scrambled for traction. She had snippets of memory from hotels and highway service plazas. The last day she clearly remembered was the morning she dropped off her son, Justin, at kindergarten. He'd cried, "Mommy!" and run back to her for "just one more hug." Her chin trembled reliving how his warm wiry body had felt in her embrace. *Who'd picked him up after school?*

A mother's terror seized her gut. *Wait. Am I still...?* Her hand flew to her belly. *Yes.* She mouthed 'thank you' to the tiny gold Fumsup! doll's head with pink sapphire eyes hanging from a chain on the rear view mirror. Deedee softly recited the first stanza of the poem it had come with:

> "Behold in me,
> The birth of luck,
> Two charms combined,
> Touchwood-Fumsup!"

"Focus on the facts, Deedee." She'd last seen her little boy on the second Tuesday in October, right after the three-day Columbus Day weekend. She hesitated a moment, then touched the phone mounted on the dashboard. A jack o' lantern with birthday candles on top flickered on the screen. *It's the 31st already?* Deedee sat up in her seat and did the math. She'd lost twenty-one days between San Francisco and...she looked at the icy darkness outside...*this God-forsaken place.*

A cacophony roared into the station's parking lot jolting Deedee back to the present. A police car screeched up alongside her, spraying gravel. She saw the prominent markings of the New Hampshire State Police. Red and blue lights slashed intermittently through the canvas of white light.

A state trooper sprang out and aimed his gun across the roof of his car straight at her head. "Show me your hands! Step out of the car now." His body heat meeting the cold air made a spectral mist rise around him.

She rolled down the window with trembling fingers. "What've I done, Trooper?" she asked, her eyes darting from the gun to his face.

"I said, step out...*now.*"

She heard a calming, firm voice inside her racing mind, *"Do as he says, Deedee."*

Her hand floated to the ignition and pulled out the key. The interior lights came on. Deedee angled the rear view mirror at herself. She recognized her ivory skin, plush lips, and perfectly oval face, but her emerald eyes and strong Celtic jaw had a hard edge to them she had never seen before. "Who are you?"

She clutched the key in her fist when the Voice answered.

"Whomever I want to be. Today I'm you."

CHAPTER 3

Laurie Locke

Saturday Afternoon | October 31st | Samhain

Laurie Locke was in her new backyard raking leaves. A storm was coming to Ashuelot Hollow, New Hampshire and with every gust, the tarp she was raking them onto rolled up like a surfer's wave into the air.

Laurie raked.

When she'd gone out to the garage to get the milk she'd forgotten in the back of her Jeep the night before, her husband Randy and their seven-year-old son Elijah were coming in. Randy placed the leaf blower against the wall. "Great hon, you're up. You can finish the yard. The game's on."

"I'm in the middle of season 3 of *The Blacklist*," Laurie opened the milk carton, sniffed, then poured some into her coffee mug.

Randy whispered over Elijah's head, *"You've been in those Grinch pj's binge-watching TV all week. It'll do you good to have a rake in your hand instead of the remote. I'm really worried about you, hon."* He put his hand on her shoulder, but she brushed it away.

Siren, Randy's Irish setter, bounded into the garage and pressed against him.

"You still love me, don't ya' girl?" He patted her soft, bony head.

"'Cause she's an airhead just like that—" Laurie stopped herself from saying more and drew Elijah to her. "Are you tired, 'Jah?" Elijah nodded against his mother's soft hip.

"All right, go watch the game with your dad." She threw Randy a look over the boy's head and said, *"You should've worried about me when you were in Cincinnati with her."* She set her mug down hard on the workbench.

Her husband stared at her with a hurt in his eyes she hadn't seen before. Randy never cried, but now his eyes appeared wet. It didn't break her resolve against him.

Elijah scuffed his boots on the cement floor.

"Let's warm up those cheeks." Laurie placed kisses all over his face.

"I love you, Mommy." Elijah hugged her a little too tightly.

Laurie winced as the shards of guilt which nature reserves especially for mothers cut into her heart. She cleared her throat. "Go tell your sister to come out." She grabbed the rake from the wall.

Randy looked at her long and hard then took off his coat. "It's windy out there. Put this on." He held it for her like a gentleman.

Laurie handed him the milk carton and brusquely took the coat from him.

Randy's voice cracked as he squeezed his son's shoulder. "Com'on Duke, let's go watch the Bucks pummel the Golden Gophers again."

The screen door to the kitchen banged shut behind them. Alone now, her sadness jammed itself down her throat like an endotracheal tube, hollowing her out. She put on Randy's coat like it was made of tissue paper. Her husband's special scent mixed with his fresh sweat embraced her.

Amy walked into the garage and saw her mother with her eyes closed wearing her father's coat holding a rake. The twelve-year-old paused with her hand on the doorknob and sighed loudly. "Mom...*Mom!* Elijah said you wanted me."

"Yeah, hi sweetheart."

"Like I can't handle you acting crazy all the time."

Laurie dragged off Randy's coat. "I...I'm fine, really."

"Whatever you say, Mom."

"Come an' help me rake, honey." She chucked her slippers to the side and pulled on the tall rubber brown boots Randy shoveled snow in.

"No way. I hate doing stuff like that."

"Sweetheart, see that storm coming? I can't finish it alone in time."

Amy took her phone out of her pocket. "Fine, I'll give you fifteen minutes."

"We need at least a half hour." Laurie shivered.

"OK, fine. Give me Dad's jacket. You take mine."

"I don't know if it'll fit me, I'm so fat now."

"Stop it Mom. See, it fits you great."

Amy helped clear the leaves, but when the alarm on her phone went off thirty minutes later she said, "Mom, I'm done," and put her earbuds back in.

Laurie watched her leave. *Nothing prepares a mother for a twelve-year-old girl.*

Laurie raked.

Last October, Laurie had still been a fitness trainer in Columbus, Ohio until Randy was forced to transfer to New Hampshire in June. She'd left her whole life behind. Her forty-three-year-old body ached, but the pain felt good.

She raked.

The tarp blew up into the air again. "Fine, Mother Nature, you win." Laurie threw the rake aside and laid on the mound of crisp leaves. She gazed at the dark sky. The clouds formed into choleric black rhinos lumbering forward—coming for her. She shuddered and pulled her eyes away.

Her hair blew in her face and she grabbed a chunk of blonde searching for split ends. There were many. She trimmed them with her teeth. Laurie had been plagued with good looks since she was a baby and had always hated the attention she received. "What an *angel* she is!" When she was thirteen, the admiration took an evil turn. "They won't believe you, angel." Laurie, the beautiful, shy little girl grew up to be Laurie the gorgeous, busty introvert. Randy said he would protect her, so she'd let her guard down and gotten pregnant with Amy. And Randy had shielded her until his father was killed.

A year had passed since her father-in-law's death and now Laurie insulated Laurie from the world by gaining twenty pounds and letting her dark roots grow out several inches until Amy asked if she was going punk. She picked up the kids from school in her pajamas and slippers, forgot to brush her teeth—only realizing it at night when she ran her tongue along the grit which had built up there all day. Like today. She scraped yellow crud from her front teeth with a ragged fingernail and flicked it away. No one harassed her anymore.

I've got to start living again. She remembered lying like that on the grass at the Surya Namaskar seminar she'd attended in Ohio the previous summer. *What was that phrase they taught us to say over and over to help us return to the Self...to help our joy unfold?* Laurie chanted, "Om Bhaskaraya Namaha...Om...Om Bhaskaraya Namaha...Om Bhaskaraya Namaha..."

There was no sun to salute. No joy unfolding, just the menacing black rhino herd closing in.

She stood and grabbed the rake with renewed vigor. "A good sweat'll do it."

Randy used to call her his trophy wife. After they were married he'd tell everyone he had his trophy "All 'Locked' up- ha, ha, get it? Randy and Laurie Locke-d together forever." Well, his key wasn't welcome in her lock anymore since he'd used it to open other locks.

The rake took on a life of its own.

She broke into a sweat. It felt good. Her feet were hot in the insulated boots.

Red and black flashed to her right. She glanced up and saw her elderly next door neighbor in a checkered flannel shirt. He held a leaf blower and stared at her feet. Dissected worm halves writhed and shiny beetles scurried for cover in the dark circular wound she had torn in the earth.

He must think I'm a maniac. She smiled her prom queen smile, and it worked because he strode over to her, an old-time gunslinger with his blower strapped across his chest. The smell of the exposed raw life blood in the circle of soil invigorated her.

"It's nice to finally meet you." She held the rake in one hand and extended the other to him. "I'm Laurie Locke."

He held the blower with both hands and shifted its weight over his old man belly. He cleared his throat, "Exeter Towne."

He hadn't taken her hand. She looked at it. Well, no wonder he hadn't wanted to touch the filthy paw she'd offered him. She let it fall to her side and saw her green Grinch pajama bottoms and Randy's muddy boots. She felt her cheeks and ears flushing.

"Having trouble with the *yard* there?" he asked. There was that quirky 'r' in the New Hampshire dialect which was left out of words like 'yard' and 'heart' but showed up in others. Laurie would always grin when a NH native said to her, "So, you taught yoga," because it sounded like, "So, you taught yog*ur*." Yep, she wanted to say, I was a yogurt instructor.

"Yes, I'm in a hurry—"

"I'd say so." Exeter Towne surveyed the damage she'd done to the lawn. "Where's the rest of your family?"

"Inside watching the football game."

"That so?" He cast his eyes to her house.

"Well, Ohio State is playing. We moved here from Dublin, Ohio. Randy and I grew up there."

"Ohio. My wife said you were from the Midwest—"

"Yeah, 'The Buckeye State.' You ever visited there?"

"Nope. Only travelin' I did was to Ko*r*ea."

"It's weird with a name like yours that you've never traveled."

"What's that mean?" Exeter Towne re-adjusted the strap of his leaf blower over his shoulder.

"Uh...well, yeah. Do you have a favorite college football team?" He obviously didn't see the irony in his name or too many others had.

"Only graduated high school. Never did college."

Laurie felt the wall between them rise. She wanted him to like her, to have a real conversation with him. With anyone. So she tried again. "All I have is this tarp to put the leaves in. It's got a drawstring. See?" She pulled at the cord to close the tarp, but it folded up into a taco shell and the leaves blew out. She beat it down with her feet. It bloated up again in the wind.

Exeter Towne stroked his trim white beard with his thumb and forefinger. "Well, I've got an extra bin you can bo*rr*ow."

"Really? Are you sure?"

"Yep."

"That'd sure make this a lot easier." She took a step forward.

He put his hand out to stop her. "No, no—you just keep on."

She watched him walk away not sure if he wanted to help her or not. She knelt and replanted as much of the ravaged grass as she could. Her neighbor came back dragging a large bin behind him. He shook his head when he saw her.

"Not much you can do about that now." He put his hand on her shoulder. No one outside her family had touched her in months. Maybe it was the positive ions in the air or maybe it was time to let out the wretchedness clogging her soul, but Laurie wept silently into her dirty open hands.

Exeter Towne quickly took his hand away and grimaced. He slid the leaf blower over to his hip, glanced around, and lifted Laurie to her feet stiffly pulling her to him. She cried into his soft shoulder. "There, there…that's all right." He tapped her back with his fingers and did not rush her. His old flannel shirt was cozy and smelled like the smoke from a campfire. When lightning cracked nearby, she pulled away.

"I was starting to think that NH stood for 'No Hug.'" Laurie wiped her eyes on her sleeve snuffing her nose. It was a bad joke. She glanced at him to see what he thought.

Exeter Towne slung the blower back across his chest. "Nope. It takes folks around here a while to get acquainted. Not like that in Ohio, I expect."

"Yeah, it's totally different there. We Ohioans are big huggers."

"That so?"

"I've tried to make friends here, but I'm kinda shy."

"I've only seen you with Tasia, the mail lady."

"Tasia's my friend."

"She's just doing her job. On the other hand, my wife Marion's off to a women's social something or other Tuesday night down to the church. We've seen your family there a couple of times. You might try that."

"I got an invitation, but I didn't think I should go."

"You should. I'll tell Marion and you can go with her. Now go inside n' lie down. I'll clean this up."

"Are you sure?"

"I'm never sure of anything. Go on in now."

"OK. Thank you, Mr. Towne."

"Exeter." He switched on the blower.

CHAPTER 4

The Marionettist

Saturday Morning 3:06 AM | October 31st

The blazing flood lights of the service station reflected off the barrel of the state trooper's rifle—still pointed directly at Deedee's forehead.

Deedee slipped the key fob into her skirt pocket. She opened the door, held her legs together like a Stepford wife, and swung them out of the car. Her red pumps crunched on the broken blacktop of the empty lot. She stood halfway up and smoothed out her navy blue skirt. Her stomach clenched.

He was talking. She didn't hear him at first. Her brain was trying to untangle the knot.

"Raise your hands now, so I can see them."

She looked from the gun to the man.

"Raise your hands above your head...*right now*." His face was a stone mask.

She lifted her hands unsteadily above her head. The trooper strode around his cruiser toward her. She felt the alien smirk return to her face. The sapience stirred deep within her and rose. Deedee's hands trembled as she fought the sudden urge to strangle the trooper. Her elbows bent—

"Don't move." He caught her slender wrists and lowered her arms. He took a step back.

"Grab his gun," the Voice said.

"You'd better put cuffs on me, Trooper. I might hurt you."

The trooper towered over her. He tightly smiled and paused before saying, "I don't think handcuffs are necessary, ma'am."

"Please, I don't feel right. *We're not alone.*" Deedee bit the inside of her bottom lip and swallowed the blood from the reopened wound.

"You are weak, Deedee...I will make you strong," the Voice said.

"Ma'am, we're the only ones out here."

"But...I hear her...don't you?"

The trooper raised his eyebrows and put his rifle on the front seat of the cruiser without turning his back to her. He spoke gently like she was a nut job. "No ma'am, I'm afraid I don't. Why do you have blood on your face?"

"I bit my lip." She stuck her bottom lip out.

He made a choking noise in his throat. "That's pretty bad." He lifted his radio from his utility belt. "Ma'am, you sit tight while I call dispatch and—"

Her body shuddered and her eyes rolled up into their sockets. She slapped the radio out of his hand. It clanged on the blacktop.

The trooper spun her around and handcuffed her, then shoved her back against the cold car.

Deedee's irises snapped back to the center. "Stop, you're hurting me."

Deedee felt another pair of eyes follow behind hers as she watched the trooper bend to pick up his radio. The hidden presence in her mind raised Deedee's right foot to kick him. She rooted it firmly next to her left. He roughly shoved the radio back in its case and planted his legs wide in front of her. Deedee fixed her eyes on the trooper's badge. She managed to slur, "What'd ya' sstop me for?"

He leaned in closer. "Have you been drinking, ma'am?" He sniffed the air between them. The trooper moved back with a quizzical look and rubbed the tip of his nose. "You smell like... like J'adore, and ...egg salad." He seemed to be thinking out loud.

She dragged her gaze up to his face. "Egg...ssalad?"

"I clocked you doing over 70 in a 50-mile-an-hour zone on black ice. You could've been killed. Why didn't you pull over?"

Deedee willed a little piece of her mind's real estate back. "I don't know."

The trooper pulled his baton out and slapped the metal rod in his palm. It clink... clink... clinked each time it hit his thick wedding band. She sized him up. He was clean-cut and clean-limbed, though not handsome. What attracted her was his cocksure stance. It seemed to come from more than being allowed to enforce the law on a deserted road all by himself. The circling wind purred against her bare legs and licked her thick fiery hair off her back.

"I need to search you," he said starting at her shoulders. He reached into her skirt pocket. "I'll keep hold of your key." He patted her hip like she was a pony.

She tried to cross her legs, but her heel slid and her ankle turned outward. He grabbed her waist to steady her, his thumb tips met at her navel. He smelled clean.

"Whoa, hold on. I'll need your driver's license."

"It's in my purse...there on the passenger seat."

He reached in and took out her license, angling it in the light. "Deedra Morrigan—"

"It's pronounced *Deer-* dree.' No one ever says it right, so I go by 'Deedee.'"

"Right. San Francisco, California. It's your birthday. The big 4-0 on Halloween. Should I say trick or treat or happy birthday?"

"Ha, aren't you original."

"It's my birthday too."

The Voice made her shiver.

"Do you have a coat, Ms. Morrigan?"

"I'm not cold."

"But you're shivering."

"The temperature's not the reason, Trooper."

The trooper's mouth did not smile, but his eyes did. He glanced toward the empty road. He had short-cropped hair like most law enforcement, but he wore the tan hat with that macho drill strap in the back which only state troopers wore. She had the urge to slip her fingers behind his head, under the taut leather.

She knew his interest would wane soon. Most men flirted with her when they met but quickly found her conversations too highbrow and ended up feeling like Neanderthals. Andrew could hold his own with her; he adored her. Guilt rushed in. Deedee twisted her diamond engagement ring to the inside of her palm, toying at it with her thumb. *Why am I acting like this? Is it the hormones? Focus on the facts.*

"What's your name, Trooper?"

"Sergeant, badge number 379." The trooper eyed her and stroked his baton. He was strong and intelligent. Just her type.

"See, we have the same taste." The marionettist raised the control bar.

Deedee looked around the empty lot. "There. Did you hear that?" Her skin twitched.

"You're going crazy, Deedee..."

He pointed behind the station. "That's the Connecticut River right over there. Otherwise, we're alone. What brought you to our side of the country, Ms. Morrigan?"

"I'm not sure."

"What do you do for a living?"

"I'm a rare antiquities dealer."

"Do you search the classifieds for estate sales?" He motioned with his baton to her back seat.

She saw the stack of newspapers spilling onto the floor. "I...don't know where those came from. I handle high-end clients. They call me."

"My wife likes antiques." The trooper stopped slapping the baton midair and looked at his ring. He straightened his back. "Ma'am—"

"Could you please loosen these a little?" Deedee showed him her handcuffed wrists.

The trooper unlocked one bracelet and cuffed her hands again in the front then took her by the elbow. "You'll need to wait in the patrol car while I run your license, Ms. Morrigan."

At that, something deep inside her opened its eyes...a cobra uncoiling itself from around the clay jar which held her soul.

"Good. Invite me in, son of Eve."

Get out of my brain!

No cars had passed the whole time they were at the service station. A colubrine wind embraced them. It pushed them toward the cruiser which was parked between two lonely arteries: the road of black asphalt and the river of black water. Cold air rippled up Deedee's skirt and made the trooper hold onto his hat despite the drill strap. He helped her into the back and folded himself into the front seat. He placed his hat on the dashboard.

"I want that hat."

The Voice had followed her into the safety of the cruiser. *So I am crazy.* Her hand went to her throat to the gold cross necklace and worried it between her thumb and forefinger.

The trooper got on his radio to call the dispatcher to run Deedee's license.

The cobra rose to strike.

Not again. Deedee sweated. Her legs slid together as she buckled herself in. Her hands and feet wanted to claw, kick—and kill. Deedee gripped the belt across her chest and squeezed her eyes shut, struggling not to move. *Please, don't let me hurt anybody.*

The Voice said, ***"Leave the hurting to me."***

The cobra struck and Deedee's sight shot inward. She saw herself sucked down a long passageway into the far recesses of her mind. The handcuffs were gone. The seat belt was gone.

Her body reacted by bracing her legs against the backseat of the cruiser. The walls of her mind were slippery sides of a well, and she plummeted downward into blackness. A cage awaited her there—Deedee's own skeleton was creating it. The tunnel filled with the roar of bones cracking and groaning as her ribs extended outward forming a white circular cage. She pressed her hands to her ears and screamed.

Deedee tumbled to a halt outside the jagged opening of the cage. A figure appeared and stood over her. It was female. The hard green eyes Deedee recognized...

...and the Voice. *"The debt is paid."* The female figure kicked Deedee hard on the chest making her stumble backward into the cage.

The bone bars fused together forming a ball of ribs around Deedee. She pulled herself to her feet in time to see the entity ascend the windows of her eyes. Deedee shook the curved bars and wailed, "Who are you?"

The despotic Voice surrounded her with the answer: *"I am Lilith."*

CHAPTER 5

Trooper

Saturday Morning 3:18 AM | October 31ˢᵗ

The cruiser lurched from side to side. Deirdre Morrigan had buckled herself up and was screaming and holding onto the seat belt. The 'cage' protected the trooper with a barrier of thick soundproof glass, steel mesh, and metal. He hoped it would hold. The woman unsettled him and now she was tripping out like he'd never seen anybody trip before. There—now she was calm and sitting quietly in the middle of the backseat staring at him.

He didn't like red-haired women, but this one pulled at him.

She clinked the handcuffs together. "*B'nay 'adam**, look at me."

Her voice was different from before, like sugar on snow. He

---

*B'nay 'adam- Hebrew for *Son of Adam*.

held her gaze in the large rear view mirror. She unbuckled the seat belt and brushed her long hair over her shoulder. She moved her fettered hands to the top button her of her white silk blouse.

"Ma'am, sit tight and let me do my job."

"Sergeant." She unbuttoned the top button. "I'll treat you to your own little vernissage."

He had no idea what that meant, but he liked what he saw. The second button eased through her fingers. He faced front, but angled the mirror at her. "Keep your clothes on, Ms. Morrigan," he said sternly into the mike.

"Are you a trooper with two *o's* or a trouper with an *ou*? I hope you're the latter...we can perform together." The woman unfastened the third button. As each one was freed he felt the heavy mantle of authority lift from his shoulders. He pulled on his collar to loosen it. The hand holding the mike lowered and his eyes fixed on her fingers, their downward motion; his handcuffs were silver bracelets glinting on her milky wrists.

"How do I compare with the females you ogle on the screen?" She undid the next two buttons.

What?! How does she know about that? He turned around and opened the soundproof glass divider. "Ms. Morrigan—"

"I know a lot about you, Sergeant #379. Your poor wife has no idea what you're into, does she? But I know *exactly* what you like." She toyed with the last button, then dropped her hands in her lap.

He could not take his eyes off her. He'd forgotten to breathe and let out a low moaning sound as if in pain. He was. The sharp plastic of her license pierced his palm. He opened his hand. The license was bloody and bent in half. He licked the cut skin and his tongue touched his gold wedding band. The metal sent out shocks of guilt which electrocuted his stomach.

What was he thinking? He couldn't let his wife down again, not after she'd finally let him back into their bedroom, if not into her heart. He closed his eyes and saw his wife's face. A new force of shame, duty, and love pushed back at the lust building in him. He shut the glass divider. The pressure in his body lowered. He flattened out the woman's license. "Continue to flail around back there if you want, Ms. Morrigan. I'll arrest you for indecent exposure too."

"How many cops does it take to screw in a light bulb? None. It turned itself in." She laughed.

He ignored her. Wait—why could he still hear her? The glass was soundproof. He straightened his shoulders. *Steady man*. He picked up the radio and pressed the button to call dispatch. Nothing happened. He tried it again. The radio was dead. He slapped it in his palm.

Ja-bang...ja-bang...ja-bang. The woman was kicking the metal divider behind him, and even though there was a two-inch gap in between the metal and his seat, he still felt the pointed toe of her heels in his back. *How was that even possible?* The trooper got out his cell phone to call headquarters. *I want to know who this lewd chick is.*

Ja-bang...ja-bang...ja-bang. He shifted in his seat to avoid her foot. She found her mark right in the small of his back. Ja-bang. That time it hurt. He rubbed the sore spot.

Silence. The kicking stopped. He was afraid to turn around. He had his finger poised above the CALL button when the whole car shuddered.

"Look at me, son of Adam," she said.

He had to look. She seemed luminous in the dashboard lights. The woman leaned forward, her breath fogging up the divider.

"Please stop..." he said more to himself than to her, but he could not move. She drew a heart with an arrow through it on the glass.

He wanted to fight back—to yell at her—to curse her—to punch her in the face—anything to stop her. He opened the glass divider. They were separated now only by steel. Her scent caught him, surged through his body, washing away the rage—along with his sense of duty and shame. He craved her, coveted her—ached to take her.

"Go ahead." She flashed him her cubic zirconia smile.

The trooper squeezed his eyes shut. He could no longer picture his wife's face. The Morrigan woman had taken over his mind's tableau.

She jabbed the back of his seat again. "Sergeant #379."

He opened his eyes.

She held up her wrists to him. "Free me from these shackles."

He put his big hands on the steering wheel and gripped hard. He croaked, "Forgive me." He could not remember his wife's name.

The trooper drove behind the gas station. He turned off the emergency lights and got out. The Connecticut River roared by in the darkness a few feet away. He didn't notice. He moved with military precision to the writhing female in the backseat. The lower half of her body was fire. He closed the door immersing himself in the flames.

CHAPTER 6

Deedee

Saturday Morning 3:24 AM | October 31st

*D*eedee watched her body ravage the state trooper from the bone cage in her mind. The bright console lights flashed across her face like a disco ball creating the same disorienting effect as if she were in a nightclub and couldn't focus on her dance partner.

Deedee was grateful she couldn't see clearly. It was a beastly coupling.

Or was it? Andrew and she had watched the breeding of horses once. At least animals had the goal of creating a new life. Deedee did not know the purpose of this. It seemed to be the opposite of procreation—it was a Cimmerian void which drew the trooper's life into it. No, this was lower than the beasts.

CHAPTER 7

Bienvenue

Saturday Morning 3:44 AM | October 31st

The red-haired woman touched the claw marks on the state trooper's bare chest. "That was the best violation I've ever received, Sergeant, so I'll let you in on a little secret. Deirdre Morrigan, or if you prefer the poodle version of her name like she does, 'Deedee,' is incognito, but I'll go by Deirdre while I'm in her skin. Don't tell anyone, okay?" She grabbed his chin and wagged it back and forth.

He didn't answer.

Lilith yanked the cross from her neck and dropped it on his chest. The religious symbol which had held no real significance to Deedee when she owned her body had little effect on its new tenant. Lilith was merely disgusted having to touch it.

She put her clothes back on and found her pumps, they were Christian Louboutins—the real crime would be to leave them behind. She held one shoe above the trooper's face. Its red heel made an unusual yet feminine weapon. She traced his eyebrows with the heel then put the shoe on. She wouldn't use the Louboutins this time—these were brand new. "Let's make this look like you were to blame, Trooper." She touched the door. There were no handles. She was locked in.

She felt around on the floor for the trooper's utility belt and found his knife. "Such a Boy Scout," she patted his cheek. She gripped the knife in her fist and hit the window with the glass breaker at the end of the handle. The glass exploded onto the ground outside. Her pinky was cut and gushing blood. She put it in her mouth and sucked. It healed immediately. She stuck her hand out the window and opened the door.

On the front seat she found her license and the Jaguar's key. Her stomach growled. Lilith grabbed the trooper's sunglasses and hat and tucked her long red hair inside it.

The interior lights of the service station shot on at her approach. She swept her hand in front of the glass door and it flung open setting off the alarm. She went inside and grabbed a blue plastic shopping basket and walked straight to the candy aisle. "This will have to do." She unwrapped a Lindt bar, devoured it, and scooped several more into the basket. She walked to the fridge where she swept an armful of iced coffees on top of the chocolate bars, then over to the counter where she tossed in a copy of every newspaper they had on the racks. She tipped her hat to the surveillance camera on the way out. Her gloves were on the ground waiting patiently for her where Deedee had thrown them. She pulled them on.

Lilith set the shopping basket and trooper's hat on the passenger seat of the Jaguar. She walked over to the cruiser, put it in Neutral, and guided the car toward the river's edge. The trooper moaned in the back seat. "You should've let me off with a warning," she said shoving the car over the muddy embankment into the dark river below. She waited until she heard the cruiser hit the rushing water, then strode back to the Jag. She shifted into Reverse spewing broken blacktop in her wake.

Lilith drove, finishing off two more Lindt bars. As she was cocking an iced coffee to her lips, she almost missed the blue sign which said, 'Welcome-Bienvenue to New Hampshire 'Live free or die.' She swallowed and said, "Très bon. Let's see if they mean that."

Deedee watched helplessly through her own eyes, now merely the back windows of a prison transport van, as her captor drove away in her beloved ruby red Jaguar...in her body...and into the night...to God knows where.

CHAPTER 8

River Water

Saturday Morning 3:54 AM | October 31st

The trooper woke to cold water blasting his bare skin. *River water*. He shot upright. The gelid river rushed in through a broken window. The front ramming bar of the cruiser was jammed into the left river bank.

The trooper's academy training took over—not fear. The break in the window was too small for his broad shoulders. He kicked the remaining shards of glass out of the frame cutting his heels though his socks. The hole was a jagged shark's mouth. The water was up to his chest, so he pulled himself through the opening, the glass teeth shredding his obliques. The pain made him double over and catch his knee in the window. He pushed with his hands and was free of the cruiser.

The river hammered into the trooper trying to claim him for itself. He held fast to the door handle, then to the back bumper, working his way around to the embankment. He grabbed onto the tangle of roots and rocks there, scraping and clawing his way up to the shore. At the top, he stood, muddy and bloody, in just his socks.

He was approximately twenty yards from the service station. The alarm system blared and blazed. The front door was hanging off its hinges, banging in the wind. He hobbled toward the building like a zombie streaker.

He staggered inside, to the back where he found several attendant's uniforms in a closet in a box. He formed his hand into a shaky claw and stiffly bent over to grab a dark blue coverall, but he lost his balance and free-fell to the floor.

He laid there for a few minutes, wavering in and out of consciousness until the needles in his arm woke him up. He scooted backward on his elbows and when he moved to lean against the wall, he cried out in pain. Deep gashes ran the length of his chest. That hadn't happened in the river. He remembered nothing before the river.

The trooper grabbed the coveralls again and maneuvered one jerky leg in, then the other. He took off his wet socks and managed to jam his feet into a pair of rubber boots. He leaned against the wall and willed himself to stand.

He was still cold. A dingy winter coat which reeked of gasoline hung alone in the closet. He dragged it off the hanger, shoved his icy limbs into it, and put the hood over his head. That was better, but external warmth wasn't enough. He needed to drink some heat. He headed for the coffee machine. He grappled for a cup and wolfed down three packages of Swiss rolls while the machine gurgled to life.

Hot coffee in his hands and sugar in his body made his brain start to work again. He only had a few minutes until his fellow state troopers arrived. What was he going to say? Tell them he couldn't remember how he'd lost his cruiser *and* his clothes? He was already under the watchful eye of his new captain for the mess he'd made back home. The last thing he remembered was holding the red-haired woman's license. What was her name? It was hard to pronounce. Damn that devil woman.

He saw her red Jaguar was gone and scowled. He couldn't recall the plate number either...*hold on.* It was coming to him: California. He swigged the last drop of coffee and crushed the empty cup into a tight ball. *Wait till I find you, sweetheart.*

The state police pulled into the service station.

The trooper steeled himself and walked to the front door. He threw the cup in the trash, pulled the hood back, and raised his hands over his head. He was met with a blinding light to the eyes and went out the door squinting.

He said in a loud voice, "I'm Sergeant Randall Locke. New Hampshire state trooper, badge number 379. I'm coming out. *Don't shoot me.*"

The beam focused on his face. The state trooper holding the torch approached him, his gun still drawn but lowered. He peered at the man in the dirty blue coveralls and his face lit up with recognition. "What the hell? Randy, is that you?"

"Geoff—I'm glad it's you, man." Randy lowered his hands.

Geoff holstered his gun. "What're you doin' out here?"

"I have no idea." Randy's body trembled in the cold wind.

"Get in the cruiser and get warm. You can tell me whatever you remember in there."

CHAPTER 9

Tophet

Saturday Afternoon | October 31st

Ari walked quickly around the back of the BMW to the passenger side door of the truck so no one in the office would see her. She wanted to peek inside the cab, but the running board hit her at chest height.

Wait. The truck was custom-painted. On the door was a family: a husband and wife, a son, and a daughter. On the cab was a house with rocks falling on it from the sky. In the front yard was a gravestone which read 'R.I.P. Tiffany, Wife & Mother'. The next scene on the truck bed was of the man cradling his young son in his arms, his mouth gaping in grief at a stormy sky. It was fearfully wrought and unsettling.

Ari peered around the back. The man and his daughter were still inside the trailer. She moved around to the tailgate. It was hard to see through the rain. Painted there was the man lying on his back, a broken sparrow. The license plate underneath read: TOPHET. *What does that mean?* She sheltered her notebook under her coat and jotted down the word along with the make and model of the truck.

The store's trailer door banged wide open. Ari ducked in between the two vehicles without thinking. Now she was trapped. She wiped the rain from her eyes and peeked out over the hood of her car. The man stood in the doorway sniffing the air. Ari felt eyes on her. She looked up and pressed against the BMW. A green-gray brutish face was painted on the driver's side door. The eyes followed Ari's. They were alive with hatred. *Calm down...it's just like a CGI effect because of the rain, right?*

The man clanged down the metal steps in his heavy steel-toed boots. He held the little girl by the scruff of her neck like a filthy kitten. "I told ya' not to talk to nobody. So stop yer bawlin'." At the bottom step, he pitched her onto the wet cement. She skidded into a puddle on all fours. "Get in the truck." He cuffed her on the back of the head and her forehead smacked the ground.

"My Lord!" Ari shot up.

The creep saw her. "You. Get away from my truck."

Ari ran and knelt in front of the little girl. "You okay, honey?"

Rain streaked her dirty wet cheeks, but she swiped at them. "Go 'way, lady."

A strong hand grabbed Ari by the shoulder and hoicked her to her feet. "Ain't you a sweet piece a meat," the man said.

The little girl scrambled out of the way in a backward crab crawl and curled up into a ball on the bottom step of the trailer.

"Don't touch me." Ari wrenched her shoulder from his grasp. She faced him, blinking in the rain, staring into the diminutive bastard's eyes. A big cat protecting her cub.

His expression instantly softened, his eyes were human—and kind, his voice full of foreboding, "Sister, thou believest that God is one; thou doest well: the devils also believe, and shudder."

"What did you say?" Ari peered into his face.

Go now...sister!

She hadn't heard him say the words, so much as she had felt them. Yiayiá's prayer rope vibrated in her pocket. Ari placed her hand over it. *What should I do?*

I warned you... His lips curled up at the sides. The creep was back.

Her temples throbbed. Ari put her hands on the sides of her head. She looked at the man. His eyes were not human anymore—the sclerae were dark bulging spheres. The golden-rimmed irises were circles of black upon black. They were identical to the eyes painted on the truck. The absolute hatred in them seared her soul, but she couldn't look away.

The man wiped his wet mouth with the back of his hand. He skirled like a bagpipe in a mixture of foreign words and guttural tones: a litany of evil. The syllables invaded her mind through her ear canals. She covered her ears. Her brain could not link them to anything it had ever heard before.

She turned to run to her car, but the man pushed her with both hands into the pallets of salt bags behind them. Her back cracked into the hard salt and the wind whooshed out of her. Ari slumped to the ground. The man tromped over to the pallet and pulled on the bags. A bag ripped and salt pellets cascaded on her. She couldn't move or scream—her lungs were empty.

The man wrenched his hands out of the pallet howling as if he had yanked them from a fire. He rubbed them on his jeans. She smelled burnt flesh. The man dropped to his knees and flailed his hands in a pothole full of rain water.

Ari stood.

The door of the trailer flung open and the young man bounded out. He saw the little girl just in time and grabbed onto the wet railing. "Whoa, I didn't see you there, kiddo. Hey, like are you okay?" He swung around her and peered into her face. He looked to her father for an explanation.

The man was hunched over with his back turned.

Ari knelt in front of the little girl, tucking her wet hair behind her ear. She flinched at Ari's tender touch. "*Call 911*," she whispered to the boy.

"All in fun?" the boy repeated.

Ari whispered louder, "*No, I said—*"

"She shoved my kid down them stairs." The man stood behind Ari.

"No, I'm trying to help her. He's the one who pushed her," Ari said to the boy.

"Like I'm gonna hurt my own kid. I should have ya' arrested, pretty lady. Yer lucky my Penny's a tough little tom boy." He slapped her on the back. Penny shot her boot out to avoid falling off the step. "Get in the truck."

"Look. I didn't do anything to her." Ari stood to look into the creep's eyes. "You're lying."

"See ya' around." He winked and brushed past her.

"Are you okay, kiddo?" The boy searched Penny's face.

She directed a well-rehearsed smile at him. "I'm a tough little tomboy, like my daddy said."

The man put his arm around the boy's shoulders. "Let's load the beast," he said leading him toward the pallets of manure.

Ari was drenched. For the first time she didn't care. Penny's limp brown hair hung in her face. Ari tucked it behind her ear again. This time the girl let her.

"Please, Penny. I need to ask you a question. The little girl painted on your daddy's truck. Is she you?"

The girl didn't answer.

"Penny, I have a little girl too. She's right over there in that car. See? Please tell me if that's you in the painting."

Penny looked over at the BMW. Dorothea peeked at her from under her blankie. "Maybe."

"Okay. I'm going to help you. Sit tight."

Ari sprinted to her car and got her phone. When she turned around, she saw the man push Penny hard on the back toward the truck. "I told ya' to get in the truck." The girl stumbled.

Ari yelled, "Stop it!" and ran to the pickup, but the man hurled the girl into the cab. He vaulted in himself and slammed the door in Ari's face. She banged on it with her fist. "I'm dialing 911!" The man swiped the phone out of her hand. It smacked her on the cheek then hydroplaned across the parking lot.

He leaned out the window. "I'll remember you." He licked his lips. Ari felt naked. He put the truck in reverse, just missing her, then backed into the wall of salt bags stacked six feet high behind her. The corner of the stack toppled to the ground. The bags burst open. White bullets of salt shot her in the back almost knocking her down. The bull truck roared off the lot expelling noxious smoke out its horns.

Ari coughed and the left side of her face pulsed in pain. Salt ate at her hands. She held her palms open to the rain to wash them clean then staggered over to her phone. The screen was cracked and only half lit.

She trudged back to the BMW. She opened the trunk where she kept a tote of emergency supplies. She draped an old blanket over herself.

For Dorothea's sake, she had to pretend all was okay. Ari eased her broken body into the front seat. Her hurt cheek was hidden under the blanket. She let out a painful breath and assumed the role of 'Dorothea's mother'. "Let's go home, moró mou."

Ari pulled the visor down and looked at her face in the mirror. A welt was forming on her cheekbone. It would leave a scar; she could deal with that, but the cast of her eyes was different. She wasn't sure how or why, but her life had changed—forever.

CHAPTER 10

Hector Apostollis

Saturday Afternoon | October 31ˢᵗ

Ari eased her car into the attached two-car garage. Her husband, Hector, stood in the kitchen doorway holding a Coke. He smiled at her.

She frowned at the Coke.

Dorothea bounded out of the car and ran to him, "Babbá! Babbá! There was a bad man at the hardware store!"

He picked her up. "What bad man, *koúkla mou*?*" His 'little doll' snuggled into his neck. Her curls always held the faint scent of his cologne.

"The bad daddy with the big truck, Babbá. He made the pink girl fall down the—"

*Koúkla mou- Greek for my little doll.

"A pink girl? Ari, what's she talking about?" Hector called out to his wife.

Ari pushed the button of the garage door opener. Normally she loved the finality with which the heavy door closed and sealed off the outside world. Today she didn't feel safe.

She brushed past her husband into the kitchen. She didn't want him to see her face yet. She started dinner. Familiar actions comforted her. Familiar arguments did too. "Where'd you get the Coke from?"

"Why're you all wet?"

"Long story. Where'd you get the Coke from?"

"Bought it myself." He puffed up his chest.

"Nice. You won't go buy the softener salt, but you will go out for battery acid."

"It's my only vice besides you."

She roughly spun the Lazy Susan around to find the pasta pot.

He waved the red Coke can at her. "It's a Coke, not cocaine."

"You are choosing it over me— over us—like a drug addict."

"Why are you trying to pick a fight with me?" He put Dorothea down. "Go wash your hands, koúkla."

"But I wanna hear what the bad man did."

"Go wash your hands," her parents both said.

Dorothea stomped to the bathroom.

"Look, I'm done being your mom." Ari wagged the long box of angel hair spaghetti at him like an index finger. "You pass another kidney stone, Hector, and this time I'll leave you writhing on the bathroom floor."

"Panayía mou—what happened to your face?" He reached for her cheek.

She let him touch her. "It looks worse than it is."

"You need an ice pack for that, *agápe mou**. Does it hurt?"

"I'm fine."

He prepared the ice pack in silence and handed it to her. She could tell he wanted to comfort her, but she wasn't ready yet. He didn't touch her again.

"Thanks." She held it to her cheek.

"Tell me what happened."

She did. Ari told him about the boy at the hardware store, the creep with the truck, Penny, the storm, the custom-painted truck, Yiayiá's prayer rope acting weird in her pocket, the salt, and her phone breaking.

He listened and watched her pace up and down the dining room twirling the long prayer rope around her fingers like a *komboloí***.

"Well, what do you think?" She rubbed her forearms.

Hector's eyes were unremarkable brown windows, but the engineer behind them worked the gears with prudence and humor. She saw in them that he didn't want to say what he thought.

"You don't believe me."

"Why didn't you stay in the car? You always stick your nose where it doesn't belong then get in over your head." He pointed at her swollen cheek.

"I couldn't sit there and do nothing."

---

*Agápe mou- Greek for *my love*.

**Komboloí- Greek for *worry beads*.

He formed his hands into claws. "Did the tigress come out again? Why didn't you let someone else fight for justice? You're a mother now. Dorothea was right there in the car, for God's sake."

"The doors were locked. I made sure she was safe. How dare you think I wouldn't protect our child above all else? You know I would, Hector."

His voice softened. "*But you didn't*. You ran off and left her in the car, and look what happened to you. What if that guy had pulled that stack of salt pellets on you? You'd be in the hospital right now, and I'd be at the police station reporting a kidnapping, not standing here arguing with you in the kitchen."

She crossed her arms. "Cowards live longer—right Hector?"

"I'm not a coward, Ari. But I do know when to fight and when to walk away. You don't."

She couldn't look at him. He had convicted her with the truth and cut through her excuses. She toyed with the prayer rope like a scolded child. She'd rather scrub public toilets with her toothbrush than admit she was wrong. "You're right. I didn't think. I didn't protect our daughter." She looked at the floor. Scratchy tears edged up her throat.

"Come here." He gathered her into his arms. Ari felt safe in his familiar embrace, so she let a few tears escape. No more. It wasn't her thing to cry.

He said into her hair, "Agápe mou, what upsets me is that a jerk hurt my girls."

She pulled away. "He was more than a jerk. You should've seen him, he was *evil*. He wasn't human. You didn't see his eyes...they were all black...demonic and hateful." She showed him her goose bumps. "See? Talking about him still freaks me out."

"Well, I dunno, Ari. I haven't seen many demons driving around Ashuelot Hollow in monster trucks, buying bags of manure...they have enough of that down there." He pointed downward. She knew he was trying to make her laugh. His hands were at waist level and he twirled them in a half circle in a doubtful gesture. Even though he was a second-generation Greek, Hector (like most Greeks), did much of his talking with his hands.

Ari wiped her eyes with a napkin. "It's not funny. You weren't there. I've never experienced anything like it before. Do you believe in angels?"

"Yes, and I feel sorry for your guardian angel. He must work overtime."

She slapped his arm. "Well then, don't demons have to exist too? To balance out good and evil?"

"Sure they do, but I don't think you know enough about the spirit world to tell me anything. When's the last time you went to church?"

"Easter."

"So five months ago. You don't even call it *Páscha**, like a good Greek girl." His hands were quiet on his hips for the moment.

"Liturgy at Annunciation is so boring. Besides, that's your special time with Dorothea." Hector smelled nice. She moved in to nuzzle his neck.

He gently pushed her away. "It should be family time."

"Okay, tomorrow we'll *all* go to church. I'll even kiss Father

---

*Páscha- Greek for *"Easter"* or *Passover*.

Leonidas' hand."

"Hallelujah."

"You need to know that I was truly frightened by that creepy guy today. You should've seen the way he threw his daughter down the stairs. That was outright child abuse. How do you explain the other stuff I told you? Like why my prayer rope vibrated in my pocket when that creep grabbed me. It's never done that before."

"Look, I think you saw an undoubtedly nasty guy, Ari. But you stay up late writing and making up stories. You're tired, it was raining hard…"

"I can't prove to you what I saw, Hector, but I know it was way out of the ordinary. If you'd helped me run errands this morning instead staying at home to watch the race—"

"God will forgive me for that. He loves racing too. After all, who could deny His hand in making an F-1 Ferrari?"

CHAPTER 11

Boogeyman

Tuesday, 5:50 PM | November 3ʳᵈ

Lilith parked the Jaguar in a handicapped spot in front of Faith Fellowship Church. At 6 PM in early November it was already dark. Beams of yellow light shone through the long narrow church windows piercing the blue black evening air. Her index fingers ticked on the wheel while the other eight remained steady, waiting to serve their mistress while she sized up their new prey.

The church's main entrance was an insult— just two plain glass doors—they could have been the entryway to any number of less spiritual establishments, like Syd's Carpet Castle down the street. The building did not reflect the Tyrant's majesty. The Cathedral of Hagia Sofia, Saint Peter's Basilica, and the Canterbury Cathedral at least aspired to.

She extended her palm toward the building. *The Spirit is weak here. Barely a whisper from the Tyrant.* It suited her purposes perfectly. It was a 'have it your way' church which served Christianity up like a sandwich at Subway. She was searching for a lost sheep...*where are you, darling?...ah, there you are...sitting by yourself...in the corner...your eyes on your small plate of appetizers...hating every bite, every calorie...hating every miserable breath you're taking...no one's talking to you...vulnerable...lonely...and beautiful: perfect for me...your name?...yes, on the name tag...how considerate of these Christians to make my job easier...Laurie...yes...Laurie Locke, I've come for you, my dear.*

She picked up the newspaper clipping and read the part she had circled: "8th Annual Women's Interfaith Fellowship Event. This will be a great opportunity to connect with women from other local churches. Come, be encouraged by women of faith, and enjoy amazing appetizers and fun activities! Time: 6 PM, Tuesday, November 3rd. Contact Marion at—"

How could the Tyrant have made such vacuous, stupid creatures to occupy Himself with—then give them free will? Many don't even believe He exists. They don't believe I exist either. I am an imaginary specter, a mere boogeyman.

She put her right hand into her, *well now anyway,* Louis Vuitton purse and caressed the soft chamois bag of Runes. Lilith felt around for the jeweled lipstick case which had belonged to Bunny. She held it to the light and admired its workmanship. This case was still beautiful, but Bunny's corpse was decomposing in a culvert in Idaho.

She touched up her lipstick in the visor mirror. The rich were predictable in their love of luxuries, so they were always her target of choice. Her logic was, if her spirit had to inhabit vile human bodies to operate in the physical realm, at least she could treat herself to a taste of the paradise she'd lost.

Lilith was putting the lipstick back into her purse when Deedee's cell phone rang. Her hand fished it out, moving of its own volition. The ringtone was the special one which Deedee's son had chosen for their home phone—the tinkling of an ice cream truck.

Deedee heard her son's ringtone and broke through the bone prison. She took control of her body. The ring tone was waning! She jammed the tip of her finger on the answer icon.

"Justin!"

"Mommy?" The young boy's voice on the other end sounded hopeful and scared.

"Yes, Justin, it's Mommy. How are you, buddy?"

"Mommy! Daddy lets me call you every day. But you never answer. Why didn't you pick me up?"

"Oh buddy, I'm so sorry. I love you more than anything in this world. You must believe me."

"Mommy where are y—"

"Justin, give me the phone," Andrew said in the background. "Deedee, is that you? Where the hell are you?"

"I—" She couldn't speak, a sob caught in her throat.

Andrew's voice softened. "Deedee, please come home. Justin needs you... I need you."

"Andrew, I'm so sorry... I don't know what..."

"Honey, where are y—"

Lilith pushed the call end button.

Lilith grabbed Deedee by the hair, shoved her back into the bone cage, and slammed the door. "Enough of you, woman."

Deedee scrambled to her feet, fists on the white bars, and screamed, "Why are you doing this to me?"

"Because I need your fleshly vessel...and this tiny, baby girl." Lilith patted her belly. "You gave them to me."

"No, I didn't. I would never agree to—"

"I would not have been allowed in if you hadn't invited me."

"Please let me go. I—"

"Close your mouth before I do—permanently. I have business to conduct here. I don't have time for this. Make no mistake, I will kill your son if you try to take control again."

Deedee shrank to the back of the cage. "No...no...no...not my baby Justin. Don't hurt my son...or my baby girl." She rent her clothes. She knew the atrocities Lilith was capable of committing. While alone in her mind's prison, she had been experiencing flashbacks of what her body had done to children and their parents along the way to New Hampshire. It was a horror movie starring herself which she didn't remember making.

"I will do to your son what is done to my sons, and I am not merciful. Are we clear, Dee...dee?"

"Yes, I'm sorry, I—please, I'll be good." Deedee knew now she had to use her strengths—her ability to be a detached and logical problem solver. She would lay low and gather facts to find a way to protect her children and take her body back—she had to—for them.

Lilith shut off the phone and shoved it into the purse. "My phone...my purse...and my body." Andrew wouldn't be able to find his wife. Lilith had uninstalled the tracking app weeks before and had switched the license plates. Her bottom lip twitched.

She wiped away a bit of saliva from the corner of her mouth. It was time to move into another body. Deedee was trouble.

Lilith got out of the car. She pulled the gloves up and smacked her palms together. The leather made a pleasing *crack*. "This should prove interesting."

CHAPTER 12

Women's Interfaith Fellowship

Tuesday 6:07 PM

Ari raced into the Faith Fellowship Church parking lot and pulled alongside a red Jaguar. It was parked in a handicapped spot with regular California license plates. Ari got out and peered into it. No disabled persons placard hung from the rear view mirror, just a tiny gold ball. *Whoever she is, she ought to make this evening more exciting than usual.*

The 8th Annual Women's Interfaith Fellowship Event was in full swing. After she hung her coat in the hallway, Ari hurried toward the sanctuary. Her boot heels clacked on the linoleum floor.

Marion Towne looked up from where she sat at the welcome table. "Hi! Welcome!"

"Hello!" Ari faked the enthusiasm back. She glanced at the list of names.

Marion handed her a pen. "Sign in here. I've got your name tag all ready. Your church's name barely fits on it. Here you go—oh my, what happened to your face, dear?"

"I fell down at the hardware store."

"That so?"

"This makes it look worse than it is." She touched the gauze bandage on her cheek. "I almost didn't come tonight."

"Well, I'm glad you did. I'll pray for your healing, my dear."

Ari slapped the name tag on her chest. *How many times had she heard that empty phrase?*

"We're all sisters in Christ, aren't we?"

"You betcha." She had to get away from Marion. "Is Tasia Papayiannis here?" Tasia was Ari's friend, not in the Facebook sense but in the true meaning.

"Let me check. Yes, she's here. Dear, I'd like you to do a favor for me. I brought my new neighbor, Laurie Locke with me. See that pretty blonde over there? She's around your age. Laurie's shy and doesn't know anyone here. Could you take her under your wing tonight? You're both ears."

"Ears?"

Marion pointed to Ari's name tag. There was an ear printed on it.

"Oh, I see."

"Why don't you first go help yourself to some amazing appetizers? The activities will be starting in a few minutes. When I'm done here I'll introduce you to Laurie."

Ari went to the appetizer table. At 6:15, the food was well picked over. The only person there was a red-haired woman with a paper cup of punch in her gloved hands. The smell of sulfur wafted into Ari's nostrils. It was faint enough for her to doubt her senses for a moment. *She smells like...like rotten eggs. That's odd, she looks soignée.* Ari decided to believe her nose. Her instincts were rarely wrong.

She looked at the woman's name tag. It read 'Deirdre.' No last name, but she was an 'ear' too. Ari reached for a piece of prosciutto wrapped around cream cheese. So did Deirdre. Their arms touched. The woman's arm was hot even through the leather glove. "Pardon me," Ari said, but the other said nothing.

The woman was surveying the room full of women. Her teeth bit into the prosciutto wrap like a guillotine.

Ari cringed. She held her paper plate like a prop so she could remain at the table and watch Deirdre navigate her way through the flock of women, more a big cat than a woman.

Marion spoke into the microphone, "Ladies, look at your name tags and see what body part is printed there. Find that table and take a seat, please."

The sanctuary chairs were set up into ten horseshoes with a round coffee table in the center of each. After Marion introduced them, Ari took the empty seat around the 'ear' table next to Laurie. She knew some of the other women by face, but couldn't remember all their names. *Thank God for name tags.*

The icebreaker task involved an orange ball of yarn and saying, 'My favorite (fill in the blank) is...or I like (fill in the blank).' No one made a move to pick up the ball.

In groups, Ari tried not to be overbearing. It was her instinct to lead, but often it created resentment. She waited a few awkward moments, then picked up the ball of yarn and juggled it between her two open palms. "My favorite color...isn't this. It's scarlet."

"Mine too," Deirdre said.

Ari twisted the orange yarn around her own fingers then gave Deirdre the ball. *Take those freaky gloves off already.*

Nervous laughter burst out each time someone said, "Me too!" and took the ball of yarn.

Silly kittens. How this is supposed to bring me closer to Christ is beyond me.

Laurie fidgeted with her long strand of freshwater pearls. So far she had nothing in common with anyone.

"What's your favorite snack, Laurie?" Marion asked.

"I can't think of one...I'm totally blanking out," Laurie said.

How am I supposed to connect with her? Be nice. Ari told herself. *Fine.* "My favorite snack is popcorn, and not that microwave junk."

"Me too!" Laurie smiled as Ari handed her the ball of yarn.

I guess she can't be all that bad if her favorite snack is popcorn. Ari smiled genuinely back at Laurie.

Laurie said, "OK, let me think. Um, I can't think of another favorite...but, um...I'm a Libra."

Ari's smile dropped into a frown. All the other women in the circle looked at each other murmuring their mutual disapproval of astrology.

Laurie looked at the floor and worked at the ball of yarn, fraying the end.

Deirdre stepped forward. "Me too." She extended her hands to let Laurie wrap the yarn around her fingers. "Mahatma Gandhi, Aleister Crowley, and T.S. Eliot were all Librans."

Laurie smiled gratefully at Deirdre who beamed at her.

Ari could hardly believe what she had heard. She looked around the circle. No one else seemed to know who Aleister Crowley was. The Satanist's only commandment had been, "Do what thou wilt shall be the whole of the Law." Ari aimed the quote at Deirdre.

"Yes, I heard Crowley say that. He also said, 'Having to talk destroys the symphony of silence.' *You* should remember that." Deirdre wiped a bit of saliva from the corner of her mouth.

Touché. Ari pulled her glasses down and did a detailed writer's scan of Deirdre for clues about her character.

When Marion announced the end of the exercise, all the women in the 'ear' group were connected together in an orange spider web of yarn. Ari wanted to release her fingers from the yarn, but the other women were playing 'cat's cradle' en masse. She noticed the many strands connecting her to Deirdre. Only one strand connected her to Laurie. *I should try again with Laurie.*

The women finally untangled themselves. "Hey, you're in the 'blue' group like I am," Ari said to Laurie peering at her name tag.

"Great, we can sit next to each other again." Laurie and Ari walked out of the horseshoe.

Deirdre tapped Ari from behind. "Her name's in blue, like mine. Ari, yours is purple." She hooked her elbow with Laurie's. "Let's go find the 'blue' ladies."

"Maybe I'll see you in the next group," Laurie said over her shoulder to Ari.

Ari looked at her name tag. She could've sworn it was blue. Yes, now it was purple. "Yeah, I hope so too." Deirdre irked her. She went to the 'purple' group and plopped next to her buddy, Tasia.

"That new woman, Deirdre, is being a real harpy to me," Ari whispered to her.

"Is she the one with the long red hair and the wild matching gloves?" Tasia asked.

"That's her. Marion asked me to take a woman named Laurie Locke under my wing tonight. But Deirdre swooped down and dragged her off."

"Well maybe that's good. Laurie's on my route. Her husband's a state trooper and he's gone a lot and they're new in town. If she sees me delivering her mail, she always wants to chat. They live next door to Marion and Exeter Towne."

"Are you ladies joining our discussion?" asked the woman sitting across the horseshoe. In her black leather motorcycle vest covered with patches, she screamed 1970s. She pushed her long gray hair back revealing her name tag which read 'Bella Delmacchio, Italian earth mother.' Bella's hair was longer than Ari's; that bothered her like it always did, but the woman had an unsightly strip of pink scalp an inch wide down the middle. That made Ari feel superior.

Unlike Ari, Bella had no qualms about taking charge, so she snatched the icebreaker question cards off the coffee table. She fired at Ari first. "The first question has several parts to it. I'll ask my fellow gray-haired lady over there. What's your name?" Bella squinted to read Ari's name tag.

She's too proud to wear glasses. Ari pushed hers up her nose. *And my hair is platinum, not gray.* "Ari."

"Okay, Ari. The second part is: 'Where are you from?'"

"New Hampshire."

"How original. And what do you do?" Bella asked.

"I'm a writer."

"Ooh, a writer. Tell us what you write."

"I'm writing a novel."

"What's it about?" Bella dug further.

"It's complicated," Tasia snorted and covered her mouth with her hand.

"Yeah, it's complicated," Ari mimicked Tasia.

Bella looked at Ari with piercing blue eyes which had lived through a lot—*such eyes are hard to say 'no' to.*

"Fine, but tell us anyway," Bella said.

Ari spoke looking around at the circle of women. "Well, I don't want to tell you. My novel is like a fetus in utero. It's not fully formed and I need to protect it until it is." She put her hands in her lap.

"Well, maybe if you carry it to term you will tell us all about it." Bella moved on to Tasia.

Deirdre wasn't in the 'purple' group. Ari wanted to know where she was from and what she did.

Bella flipped over another card. "Ari, maybe this question won't be too *'complicated'* for you."

All the women in the circle looked at Ari. "I didn't hear the question."

"I haven't asked it yet," Bella said smiling but only with her mouth.

The women laughed uncomfortably.

"Ask me." Ari had steel in her voice.

"What is your spiritual gift?" Bella aimed her probing eyes once again at Ari.

Ari met her gaze. "Snark." She steepled her fingers under her chin.

Bella straightened the cards then slapped them on the table. "Next activity, ladies."

The last round of the event was based on age. "Lead me to the gallows," Ari said to Tasia as they walked down the aisle between the horseshoes. They passed the women in their 20s, the ones in their 30s where Tasia went in and sat with all the other women in their Bible study group. Ari was a decade older than her friends with young children too. She mimicked hobbling on with a cane making Tasia and the others laugh, but she straightened up when she reached the women in their 40s horseshoe. That peculiar but intriguing woman, Deirdre was there. *She's in the wrong group—no way is she in her 40s.* Laurie and she were engaged in an animated conversation.

Ari felt out of place. Why did she always feel like an outsider? The other women in the group sat there half smiling at one another. All stuck in the purgatory of the reproductive life cycle, in between the young women in their 20s and 30s, and the older women in their 50s and 60s and beyond. Her group was the last bastion of estrogen.

Ari sipped her punch and interrupted Deirdre and Laurie's powwow. "So what's your story, Deedra?"

"It's pronounced '*Deer*-dre'," Deirdre said.

"Forgive my ignorance, '*Deer*-dre.' It's a pretty name. Where does it come from?"

"It's Celtic." Deirdre looked away.

"What's it mean?"

Deirdre looked at her. Her eyes penetrated Ari's with a darkness which seemed otherworldly. She held her gaze for a few long moments—more than was socially acceptable. "It means 'mysterious and sorrowful' or simply 'fear' in Celtic." Her voice was dark chocolate ice cream.

"I think names are important. We Greeks bestow on our children the names of saints. They make great role models."

"You are not named after a saint. 'Ares' is the Greek god of war. A great role model indeed, but it's not your given name, is it?" Deirdre touched Ari's bandaged cheek.

Ari felt a transference of energy from Deirdre's fingers. Deirdre looked into her eyes for a moment or two before she drew away. Ari touched the gauze patch.

"Your given name doesn't suit you." Deirdre folded her hands in her lap.

Deirdre and Ari were like pole repelling magnets.

Ari leaned back in her chair and crossed her legs. "My parents christened me 'Areté' because in Greek it means—"

"*Virtuous* friend." Deirdre drew out the first word to the fullest, mocking Ari.

"Wow, no one has ever known what my name means," Ari blurted out. She was offended yet oddly excited about having the attention of such a fascinating creature.

"I think Areté is a pretty name," Laurie said.

"I don't think I've earned it yet," Ari said without thinking. She took a sip of punch and wished it was a stronger concoction.

Deirdre moved her chair closer to Laurie, sidling up to her. She whispered in Laurie's ear and Laurie laughed out loud.

There was a short stack of questions on the table. Ari picked them up. "This one says: Do you speak a foreign language?" The women stared at Ari and shifted in their seats. This was clearly no Tower of Babel.

Ari said, "I wish I spoke Greek better like my parents do."

Deirdre said, "I'm fluent in Greek and in twenty-five other languages as well. It's necessary in my line of work."

"That's amazing. Which ones?" Laurie asked.

"Icelandic, Hebrew, Arabic, Navajo, Mandarin, Gaelic..." Deirdre proceeded to rattle them off like they were items on a shopping list, not difficult languages to learn.

All the women gawked at Deirdre.

"That's impressive. What exactly do you do?" Ari leaned forward.

"I'm a rare antiquities dealer." Deirdre folded her hands on her lap. Laurie folded hers.

OK, I'll play stupid for a bit to draw Deirdre out, Ari thought. "How do you find cool antiques? Do you go to a lotta yard sales?"

Deirdre eyed Ari. "No, I do not. However, occasionally I hold estate sales for wealthy families."

Ari set her own eyes on dead bolts, and stabbed a verbal fork at Deirdre. "You auction off dead people's stuff? So you're a hearse chaser then."

Deirdre cracked one of her knuckles. "I work with museums and private collectors. Families call *me*. I do not have to *chase* anyone." Her eyes were cold polished jade.

Marion announced on the mic the evening was over. The women bowed their heads and Marion said a closing prayer. "Good night, ladies. Thanks for coming. God bless you all!"

Ari and the other women stood to leave, but Deirdre and Laurie sat huddled, all snuggled together. *How chummy.*

Tasia came over and stood next to Ari. "*Páme*.*"

"*Oxi, prépei na méno ethó**,*" Ari said under her breath, pointing her eyes at Deirdre and Laurie.

"*Yiatí***?*"

Ari stood and whispered in Tasia's ear. "*Káti then paéi kála me aftín.*"

"*Ti? What?* Speak English."

"*OK. I said something's not right with that woman.*"

"Which one? Laurie or the redhead?"

"*Keep your voice down! The redhead, Deirdre.*"

"What'd she do again?"

"*Look, she's a smooth operator and she's got an agenda with Laurie. I want to learn what it is.*"

"Your writer's curiosity always gets you in trouble. Remember how you got that?"

Ari touched her cheek. "Yes."

---

*Páme- Greek for *Let's go.*

**Oxi, prépei na méno ethó.- Greek for *No, I must stay here.*

***Yiatí- Greek for *Why?*

"Be careful Ari. I can't stay, I need to put the kids in bed. I know Yiannis'll still have them all up when I get home and I have to cover Sally's route tomorrow." Tasia heaved her heavy purse onto her shoulder like a mail bag. "Text me if you uncover Deirdre's evil plot."

"Go home." Ari playfully guided her toward the door. She turned her attention to Laurie.

"Your children are how old?" Deirdre asked Laurie.

"My son, Elijah, is seven and in the second grade. He plays in three soccer leagues." Laurie beamed with pride.

"He must be a good player." Deirdre beamed back.

"Yeah, he must be," Ari interjected.

Deirdre's face tightened.

"He sure is. Last year he did summer training with the Columbus Crew."

"I've heard of them." Ari scooted her chair next to Laurie.

Deirdre narrowed her eyes at Ari.

"The Crew's coach wanted us to leave Elijah in Ohio with my parents when we told him we were moving to New Hampshire. But I couldn't leave my little boy behind. The coach was upset, so was my son."

"What about your other child?" Deirdre turned to face Laurie.

Laurie's face immediately changed into a frown. She worried a pearl on her necklace between her thumb and index finger. "Well, my daughter Amy's twelve and in the seventh grade. You know how girls at that age can be cliquish and cruel, and Amy's gotten in with the wrong crowd here."

"What about the girls in the church youth group?" Ari asked.

"Those are the girls I'm talking about. After school they want to hang out at the mall, doing God knows what. They're not studying at the café there like they say they are because Amy's grades have slipped from all A's to C's."

"You need to look in Amy's book bag the next time she comes back from the mall. I'm picking up a vibe that she might have a case of sticky fingers." Deidre played her hands in the air.

Laurie sat back in her chair. "Amy would never steal. She's still a good girl…it's just that she and I fight every day. She wasn't like this back in Ohio."

"It's puberty. She'll grow out of it," Ari said.

Deirdre patted Laurie's leg. "Let's take your mind off all that. How about dinner after church this Sunday? Does your family have a favorite restaurant?"

"No, we're new in town. Do you know anywhere good, Ari?"

"Pommes Frites is informal and fun. They're famous for their hand-cut fries."

Deirdre said, "Fine, it'll be a good place to take your kids, Laurie."

"You wanna come too, Ari?" Laurie asked.

"Sure, we'd love—"

Deirdre squeezed Laurie's knee. "Well, not to be unkind, but I wanted only *our two families* to go, Laura-lee. My husband, Samuel is coming up tomorrow and I think he and your husband, Randy would indubitably hit it off."

"How do you know my husband's name?" Laurie asked.

"You mentioned his name earlier."

"I don't remember talking about him tonight..." Laurie's eyes moved like they were reviewing an internal slideshow of the evening.

"So...*our* husbands can share a beer." Deirdre pointed her finger between herself and Laurie.

"*Randy can't drink,*" Laurie whispered.

"Well, he can have a soda. Does your husband forbid *you* from imbibing?" Deirdre asked.

"Well, no." Laurie bit her lip. "I haven't had alcohol in over *a year*. Not like he's noticed my sacrifice..."

"You *deserve* to have fun." Deirdre patted Laurie's knee again. "Let me add you to my contacts."

Ari got out her phone too. "I'll give you mine too."

"Deirdre, you don't *really mind* if Ari comes too, do you?" Laurie asked.

"Sure." Deirdre's fingers were arched into claws on her phone.

Laurie got up to leave.

"I'm so glad to meet you both!" Laurie hugged Ari, then Deirdre.

Yuck. It must be like hugging Cruella de Vil.

"It was lovely meeting *you*, Laurie." Deirdre broke away from Laurie's embrace and straightened her blouse.

Laurie left, but halfway to the door, she turned around and waved and smiled, eyes and all.

Ari waved back. Deirdre smiled and picked up her big red purse. She looked at Ari. For a second, Deirdre's eyes reminded Ari of the man at the hardware store. The hair on her arms stood up. It was the same evil—deep, ancient, and determined. Well, thank God, so was she—determined, that is.

"Deirdre, may I have your business card?"

"They're in my car."

"Maybe you could give me one on our way out. I think I'm parked next to you. The red Jaguar is yours, isn't it?"

Deirdre put on her coat. "Yes, it is."

"I'll be right out. My coat's in the hallway."

Deirdre's pumps clicked down the linoleum hallway toward the entrance.

Ari got her coat. She pushed through the heavy front doors grasping her collar against the cold wind. Her car sat alone in the parking lot. "Nice," she fumed.

She got into her car. Her face felt different. She pulled the visor mirror down and peeled off the gauze bandage. The swollen gash she should've had stitched was gone. She probed and rubbed her cheekbone with her fingers, stretching the skin tautly. She had her perfect, flawless skin back. *Just like Dorian Gray.*

CHAPTER 13

The Ashuelot Hollow Inn

Tuesday Night | November 3rd

Back at the Ashuelot Hollow Inn, Lilith stripped out of her clothes. She shoved them in a trash can, all but the Louboutins.

No amount of detergent could remove the stench from her clothes after she'd been inside a church. The body, the purse, and the pumps, all made of skin, could be sanitized. Lilith stepped into the shower and opened the jar of turmeric, lime, and sugar she always had with her. She dipped her fingers into the yellow paste and rubbed it on her face and shoulders and all the way down to her shoes. The turmeric's familiar musty aroma soothed her. She scoured the tender skin until it chafed red. She reveled in the pain. Any corporeal sensation she had while incarnate was exquisite, because as a disembodied spirit, she felt nothing. Steaming hot water washed away the yellow paste. She inhaled the yellow vapor to cleanse the lungs as well.

She got out and dried her limbs. She stuffed tissues into the pumps to keep their shape. She wiped the steam from the large bathroom mirror, and looked at the vessel she was obliged to use. Even after several millennia she did not feel at home in a human. Her own soma had been magnificent! When she gazed into the mirror she could see the aura of her true form surrounding the pathetic husk she was confined in at the moment. She moved her fingers down the pure white skin of her torso to her navel. The flames of fire began there. Oh, how she had once moved with those caressing flames over the earth, a beautiful fiery mermaid. Impossible with legs. Mankind plodded about like oxen in untilled fields.

At least this human woman had red hair much like hers had been. Lilith unwrapped the heavy wet tresses from the towel and finger-combed them while she walked to the kitchenette. She poured herself a glass of the Bushmills 21-year-old single malt Irish whiskey she always had with her. She lifted the glass to her nose. The familiar rich toffee and dark mocha notes comforted her. She sipped it by the open balcony door. The cold air made her moist reddened skin bump up, returning it to its original milky white color.

She stared out into the autumnal night and smiled, wishing she could've been there when Ari had discovered her face was all healed. She took another sip. She was drooling again, and swiped the errant saliva from her chin. *What disgusting creatures humans are.*

Lilith was antsy. She was always a bit off after being in a church. Hunting would fix that.

She shrugged on black jeans, a black cashmere sweater, and her gloves. To catch prey she'd need props. She slid the phone into her back pocket and grabbed the bottle of Bushmills, then strode down the hallway in her bare feet combing her damp hair with her fingers.

The hallway stank of all kinds of human filth. As she passed one room, she paused. She closed her eyes and inhaled. The energy in the room was lusty but intermingled with a strong scent of innocence. In Room 236 were a man, a woman, and *a male newborn*.

CHAPTER 14

Room 236

Tuesday Night | November 3rd

Lilith knocked three times on the door. The TV inside paused and she heard shuffling. A man's voice with a croak in it asked, "Yes, who'sss there?"

Good. He was drunk. "Deirdre." She saw him peer at her through the security hole. She smiled with her teeth and shook her semi-wet hair.

The man opened the door with the lock loop still attached. He rubbed his eyelids. "Are you kidding?"

Lilith raised the bottle. "I don't like to drink alone." She tossed her weight from one foot to the other. His eyes went to her breasts as they bounced unfettered under her soft sweater.

"Deirdre, huh? Damn. I can't. My wife's asleep in the next room." He pressed his lips tightly.

"Doesn't the bedroom have a door?"

"Well, of course there's a door."

"Close it. I promise she won't hear a thing."

"Hang tight."

She heard an inner door close.

The man in Room 236 fumbled with the lock latch. He opened the door grinning like a little boy with a new matchbox car. He had a slight gap in his front teeth. "I'll put a shirt on."

She eyed him over. He sucked in his stomach. She tapped on the bottle. "Bushmills 21-year-old single malt. I'll take a drop of water, if you've got it."

"Come on in," he waved her into the room.

Lilith brushed against his curly chest hair with her shoulder on the way in. "I treasure hairy men." They reminded her of Samael. The man in Room 236 tensed at her touch, like Deedee's husband, Andrew, had the first time.

"My wife says I look like a beast."

"Oh, I love those too."

CHAPTER 15

Deedee In Room 236

Tuesday Night | November 3rd

The man in Room 236 looks like Andrew: athletic and successful. Is that why Lilith targeted my husband? I remember the first time we met her, that must have been her, but she was in a man's body then. Our minds are touching now, blurring the boundary between her memories and mine of that weekend. Are we that close? I can see our first encounter through her eyes, from her vista like I'm watching a movie with the scenes spliced together. Yes, it must be Lilith because I didn't play pool with Andrew in San Diego. There he is shooting pool by himself at the Hyatt. How terrible, yet fascinating to be privy to Lilith's thoughts this way...

Lilith had walked into the hotel bar that June looking for Deedee. She'd been in a man's body since Christmas, a neo-natal surgeon's named Dr. Thomas Ludleon. *See, I was right.* Lilith had taken him over to gain access to the neo-natal intensive care unit. What a deliciously amusing playground that had been. *I don't want to see that...no...* Dr. Ludleon's body now lay tied by the legs to his yacht's anchor in the San Francisco Bay.

As 'Dr. Thom', Lilith had asked to join Andrew's game. In the course of the evening the conversation had moved to infertility treatments because Andrew and his wife, Deedee, were having trouble conceiving a second child. *Andrew, why'd you tell him that? It was a private family matter.* Deedee had been up in their hotel room minding their sleeping child, Justin, while the men played pool.

Deedee was a Celtic redhead and a rare antiquities dealer. For Lilith, bodies were simply tools to use, and men and Celtic women were best suited for her purposes. The female flesh of other races often deteriorated quickly when she inhabited them resulting in unpleasantness. Hardy Celtic women could withstand her energy when she was inside their bodies. But the Celts had become assimilated into the Irish population and it was difficult to locate a good specimen. So Lilith cultivated her own supply of suitable bodies, by promising women special powers in exchange for their babies. A child was marked at birth, then allowed to grow to maturity until the demon had a need for its vessel.

Deedee was such a child. Unbeknownst to her, her mother, a sorceress, had promised her unborn baby to Lilith, the Queen of the Night, and had baptized her with the name Deirdre Ethane Morrigan. *This is my mom's fault? I don't worship Satan. I'm a spiritual person.*

Andrew had supplied the access Lilith needed to take over Deedee.

Now Deedee's point of view took over the movie reel... *At the breakfast buffet early the next morning Andrew looked embarrassed when Dr. Thom said, "This lovely woman must be your wife, Deedee."*

Deedee flushed as he sat next to her. "Nice to meet you. Andrew told me you beat him four to three at one-pocket last night. I'm impressed. That's a rare occurrence."

"He was a formidable opponent. We played until late. I'm sorry I kept him from you and your son."

"We were fine. We watched a movie, then fell asleep afterward, didn't we, buddy?"

Justin answered with his mouth full of waffle, "Yeah, Mommy lemme get a movie in the room...an' stay up till nine!"

"That's pretty late for a five-year-old." Dr. Thom tussled Justin's blond head. Deedee cringed.

Deedee motioned for her son to not talk with his mouth full. "Yes, unfortunately we spoil him because he's the only one we've got." She glanced at her husband.

"This is for you, my dear." Dr. Thom handed her a tiny box.

She opened it. "Oh...It's a Fumsup! doll charm from the Great War. I've never seen one in such excellent condition."

"This one is 15-carat gold, from 1916, an original piece made by the jeweler who invented them—" Dr. Thom wiped a bit of saliva from the corner of his smiling mouth.

"—J.C. Vickery. Oh look, how cute! It has pink gemstones for eyes."

"Those are sapphires...they're pink for a reason."

"Then this is rare and expensive, Dr. Ludleon, I can't accept—"

"Please call me Dr. Thom. I think you will appreciate its value in more ways than one. It will help you conceive a baby girl."

Deedee couldn't speak.

"May I see it?" Andrew took the one-inch high doll and raised its moveable arms up and down. "See Deedee? It's giving us the thumbs up to try again."

Dr. Thom handed Deedee a little folded piece of paper. "This charm has a 100% success rate, but you and your husband must follow these instructions exactly for it to work. Call me if you have any questions. Here's my card. I must go. I've got a procedure scheduled this morning. Let me know when the charm works. I want to add your success to my results."

In Deedee's analytical mind the pieces fell together, but it was her heart that reacted, clenching itself hard in her chest. Her hands went to her belly. *Oh, God...I did this to myself.*

"Yes, you did," Lilith said.

CHAPTER 16

Baby's Breath

Tuesday Night | November 3rd

The man in Room 236 was talking. The first action she always took was to silence them.

Lilith returned to the present from the mutual memory with Deedee. "What did you say?"

"I asked you how you take your whiskey." He pointed to her glass.

"Neat, with one drop of water."

"Well, we have that in common." He sat on the couch and polished off his drink. "Aah...fill 'er up, gorgeous." He handed her the glass.

She poured him a full glass of her Bushmills. "I'll put a drop of water in this for you."

The man watched her walk to the darkened kitchenette. Lilith ran her hand along the door to the adjoining room. She deeply inhaled, "... *an eight-day-old baby boy*," and licked her lips. *I'm just in time.* That thing on the couch interrupted her reverie again. "What is it?" she asked harshly. She controlled the pressure of her fingers to not break the glass. "What did you say?" she asked tempering her tone.

"Like was saying...I like being waited on. My wife never does that. God, you're hot...Deedee. Can I call you Deedee?"

Lilith's shoulders tensed up. She turned on the faucet but didn't add tap water to his drink. She spat in it.

She walked back to the man, stirring the drink with her index finger. "My name is Deirdre." She handed him the glass and licked her finger.

He sipped his drink. "This is the good stuff." He surveyed her body. He made no attempt to hide his interest from her. He was arrogant as Adam. "What's with the gloves?"

"I have sensitive sk—" Her phone rang. She pulled it out of her back pocket. It was Samael. "I have to take this."

She spoke to him in Gaelic. "I need you in New Hampshire tomorrow."

"Brilliant. The want of you pains me," Samael said in his Received Pronunciation British accent.

"I'm not alone."

"Who's—"

"I don't have time for your jealousy, husband. Are you still in New York?"

"Of course."

"Drive up here tonight. The Ashuelot Hollow Inn, Suite 254. I have need of you." She hung up.

The man's shoulders drooped. "What language was that?"

"Gaelic."

"That explains the Irish whiskey. Was that your husband?"

"Yes. He wasn't alone either. We have an open marriage."

"In that case," he leaned back on his elbows and patted the couch, "come over and sit with me or on me, whichever you prefer—babe."

Lilith drained her glass, walked over, and set it down hard on the night table next to him. "No man commands me, *b'nay'adam*." Her voice rose as she spoke.

"Hey, keep it down or my wife'll hear us." His eyes darted to the closed door between the two rooms.

"Your eight-day-old son might wake up."

"How...how do you know how old he is? I never s—"

"I'm a psychic, and newborns have strong auras, but that blue baby blanket over there did help." She pointed at the crocheted blanket draped over the armchair.

The man's nervous laugh changed into a mocking one. "Oh, I get it. How much are you gonna charge me per minute?"

Lilith removed her gloves, finger by finger.

"Time to take the gloves off?"

She slapped him hard across the face with the gloves.

He held his reddening cheek. He set his glass on the night table. His eyes were flint. "So you wanna play rough, huh?" He lunged at her.

She pushed him onto the couch and crammed a glove into his mouth. The man in Room 236 thrashed under her. He was no match for her superhuman strength. His eyes were wide open like those of snared prey.

"Oh, you're not laughing anymore? You could have called a psychic hotline. They would have told you I was coming. We're plugged into the same network."

He pleaded.

"If you think I came here for you, you are mistaken." She kicked the lamp on the side table to the floor. The room went black.

Lilith worked quickly on the man in Room 236, unhindered by the familiar cloak of darkness in the room. She got off the couch and took the glove out of his mouth—he was quiet now—and folded it and its mate into her back jean pocket. Her *raison d'être* was in the bedroom and she wanted to savor every moment of it with her bare hands.

She walked over to the adjoining door and placed her fingertips on the doorknob. She gently turned it and pushed. The air which had been sealed in for several hours, rolled in a delicious aroma of mother's milk and baby's breath over her. Lilith inhaled deeply into her borrowed lungs and held it there. She felt alive. This was why she endured humans. To do this. *To them.*

The man in room 236's wife and baby son were asleep. The baby was next to the bed in a portable crib. The mother was quietly snoring with her back turned to her infant. Lilith went to the baby. She peered down at him. His pacifier had fallen from his mouth. She slipped it in her pocket then picked a pillow off the bed.

CHAPTER 17

Samael

Early Wednesday Morning | November 4th

Samael maneuvered around the four police cars, fire engine, and two ambulances surrounding the front entrance of the Ashuelot Hollow Inn. At 6 AM they lit it up like an electronic dance music festival.

Samael strode into the lobby. A drama was playing out which he had seen innumerable times: police officers surrounded a woman who was renting her clothes and wailing over the loss of her firstborn son. The distraught mother cycled between lamenting "Why my baby?" to screaming, "I will never forgive you for this!" to a schmuck standing next to her in his robe and boxer shorts who kept saying, "I'm so sorry…honey, I don't know why I…I fell asleep on the couch." That was the father.

Paramedics held bandages and antiseptic. They huddled around the father. "Sir, we need to stop the bleeding on those...those wounds on your chest. Please. You've lost a lot of blood." One paramedic whispered to the other, *"Look at those gashes. What could do that? It looks like a wild animal attacked him."*

Samael raised an eyebrow. He knew *who* could do that.

A stern policewoman stopped Samael. "Excuse me, sir. You can't go upstairs now. We're conducting a search of the building."

"I have a breakfast meeting." Samael smiled with alabaster teeth.

"May I have the room number and name of your colleague?" The police officer tapped her pen on her clipboard.

Samael was unused to being questioned. His smile was all he ever needed to gain access anywhere. The body he was in now had ocean blue eyes and thick black Superman hair. Its superlative handsomeness had disarmed every woman before this one.

"Your inquiries bore me, officer." Samael waved his hand in front of the policewoman's face; it went blank and she dropped her pen. He went upstairs unhindered.

Lilith let Samael into Suite 254. The curtains were open to the pre-dawning sun; it had an eerie twilight effect on the room. She was as radiant as ever in her new body with the full head of cascading red hair and in a scarlet satin robe—her favorite color. The robe was untied. He was instantly enslaved.

She chuckled. "Husband, I appreciate your sense of humor in acquiring this body. Nice touch." She kissed him on the mouth, biting his bottom lip before she broke away. "And you kiss better than he did."

"I do everything better than he did, darling." Like a simmering pot on the stove, Samael's jealousy for Lilith was always right under the surface of whoever's skin he was in.

One could not detect the evil residing in Samael, judging by his impeccable outward appearance. He preferred to take over the bodies of athletic men in their early forties. He liked the maturity of their faces and the earned virility of their bodies. His vanity was apparent in his manicured nails and in the custom-tailored suits he always wore—unless he was sailing, or playing polo, or any other sport he excelled at.

"What did you do with the little boy?" she asked.

"Grandma," he said.

"We haven't done this in a long time. The irony is delicious."

"Look at all the work he's put into this body." He lifted his shirt.

She ran her fingertips down one side of his three tight abdominals, twirled her index finger in his navel, and up the other side. "Yes, I remember these."

Samael jerked down his shirt. Lilith always knew how to heat his jealousy into a full rolling boil.

"Are you hungry?" She led him by the hand to a cart near the bed.

"I'm ravenous." He grasped her forearm.

"Food first." She pulled away and sat next to the cart.

"As long as I get both."

He sat on the edge of the bed. She hand fed him pieces of fresh fruit and bites of chocolate crepes filled with cream.

"My fiery one, this body is unsurpassed in its resemblance to your true form. I am eager to revel in it." He licked the sweet cream from her fingers.

She fed him a ripe strawberry. "Put the 'Do Not Disturb' sign on the door."

CHAPTER 18

Friend Potential

Saturday Afternoon | November 7th

Ari sat bolt upright on the couch, her hand on her pounding heart. She wiped the drool from her cheek. In her dream had been the creepy pickup truck guy again. He'd grabbed her, but she couldn't free herself from his grip, couldn't pull away, like when you can't run in a dream.

The nightmare was bad and worsening. For two nights in a row she'd woken up at precisely 3 AM flailing her arms and kicking Hector. He'd held her and comforted her, but she couldn't go back to sleep. She'd conked out on the couch in the middle of the afternoon.

This time Laurie and Deirdre had been in the dream too. Ari could see both of them grinning while the creep assaulted her.

She had to call Laurie right now.

Laurie answered the phone. "Hi. Did you butt dial me?"

"No…it's Ari Apostollis. Laurie is that you?"

"Yeah, this is her. Sorry, I thought you were somebody else."

Ari silently corrected her poor grammar. *This is she.* "It's me, Ari, from last Tuesday night at the Interfaith event at the church. I just wanted to say hi."

"Hi."

"How've you been?"

"Good."

Well. There was silence on the phone for a few moments.

"OK…So, are we still on for lunch at Pommes Frites tomorrow after church?"

"I guess so. In fact I just got off the phone with Deirdre and she asked me the same thing."

"She just called?"

"Yeah, I thought you were her."

A chill rippled through Ari's body at the synchronicity of the nightmare and Deirdre's phone call.

"Ari, are you still there?"

"Uh yes, I'm here. Sorry, I zoned out for a second. You said Deirdre's coming?"

"Yes, she is. So I guess you can come too. To be honest, I've been having second thoughts all week about going. Deirdre just convinced me to go."

"I'm glad. Come on, it'll be fun to rub elbows with the rich and famous…at Pommes Frites."

Laurie chuckled. "You're right. I'm stuck here all the time. My husband has to work the night shift *again* tonight."

"Well, I'm home alone too with the kids because Hector's playing soccer with his buddies. Some Saturday night, eh?"

"Yeah, it sucks."

"Say…you wanna come over?"

"Nah. The kids are crabby…I'm in my sweats."

"Just come as you are, and bring your crabby kids."

"Oh, I dunno…"

"Oh, it'll be fun. You said the other night that popcorn was your favorite snack. I'll make red kernel Amish popcorn *from Ohio* for the kids, and you and I can have grown up food. I baked bread today and that would go great with brie and a glass of Cabernet Sauvignon or Chardonnay. Whatever you like."

"Geez, that sounds good. I haven't had a glass of wine in forever. OK, we'll be there in a half hour."

"Wonderful. I'll text you my address. See you in a bit, God willing."

* * *

Laurie hung up. "God willing?" *That was a weird thing to say—like I might die on the way there or something*. She called from the bottom of the stairs to the kids up in their rooms to get ready to leave.

Amy yelled from her bedroom, "Where're we going, Mom?"

"To Ari's house."

"Where?"

"Come down here so I can talk to you."

Amy stood at the top of the stairs. "Who's *Ari?*"

"A woman I met at that church event I went to on Tuesday night."

"Great. A *church lady*. I'm not going." Amy started back to her room.

"Amy, please. I can't leave you and Elijah alone at night—you know that. Com' on, honey I finally got invited somewhere…"

"I'm in my pajamas."

"Ari said you could 'come as you are', so you're fine."

"How magnanimous of her. Does she have any kids my age?"

"She has a five-year-old daughter."

"Oh *great*. You want me to babysit *two* brats."

Elijah passed his sister on the stairs. "I'm not a brat. Wait, Mommy, did you say a girl and a kindergartner? I'm gonna bring my Switch."

"At least she's only two years younger than you, Elijah. What am *I* supposed to do over there?" Amy said.

"Amy, bring that book you're reading. Ari said she made the best Amish popcorn…"

"Amish popcorn! Com' on, Sis, Mommy's right. We never get invited anywhere."

"Fine, I'll go, but I don't have to be pleasant." Amy shoved her brother away.

"When are you lately?" Laurie asked under her breath and grabbed her purse.

* * *

Laurie pulled her Jeep Compass into Ari's driveway. 72 Chestnut Circle was what it sounded like—a cheery yellow Dutch colonial on a cul-de-sac lined with chestnut trees.

The sun was setting behind the mountains, and in place of its warmth, the autumn chill gathered up the reins and drove all the day creatures of the valley to their homes. Laurie urged her children out of the SUV. The street was still. She felt she was breaking curfew.

Ari opened the front door as widely as it would go, "Hello! Come on in."

Laurie handed her a bag of apples. "I had these. They're local."

"Thanks. They'll go great with the brie."

The Locke's took off their shoes because Ari offered each of them an appropriate pair of slippers, then invited them into the tidy family room. A cozy fire was lit.

"Amy, you may hang out in the den upstairs if you like and watch a DVD or read, *away from the little kids*," Ari whispered behind her hand.

"Thanks Ari, I always bring a book with me when I think I'll be bored—" Amy tossed a glance at her mother, "I mean, when I have free time."

"I prefer young people call me Mrs. Ari, OK?"

"Uh, sorry." Amy widened her eyes, but kept her face a mask. When Ari bent to line up the shoes, Amy whispered to her mother, *"See? She's the 'church lady'."* Laurie shushed her.

Ari stood and looked between Laurie and Amy. "So…I'll bring you up a bowl of hot buttered popcorn and a soda. Sound good?"

"Sure." Amy trudged upstairs.

Elijah stood beside his mother shifting from one foot to the other.

Ari said, "Well, Elijah you can play with Doro—" Dorothea bounded into the room and jumped right in front of Elijah.

"Hi! Do you wanna play with my new castle? It's got knights n' horses and a draw bridge." She beamed at Elijah.

He looked at her like he wasn't sure he wanted to play with a girl, much less a five-year-old. "Where is it?"

"Come see." Dorothea dragged him into her room where a four-foot-high castle stood. It was magnificent.

"Wow," was all Elijah could say.

Ari served all the kids popcorn and soda. She found Laurie by the fireplace warming herself. She brought out a silver tray with two crystal wine goblets, a full bottle of Cabernet Sauvignon, a plate of brie, apple slices, and bread. "OK, the kids are all set. Now you and I can sit in here and have a glass of wine, *in peace*."

"That sounds great," Laurie said.

She poured Laurie a generous glass. Laurie took it from her like a child who was afraid she might drop it, gripping the stem in her fist. Ari poured a glass for herself saying under her breath, *"I've never seen anyone hold a wine glass like that."*

Each woman took a long sip and in unison said, "Ah, that's good." They laughed and there was silence for a few awkward moments.

Ari never bothered with small talk. "So, what's your story?"

Laurie stopped with the glass still pressed to her bottom lip. "What do you mean?"

"What's going on in your life?"

"Oh, well not much anymore. Back in Dublin, Ohio I used to work at a gym as a fitness trainer. I taught Pilates and yoga. Now I'm just a flabby housewife."

"You're far from flabby Laurie," Ari said truthfully.

Laurie grabbed the roll of fat which had bunched up at her waist and jiggled it. "I didn't used to have this. Randy teases me about it."

"What's he do?"

"He's a New Hampshire state trooper." Laurie dropped it neutrally like she always did and waited for Ari's response. It could go one of two ways: either Ari would think it was thrilling to be a trooper's wife (potential friend then) or terrifying to be married to a man in constant peril (no chance of hitting it off.)

"Oh, that's wicked cool," Ari said.

Friend potential! Laurie sat a little straighter.

"Does Randy know that state trooper who fell into the river last week?"

Laurie slumped back into the pillows on the couch. *This is gonna ruin it now.* "Actually...ah...he was that trooper..."

"Wow...I cut that one out of the newspaper. It's a miracle he's still alive."

"He's still pretty banged up from it."

"I hope you don't mind talking about this. It'd be exciting to be married to a state trooper. My husband's a mechanical engineer." Ari faked a yawn.

Well, maybe this isn't going south. "It's not boring, that's for sure."

"Have they found his cruiser yet?" Ari hunkered down.

"Yeah, they did. It was swept down river half a mile. They've been combing through it to try and find out what happened that night because Randy blacked out."

"Have they found anything?"

"No, not much. It doesn't look good for him that he climbed out of the back window with only—I shouldn't be telling you this. Randy told me not to say anything."

"I promise I won't tell a soul. I'm a writer…I love this kind of stuff."

"You're not gonna *write* about this, are you?"

"Of course not. But I do have insatiable curiosity."

"You swear you won't tell anyone?"

"I'm like the grave, don't worry."

"Okay, that's good enough. I'm relieved to have someone to talk to, the kids don't know, and I didn't even tell my mom. She's already pissed at Randy for getting transferred here."

"I'll bet she just misses all of you. So…what happened?"

"Randy cut himself on the broken glass, right here. Because he climbed out with only…oh…" Laurie held her glass in both hands now.

"With only…?" Ari leaned in.

Laurie blurted it out, "With only his socks on."

"What? *That* wasn't in the paper. It's amazing he didn't freeze to death. Speaking of freezing…" She got up to add a log to the fire.

Laurie took a long sip and put her glass down. She ran her fingers through her pearl necklace. *Should I tell Ari about the symmetrical claw marks on his chest too? Maybe she could help me figure out what to make of them.* Tears welled in her eyes. *No. What would she think when she meets him tomorrow?*

"Was there anything else weird about that night?"

"I need to use your bathroom." Laurie stood facing away from Ari.

"Down the hall to your right."

Laurie came back a few minutes later, longer than a normal bathroom break should have lasted. "You all right?" Ari asked.

"I'm okay. I'm just tired of being in limbo. I wish someone would tell me what to do." Laurie slumped onto the couch.

"Eat. You'll feel better. Try the brie while it's still warm and gooey." Ari offered her a plate.

"Thanks." Laurie ate. She finished her wine. The warming Cabernet, food, and the toasty fire were having their intended effect on her. Her shoulders relaxed.

Ari filled Laurie's glass half full. "I have to ask: had Randy been drinking that night?"

"No, thank God. They tested him of course. It's still hard for me to accept that my husband has a drinking problem."

"Oh."

"He didn't always. Right before Christmas last year his father was killed in a car accident on the I-270 Columbus outer belt. Randy was the first state trooper at the scene."

"That's horrible! Your poor husband." Ari sat and hugged a pillow.

"They had to use a *backhoe* to extract his father's body from the wreckage." Laurie pressed her knees together.

"How does anybody cope with such a tragedy?"
"Apparently with booze and there was…a woman."

"Oh no."

"I can't believe I'm telling you all this. You're such a good listener. Look, Randy says that this woman seduced him in Cincinnati and it was only a one-night stand…that 'it didn't mean anything,' but I'm still hurt."

"Of course you are. Has he been faithful since you moved here?"

"I think so."

"That's good. Hopefully his drinking problem *and* his woman problem were both temporary. Perhaps they were his way of dealing with the sudden loss of his father."

"I hope you're right, because I was ready to leave him last year. I'm sticking it out for the sake of the kids."

Ari sat on her haunches. "My parents are divorced and I never want my child to go through that."

"Mine are too. I never want my kids to go through that either."

"I think it's easier to deal with a death in the family than a divorce. At least you bury the dead and move on. A divorce is like a zombie rotting on the dining room table. It lies there staring at you with glassy eyes, an unwelcome guest at every holiday, birthday party, graduation, wedding, birth, baptism, and funeral. Its stench permeates everything, reminding you of the past when your family was whole."

"And safe. Certain relatives shouldn't be trusted any more than a zombie should be." Laurie pulled at her necklace again. She saw Ari's eyes register that she had understood the real meaning of her comment, then look like she was filing it away in her brain. *I've said too much. Can I trust her? I want a friend so bad.*

Ari sat back on the couch. "I think we've crossed paths for a reason."

"Me too." Laurie smiled at her with her whole face.

Ari smiled at her in kind. "I appreciate your candor. You know, there was a time when I was angry with my husband too."

"Well, I don't get mad too often." *Yeah right—remember raking a hole in the backyard?*

"Well, I was *crazy mad* when I couldn't get pregnant. The doctors said it was Hector's 'fault' because he worked around machines that radiated his, you know..." She pointed down there. "Anyway, I was furious he hadn't protected himself and he'd taken away our dream of having a baby."

Laurie shook her head. "Oh, you poor thing."

"I was. I became a thing obsessed with pregnant women. They seemed to roam the planet like locusts—they were *everywhere*. When I saw one, my heart would harden and I'd rail against God for His injustice. Moms with three, four, maybe five kids. It wasn't fair. I'd fantasize about borrowing one of their virile husbands for a night, not in a sexual way, more in a *The Big Chill* way."

"I loved that movie."

"Me too. I'm telling you all this because my marriage is far from perfect."

"I have to ask. You have little Dorothea now. How'd you finally get pregnant?"

"I had in vitro fertilization four times. Dorothea's name means 'a gift from God.'"

"Wow. What a story..." Laurie swallowed the little pool of wine that was left in her glass.

Ari got up and stoked the fire again. "What we say here, stays here. Deal?"

"Deal. I do miss talking with my girlfriends. Guys just aren't the same, are they? When I try to tell Randy how I feel, he suggests I go work out or call my mom."

"Mine's an engineer, so he wants to fix me instead of listening to me. It drives me nuts. Like this book he gave me before I got pregnant." Ari handed a book from the shelf to Laurie.

"*The Love Dare*?" Laurie flipped through the pages of the well-worn book.

"Yeah, it 'dares' you to love your spouse again."

"Hmm..."

"I know it sounds weird, but it worked. I learned how to love Hector even when I didn't like him. Love's not a feeling or pheromones, it's a verb, an active verb. I did the exercises in it, but you may borrow it if you want."

"Thanks." Laurie tossed the book on top of her purse on the floor. "I'm tired of talking about my problems."

"What did you think about the Women's Interfaith Event on Tuesday?"

"It was nice meeting so many friendly women, especially Deirdre."

"I thought Deirdre came on a little strong. Had you met her before?"

"No, that was the first time. What was she doing there anyway? She must be rich and she speaks like a million different languages—I guess I should be flattered she wants to be my friend."

A spark flew out of the fireplace and landed on the carpet. "Oh!" Ari jumped up and picked it up with her fingers and flung it back in.

"Did you burn yourself?" Laurie stood.

"Nah, I play with fire all the time, just ask Hector." Ari laughed it off. "So tomorrow, lunch at Pommes Frites after church, right? Ours ends at 11:30."

"Sounds good. Now we really have to scoot. It's way past the kids' bedtime." Laurie got off the couch.

They all went to the front entryway and said their thank-yous and goodbyes. Amy brushed past her mother to go upstairs.

"Where are you going?" Laurie shot Amy a look.

"Forgot my book."

Laurie hugged Ari knocking her glasses askew as Amy passed behind them. "Sorry." She ushered her children out the door.

Ari waved. She went inside and squatted next to the fire. She pushed the orange coals around with the poker. "What fire am I playing with now?"

CHAPTER 19

Amy

Saturday Night | November 7th

As soon as the Jeep pulled into the garage Amy bounded into the house. She tripped on the top step and landed face first on the kitchen floor.

Laurie found her on her hands and knees scooping fine white powder off the terracotta into a round box. "Where'd you get that?"

Amy glowered on the floor clutching the Lady Esther face powder box in her hands.

Elijah slipped between the two females on the way to his bedroom. "'Night, Mom."

"I'll be up in a minute, 'Jah. Amy, did you take that from Ari's house?"

Silence.

"Well?"

More silence.

"Deirdre told me to watch out for your 'sticky fingers' and I said you'd never steal. I said you were a 'good girl.' Dammit Amy." Laurie flexed her fingers.

"Who cares? What about how I feel?"

"Fine. How do you feel, you little thief?"

"Like a prisoner! You don't let me go to the mall with my friends anymore and that's all there is to do in this stupid town. I miss Ohio. And yeah, when you finally let me out of solitary confinement, you take me to a stranger's house, then forget about me for two hours. *Excuse me*, for getting bored."

"Well, *excuse me* for having a good time for once. I thought you'd be happy reading and eating popcorn, and I—"

"You don't think about me at all, anymore, Mom. I miss Grandma, she always had time for me."

"I know, I miss her too…"

Amy could hear the break in her mother's voice. She didn't dare push any further. Her mom might start crying again, then spiral downward into another depression that could last for weeks. Amy recited her mantra, *'that perfect girl is gone.' Mom, you made her leave.*

Right after Amy's grandfather died in the car wreck, *Frozen* was released on DVD. It was the only present she got that Christmas. She played it every afternoon to fill the lonely house with happy voices after her mother, still in her pajamas, had gone back to bed after picking her and Elijah up from school. Elsa and Anna kept her company all those long hours she was left to fend for herself and her little brother while their mother was checked out upstairs.

Amy's English teacher at her new school had suggested she read the fairy tale her favorite movie was based on: *The Snow Queen*. In it Amy found a way not to be weak like her mother—she had willed a bit of glass from the wicked hobgoblin's mirror into her heart to keep it hard like a chunk of ice. It didn't always work. Like right now. *I love you mom. I want you back the way you were.*

Her mother held her hand out. "Amy, I said give it to me."

Amy scooted on her bum to the oven door and hid the box behind her back. "Please let me keep it. It's like Grandma's."

Laurie's voice softened a little. "Look, I know how much you miss Grandma, but it's not yours."

Amy's bottom lip trembled. "Did you hear *anything* I said?" *Don't cry, don't cry, don't—*

"I did, but I still need to do my job as your mom."

Tears brimmed in Amy's eyes. She wiped them away. *Stop it. Don't be like her.* "What would you know about being a mom? You're the worst mother in the whole world!"

She got up to run, but Laurie caught her arm. "Amy, honey..."

Amy shoved the box into her mother's chest. "Here, take it." The tears spilled over her bottom eyelids. "You don't care about us. No wonder Daddy's gone all the time." She ran to the stairs. Midway up she turned around and shouted, "I hate you!" and slammed the door to her bedroom. Alone now, Amy wanted comfort from the same person who had hurt her. *I want my Mommy.* She fell on her bed crying and hugging her big Raggedy Ann doll.

CHAPTER 20

Fireball

Saturday Night | November 7th

"I hate me too," Laurie said after her daughter. She walked into the living room and flumped into her favorite armchair. She cradled the Lady Esther box in her lap. She took out the powder puff. Childhood memories of good times with her mother sprang to life one after the other in a slideshow in her mind. Laurie placed the puff back into the box and slid on the circular lid. *Mom, I'm turning into you. I'm not there for Amy like you weren't there for me when—*.

Her hopelessness grew with each breath, all the raw flailing emotions twisted into a tightly-braided whip of self-loathing. "God, what have I done to deserve this?" She shook her fist at the ceiling. "*Damn me*... and *damn You* for bringing me to this stupid town." She threw the box at the stone fireplace. Powder blew all over the hearth. A whirlpool of tears welled in her throat. "I can't do this anymore." She hung her head between her knees; sobbing, sniffing, succumbing.

After a while Laurie couldn't breathe through all the mucus. She went upstairs to the master bathroom to blow her nose and put on her pajamas. She saw her red swollen face in the mirror. "Girl, look at you." On the counter was her bottle of Valium. Her eye was drawn to the Jacuzzi in the corner. It lingered there forming a dreadful, final self-portrait. *What if your kids found you like that?* She scowled at her reflection. "You coward. You can't do that to them." She roughly flipped the light switch off. She wanted to forget, to be numb.

She walked past Amy's bedroom. The door was closed. She put her ear to it. The room was quiet. Elijah lightly snored down the hall. *Good. I can't be anybody's mother right now.*

Laurie went downstairs to the kitchen and rummaged around for the bottle of Fireball she hid behind the oatmeal that nobody ate. She filled a crystal highball glass with ice. Ari's book was on the kitchen table; she took it, the glass, and the full bottle of cinnamon whisky into the living room setting it all on the end table.

She pulled out the Peter Cetera CD, selected the song she wanted, and sat in her armchair. The old CD crackled a little as the song played. She poured the Fireball into the glass and drank. It seared down her throat. She welcomed the burn.

Laurie sang about the glory of love to the dancing devil on the Fireball label. She took another sip.

Everything Amy said is true. She closed her eyes and pictured Amy as a little girl doing yoga on her little mat, playing with fireflies, making up songs which always started with 'I love my mommy, oh yes I do…'

Laurie choked back the tears and picked up *The Love Dare*. She flipped through it. A few pages had smiley faces drawn on them. *I hate your happiness, Ari.* She closed the book and set it on the table. She drained the glass holding the ice back with her teeth, swallowed, and filled it again. She took a long sip and held the cold crystal in her lap.

The tears threatened to overtake her again. She walked over to the fireplace and picked up the powder box. She set the box on the mantle next to her 8x10 wedding photo. She touched Randy's younger face; ran her finger across the ornate frame looking wistfully at her wedding dress. "You were my knight in shining armor." She sang their wedding song, her voice choking in her throat.

Laurie took the photo back to the armchair. She hugged it and closed her eyes.

CHAPTER 21

The Glory of Love

Saturday, 11:57 PM | November 7th

Randy Locke came home around midnight and laid his newly-issued state trooper's hat on the kitchen table. A light was on in the living room. He stalked, like the protective house wolf he was, around the corner. He relaxed when he saw Laurie asleep in her armchair. A highball glass sweated on the table beside her. The stereo was on. He ejected the CD. *The Glory of Love*. The song they'd danced to at their wedding.

He noticed the intense powdery mother-in-law smell in the room. *Damn, is her mom here?* He saw the ivory dust all over the fireplace. *What the hell happened?*

Randy walked over to his wife. She held their wedding photo. His belly fluttered. *What's this?* He picked up *The Love Dare* and flipped through its pages. Two guys at church had talked about how taking the 'love dare' had saved their marriages. He had considered buying the book and secretly doing the exercises. Now here it was. A light-hearted feeling spread to his tingling limbs. Next to the book was a bottle of Fireball. He lifted the highball glass and sniffed it.

Several drops of condensation slid off the glass and landed onto Laurie's hand. She jolted awake and saw her husband with the glass near his lips. "What're you doing?"

"I wanted to see what you and the devil've been up to. How many of these did you have?"

Laurie peered at him. "Enough to forget what a bastard I married." She stood and snatched the glass out of his hand, but fell back into the chair. Whisky sloshed onto her blouse.

"Whoa, take it easy there. Let's get you up." He tried to lift her by the elbow, but she sluggishly shrugged him off.

"Don't talk to me like I'm a perp." She pushed herself up with the arm of the chair. "See? I'm fine."

"What brought this on?" he said to her back as she shuffled to the kitchen.

"We all went over to Ari's tonight and now Amy hates me. So now you both hate me."

"I don't hate you, hon. Who's Ari?"

"Yes, you do. You're never home. Because I'm horrible...I'm a horrible mother, a horrible wife." She stopped and leaned against the wall in the hallway.

He stepped in front of her. "Hon, stop it. You're not horrible, however, you are intoxicated. Let me take you upstairs to bed so you can sleep it off."

"Just leave me alone." She pushed past him to the kitchen.

"Who the hell is Ari?" He watched her walk down the hallway.

She didn't answer him.

Lately he was used to being ignored. It hurt him more than she knew, but he never showed it. Even though Laurie rarely said "I love you" to anyone, not even to their children, she showed deep affection for those she loved by taking care of them. He used to find little notes and dinner covered up waiting for him on the counter. That was before his dad died. Before the black time. Now she could barely stand to be around him, much alone feed him. Sustain him. Support him. He didn't have the right to expect anything from her—he knew that, but he was tired of being sorry. *It's been over a year. When will you forgive me?*

He walked into the kitchen. She was washing the highball glass. She was beautiful, as usual, even with the extra weight. It pained him not to be able to come behind her and caress her hips and move along her curves. She used to respond by pressing back into him. Now when he tried, all she did was stand still and wait for him to stop touching her like he was her dirty uncle. It was humiliating. It had taken them years to work through what that scumbag had done to her.

Randy still didn't understand how he had cheated with that brunette in Cincinnati. How could he have done that to the woman he loved? He didn't remember the act at all. But there was evidence all right. The brunette had taken a video of their coupling with her cell phone. She'd shown it to him after he'd woken up broken in a strange hotel room he didn't remember entering, with a red silk scarf tied around his neck. He violently rolled his shoulders as if his uniform was suddenly crawling with ants.

After he'd told Laurie about Cincinnati, she'd closed herself to him, body and soul. All they'd had since was one time when she'd lain there unmoving and hadn't looked at his face. He'd felt like a john.

He leaned over Laurie and smelled the top of her head. He breathed in her hair's scent. It was dirty enough to smell like her but still clean enough to look good. He loved that. She held the crystal in her hands, the water running over it. He put his hands on her hips and she tensed a little when he ran them lightly along her body to her elbow, then up to her shoulders. He pushed her hair out of the way and breathed her in again. She set the glass in the granite sink like she was afraid it would break. "I miss you, Laurie," he whispered into her ear, into her hair, into her neck. "I miss you...I miss us...I miss everything."

She said, "Maybe you should stop..." her voice catching in her throat.

"Hon, remember how good we were together? I need you. We need to be one again." She was letting him in. He pressed himself against her. She pushed back into him. He took the chance, "I love you, Laurie."

She shut the water off and turned around to face him. She touched the gauze bandage above his eye that covered the stitches there. Did he see compassion in her eyes? Yes, and passion. Her face was flushed, and in her eyes he saw a glimpse of her old love for him.

Whiskey lingered on her breath. Would one drop, one vapor of it in his mouth knock him off the wagon? He didn't care. He put his strong hands behind her head, in her hair, and pulled her face to him. She surrendered to his kiss.

CHAPTER 22

Pommes Frites

Sunday Afternoon | November 8th | Synaxis of the Holy Archangels Michael and Gabriel

Lilith and Samael knew they had found the right place when they were within twenty meters of it. The air outside Pommes Frites hung heavy with grease. They stood on the sidewalk a moment.

"I cannot eat in this foul place." Lilith squinched up her nose.

"Keep your eye on the prize, darling. Now take a deep breath." Samael opened the front door for his wife.

Lilith stepped inside. It was loud. The noise came from several troops of human apes having lunch. They would put her prey at ease, so she would endure the katzenjammer and the kids.

They were early. They'd left church after the worship team's rock concert.

Lilith had texted Laurie:

I'll meet you at Pommes Frites

Lilith stopped a passing waitress, "Where is the reserved table for the Morrigan party?"

"Over there." The girl pointed to a long table in the corner cloaked on three sides by red curtains.

"Come with me, girl." Lilith walked to the alcove. She swiped the table with her finger. "Clean this filth now."

The girl picked up the *Reserved* sign, sprayed disinfectant on the table in an angry arc, and ran the cloth vigorously over the table.

"The chairs too," Lilith said.

The girl wiped them and slapped the last chair with the rag.

Lilith checked her seat. "That will do." The girl huffed off.

"Samael, bring me a strong dark ale."

"Of course." Samael kissed the back of her hand.

Lilith sat and got out her cell phone to play her favorite word game.

The front door opened and she looked to see who it was. Ari, a man, and a little girl were scanning the tavern. Lilith went back to playing the game.

Hector held the door of Pommes Frites for Ari and Dorothea. Yiayiá's prayer rope shuddered in Ari's jacket. She shoved her hand in her pocket. Deirdre was in the back. "Deirdre?"

Deirdre didn't look up from her phone.

"Hi. So—"

"Yes! Triple word and triple letter 'j' for 'judge'. You lose again, Naamah 48."

Ari held the rope in her palm. "Excuse me, Deirdre." She finally looked up. "Hi. Is this the table you reserved for all *nine of us?*" Ari tried to hide her annoyance. She wasn't good at it.

"You weren't invited."

"Laurie told me again last night that she wanted me to come. I had her and the kids over to my house." Ari ran her finger along the back of the chair and examined the seat. "Wow, this is the cleanest I've ever seen this place. I usually have to wipe everything with a handy wipe." She draped her coat over the chair opposite Deirdre.

"I had the girl do it."

"That was nice of you, but we're going to need a little more room." Ari shoved the red side curtain to the back.

"You saw Laurie yesterday?" Deirdre touched her lip.

Ari noticed her mouth twitch. "Yes, we really hit it off." She flagged down the waitress. "Excuse me, Miss. We need another table over here. May I take this one?" She was already dragging the extra table against the longer one. "Agápe mou, help me with these chairs," she said to Hector.

"Please make yourselves comfortable," Deirdre said, her top teeth poised on the bottom ones. Ari situated Dorothea at the far end.

While Ari was arranging a sketch pad and crayons in front of her daughter, Deirdre stood and extended her bare hand to Hector. "Ari, this fine Mediterranean speci*man* must be your husband."

Ari said, "Uh-huh." She was in 'mother mode' and not listening.

Hector looked at his wife then back at Deirdre. "Well, if you mean me, yes, I am. I'm Hector, and that's our little girl, Dorothea." Hector shook Deirdre's hand in a normal way at first, then more roughly like he was shaking a strong man's.

Ari saw her husband was holding Deirdre's hand—*she's not wearing her glove!* More jealousy jolted up in Ari than she had ever felt. Her husband's intelligent dark brown eyes were now focused on that Deirdre woman's green lucent ones. Ari elbowed him. Hector let go of Deirdre's hand and shook out his own.

"*Hector, what's wrong with you?*" Ari said under her breath. Samael returned and stepped between Hector and Deirdre. He set two dark frosted mugs on the battered wooden table.

Her prayer rope quivered. Ari did not notice. She stood—and stared. It was like Superman had joined them. He was a gorgeous man, the type you rarely see up close, but when you do, you can't help but act like a star-struck idiot with your mouth gaping open because he is *painfully* handsome, and oh you are embarrassed to stare, but you must.

Superman moved to kiss Ari on the cheek. She took an involuntary step backward.

He smiled at her. "Don't be shy, love. Two kisses, one on each cheek, that's how we greet each other on the Continent. I'm Samuel, Deirdre's lesser half."

He has a British accent too. The way he'd said "half" made Ari want to disintegrate right there even though her amygdala struggled to put her into flight mode. She froze. Samuel plied her with a Shakespearean sonnet, "tis but a kiss I beg, Why art thou coy?"

Ari still wanted to run away, but she hesitated.

"We'll do it the Yankee way." Samuel extended his hand to her.

She let Samuel take her left hand in his—*how can I not, now that he's quoted "Venus and Adonis"?* He grasped her hand, palm to palm folding his fingers around her wrist. Ari's body warmed and flushed.

Hector didn't like the look on his wife's face. He brought his hand down on Samuel and Ari's to sever their connection. He shook Samuel's hand. "I'm Hector, her husband."

"Samuel." He clapped his hands together like he'd just won an argument. He looked from Hector to Ari. "You never told me your name, love."

Ari was lost in her inner desert.

"Did you hear me, love?"

"Huh? Uh, my name's...uh, my name's—"

"Ari. *My wife*, Ari," Hector broke in. "Sit down." He pressed on Ari's shoulders. He whipped his red Ferrari key chain back and forth like a *komboloí* in his hand.

A head bumped Ari in the leg. Dorothea was crawling around under her mother's chair. Ari's mother instinct brought her back to her senses. "Dorothea! Get off the floor."

"My yellow crayon rolled under your chair, Mamá. How'm I gonna color the sun?"

Ari found the crayon. "Here it is. Oh, look you." She cleaned Dorothea's hands with a handy wipe. As she did, she tuned into what Samuel was saying to Hector.

"I see you like Formula 1 too."

Hector put his free hand on Ari's shoulder.

"—I'm a Ferrari man as well. I've raced practice laps against Alonso and Massa. A perk for sponsors of the team." Samuel held his arms out like he was turning a steering wheel around a chicane.

The key chain stilled in Hector's palm. He stared at Samuel. "You've raced at Maranello?"

"Many times. Deirdre and I have a villa in Modena. We go there every summer, don't we darling?"

"Yes, Enzo lured us there years ago. He always said that in northern Italy *la vita è bella*, to anyone who would listen." Deirdre raised her mug.

"He was indeed '*il Grande Vecchio.*'" Samuel raised his beer in a toast.

"The Great Old Man..." Hector said more to himself than to anyone else.

"Let's get you a pint and ask the owner to turn the channel to the race. It starts in fourteen minutes." Samuel turned Hector around by the shoulder toward the counter.

Hector shrugged his arm off.

"Can you bring me one too, agápe mou?" Ari asked.

"Sure."

Ari looked across at Deirdre who had resumed the game on her phone. After a minute of silence, Ari got out her prayer rope and entwined the 90-bead long hematite chain around her fingers.

Deirdre's eye caught the movement. "How quaint. Are you praying?"

"No...not hardly. It's a family heirloom."

"To whom did it belong?"

"My yiayiá." Ari appreciated Deirdre's good grammar in spite of herself.

"May I see it?"

"I guess so. Please be careful with it." She put the prayer rope in Deirdre's palm.

"Oh!" The rope jolted out of Deirdre's hand onto the table. She shook her hand.

Ari snatched the prayer rope off the table.

Samuel heard his wife cry out and came over to investigate. "What's happened, darling?" He saw the prayer rope in Ari's hand.

Deirdre hissed under her breath. *"It burned me."*

Samuel grimaced. *"Why did you touch it?* I'll fetch you some ice for that."

The prayer rope seemed to nestle itself in her palm. She looked over at Deirdre. *How could this burn you?* Ari tucked it tenderly back in her jacket pocket.

Samuel returned with a glass of ice. Deirdre held the cubes in her hand, and sat back mumbling under her breath.

Laurie showed up. "I'm sorry we're late! I had to go home and pick up Randy. These are our kids, Amy and Elijah."

"Come sit next to me, Laurie. Children down there." Deirdre pointed to the end of the table. "This is Samuel. Hi, I'm Deirdre. I'm delighted you could join us."

"Hello." Randy shook Deirdre's hand.

Deirdre lightly touched his battered cheek. "You still look a little beat up."

Randy flinched. The cut, newly released from its stitches, stung when Deirdre touched it. The fingernail gashes on his chest flamed and throbbed. He grabbed Deirdre's wrist holding it in mid-air between them. "*You.*"

"Easy Trooper...I was trying to help you feel better. Are you going to arrest me for public display of affection?" Deirdre looked around at those present and smiled.

Laurie and Samuel laughed uncomfortably.

Randy turned bright red. He let go of Deirdre's wrist.

"I hope you *do* arrest me. I like cold metal on my skin." Deirdre rubbed the insides of her wrists together like she was applying perfume. "Laurie told me you had, well what can we call what happened to you? *An encounter* last weekend. Tell me, have they found your cruiser?"

"Yes, they did. A hundred feet downstream from where it was *pushed* into the river."

"You survived."

Randy cleared his throat. He found his voice and his verve. "Yes, I did. *Deer-dre* Morrigan, right? M-o-r-r-i-g-a-n?" He stood at military ease but with his hands on his hips.

"And what about your state trooper's hat? Have they found it too?"

Randy froze.

Ari had been watching the volley between Randy and Deirdre, but when he knew exactly how to spell her last name, well, that made her ears perk up.

Laurie touched Randy's elbow. "You said D*eir*dre's name correctly. I keep saying it wrong."

"I've heard that surname before, hon."

"Do sit and give us all the intimate details about the criminals you apprehend. Perhaps one of them has your hat." Deirdre put her glove back on.

Randy squeezed his hands into fists at his sides.

Laurie felt his bicep tense and tried to look into his face. "Are you okay?"

"Yeah, I'm fine." He relaxed his fingers.

Samuel patted his shoulder. "Let's fetch you a pint, shall we?"

Randy looked at Samuel like he'd just noticed him. "Wouldn't I kill for a b—" He looked at Laurie. "—a root beer," he grunted. He stalked off to the cooler. Samuel followed.

"*He's so macho,*" Deirdre whispered to Laurie like they were talking about a high school crush.

"Yeah, I know…" Laurie blushed.

Ari saw Deirdre roll her eyes behind Laurie as she pulled out her chair.

Elijah sat next to Dorothea and turned on his Switch. "You bring yours?"

"Yep." Dorothea pushed her crayons aside. They synced their devices and played a game together.

Amy stared at the 'black mirror' of her cell phone with earbuds in rapidly moving her thumbs every few seconds.

Ari said, "Why aren't kids content to color on the menu anymore?"

Their order was called out and they settled into their greasy but delicious hand-cut fries; dipping them into the specialty sauces that Pommes Frites was famous for. No one talked.

Ari shut out everything except her beer and basket of fries. Her brain was working.

She felt a tap on her arm. Laurie was waving an empty mug in her face. "Hel-*lo*... *Ar*-ri? Deirdre and I want another round. You want one too?"

"Fill 'er up."

Randy grabbed Laurie's elbow as she passed by him. "Hon, two?"

Laurie leaned over, *"Hon, you know I'm more fun when I'm a little drunk."*

He let go of her.

Deirdre smirked at Randy, her pearlescent teeth showing.

He eyed her for a moment then said in a low voice Ari heard, *"You better stop this bs right now."*

"I'm just hitting my stride, Sergeant #379." Deirdre turned her back to Randy and held Ari's gaze as she bit into a fry.

CHAPTER 23

Iden

Sunday Afternoon | November 8th

The food was eaten, the children were all staring at screens, and the big children—the husbands—were watching the Brazilian Grand Prix; now the wives could talk.

"So how long have you and Samuel been married, Deirdre?" Ari asked.

"It seems like forever." Deirdre feigned fatigue.

"No seriously. How many years have you two been together?"

"Must we discuss our husbands?" Deirdre smoothed her paper napkin flat in her lap.

"Nope. So where're you from?"

"All around. I recently bought another house—a condominium on Fifth Avenue."

"No, I mean originally. Where were you born?"

"*Another* house?" Laurie asked.

"This one in New York makes seven. Now I have a *pied-à-terre* on each of the seven continents," Deirdre said.

"Wow," Laurie said like she had no idea what a *pied-à-terre* was.

Ari did. "*A foot on earth,*" in French. She noticed how Laurie held her beer mug in both hands like a kid would. *Laurie can't hold her own with snobby Deirdre. But I can.* To Deirdre she said, "Unless you have a domicile in Antarctica, you have one too many. Many geographers refer to only six continents because Europe and Asia are one solid land mass."

Deirdre continued unfazed. "I am from a land called 'a place of delight' in a foreign tongue. It was beautiful, befitting of its name."

"If the 'foreign tongue' you speak of is Hebrew, then you claim to be from Eden," Ari said.

"Yes, you are close. In the old Celtic language, Eden is spelled with an 'I', so it's I-d-e-n. It was a village in Ireland."

"I'll look it up." Ari laid her phone on the table in front of her and swiped up.

Deirdre put her hand over the phone. "You cannot. It is no more. Know that this is a painful memory for me. However, you may ask me what you wish, but you will share in my sorrow with your knowledge of it." Their eyes locked on each other, Deirdre drew her hand back.

Ari put her phone away. "So if you miss it, why'd you leave?"

Deirdre looked out the window into the distance for half a minute. When she turned her face back to Ari and Laurie, her eyes brimmed with tears. "At a young age I was given in marriage to a man I had never met. He was kind to me in the beginning.

I believed he loved me. I opened my whole being to him like a flower lifts its petals to the sun." Deirdre dabbed her eyes. "Forgive me."

Laurie said, "It's OK. Sometimes it's best to let sleeping dogs lie."

Ari sipped her beer and pointed at Deirdre's. "Take a shot of courage, Deirdre, 'cause I'd honestly like to know how this great love affair went sour. Do you think you could press on for us?"

Laurie said, "Ari, can't you see how hard this is on her?"

Deirdre smirked at Ari when Laurie wasn't looking. Deirdre's pitiful mask was back in place the second Laurie looked back at her. "It's okay, Laurie. I want to tell you. I left because a tyrant ruled my birthplace. He allowed my husband to abuse me. My beloved husband saw my vulnerability as a weakness which he exploited. I left Iden to preserve my dignity."

"You were mistreated...but you escaped." Laurie put her mug down but held on to it.

Deirdre lowered her voice. "Yes, I did. We had been equals for so long."

Laurie put her hand around Deirdre's. "Certain men take advantage of a woman's admiration and inexperience."

Deirdre put her other hand on top of Laurie's. "You *do understand*, don't you? I am sorry you do."

"At least we have that in common now besides being Libras." Laurie smiled weakly.

Randy called out to his wife, "Hon, you okay?"

Laurie pulled her hand away from Deirdre's.

Ari was glad. "What happened after you got away from your husband?"

Deirdre said, "I fled to the Reed Sea. My husband appealed to the tyrant to bring me back, so he sent his guards out to find me. They overtook me in the midst of the mighty waters."

"What did the guards do when they found you?" Ari asked.

"Demand I return to my husband and submit to him."

"They wanted you to go back to that abuser?" Laurie leaned in.

"Yes. I refused and they made ready to drown me in the sea."

"Well, obviously they didn't. So how'd you wriggle out of that tight spot, may I ask?" Ari raised her eyebrow.

"I made a pact with the guards and they left me alone," Deirdre said.

"What on earth did you agree to?" Ari asked.

"I can't disclose that to you. If I do, the pact will be broken. I am better off now. However, the tyrant gave my husband a new wife when I did not return to him. What a thorn in his side she has been! She led him further astray than I ever did. She angered the tyrant and he kicked them *both* out of Iden! Ha." Deirdre clapped her hands together. The loud crack the leather made caused everyone in Pommes Frites to pause and look at her.

"So have you stayed in touch with your ex-husband?" Ari asked.

The cacophony of the tavern resumed.

"I know where he is."

"Do you ever wish you could go back to Iden? Without him, I mean," Laurie asked.

"Yes, I do." Deirdre wiped her eyes then folded her napkin into a square in her lap.

"I'd love to hear your ex-husband's side of the story. It sounds to me you left out some important details," Ari said.

"You may think what you like. No matter. Forgive my vulgarity, but I got wise and I got rich. I resolved to never be dependent on a man again." Deirdre looked over at Samuel. He blew her a kiss. "Samuel worships me."

Laurie said, "I've never been independent."

"You must be as rich as Croesus," Ari said.

"I met him in Lydia eons ago—uh, I mean I met a man with the *same name* years ago in Greece," Deirdre said.

"I was gonna say, you must be over two thousand years old if you've met the real Croesus." Ari steepled her fingers under her chin.

"Who's Croesus?" Laurie asked.

"He was a king who ruled in the sixth century BC in Lydia, an ancient kingdom that's now Turkey. He was wealthy, like her apparently." Ari pointed her thumb at Deirdre.

"She has a good reason. Let's talk about your new condo. Did you move in yet?" Laurie asked.

"Soon. Samuel drove up yesterday from the City." Deirdre turned toward the men. "Excuse me a minute, darling. How long until 5th Avenue's done?"

"We're waiting on the Spanish hand-carved bedroom suite you 'just had to have.' I received an email yesterday which said it should clear customs by the middle of this week," Samuel said.

"That's wonderful," Deirdre said.

"Only the best for my wife." Samuel nodded to her.

Ari wanted to throw up. *Look how Laurie's holding her head in her hands, elbows on the table, like a little kid at story time. I'll bet that's what this is—a fairy tale.*

Deirdre said to Laurie. "You practice yoga, do you not?"

"Yes, I used to. How can you tell?"

"I have a sixth sense. Maybe we can go to a fitness facility together."

"I'm beginning to think you do," Laurie was holding her mug weirdly again.

"Laurie's a personal trainer," Ari said.

"You are? Then you *must* help me tailor my workout. It's a bit weak in strength training."

Ari rolled her eyes.

Laurie sifted the pearls of her necklace through her fingers. "I'm really flattered you want me to help you, but I haven't been to a gym since I left Ohio."

"We can use the gym at my hotel. I peeked in there the other day. They have apparatus of all kinds. A peculiar half bubble-like one gave me pause."

"You mean a balance trainer? Is it blue?" Laurie perked up.

"Yes, there are two, one for each of us unbalanced gals." Deirdre waved her arms in the air making woo-woo sounds.

Laurie laughed. "All right, I'll be your personal trainer. But only as your friend, okay?"

"Well, at least let me gift you a new yoga mat."

When the discussion moved into the spiritual benefits of yoga, Ari couldn't stand it anymore. She excused herself to go to the lavatory.

On her way back she dug around in her purse trying to find her lip balm. She ran into a chair. She looked up and stopped in her tracks. Deirdre sat between Hector and Samuel watching the race on the big-screen TV. A thick forest of green jealousy rose in Ari's body as she took in every detail. She clenched her fist around the lip balm. Deirdre had her arms draped over the backs of both men's chairs. She was saying something to Hector. Her mouth was too close to his ear.

Deirdre gave Ari a look which seemed to say, *"You can't stop me, so stand aside."*

The bottom fell out and Ari dropped into a cold dunk tank of betrayal, fear, shame, rage, and hurt. The lip balm cap popped off from the pressure of her grip. Beeswax balm squeezed out of the hard plastic tube like solid pus from a boil. She let it fall. *I'm a huge coward after all.* All those times she had bragged she would defend her territory if she ever found her husband *even flirting* with another woman, dissolved instantly in the reality of it. Now all she wanted to do was...*RUN.*

She turned and banged into a chair, then into the one after it. She shoved it out of the way. Ari was dizzy and seeing spots by the time she made it to the back of the tavern. A block of wood held the side door ajar. She pushed open the door and found herself in an alleyway in between two greasy brick walls.

CHAPTER 24

Sansennoi

Sunday Afternoon | November 8th

The air in the alley was thick with fryer exhaust and sour. Ari walked briskly past the garbage bins of rotting food to the front of the alley holding her scarf over her nose. She sat in a wrought iron chair in front of Pommes Frites. It felt good to have the sun on her face.

She put her hands into her jacket pockets. Yiayiá's prayer rope. She pulled it out. Why had Yiayiá wanted me to have this? At the end of her life, the family said Yiayiá had 'hardening of the arteries' which was what they politely called dementia back then. But Yiayiá had always been lucid with Ari when they were alone. It was only when the other family members were around that Yiayiá forgot people's names or put her clothes on backward. Was she faking it?

She remembered the day Yiayiá had given the prayer rope to her. She was five and had come home from her first day of kindergarten—with a black eye no less. Her mother's hugs and ice pack had helped, but she'd needed Yiayiá's wisdom. She'd run up the stairs and found Yiayiá asleep in her soft armchair. Ari could still see the floral pattern of the chair and smell the Lady Esther powder which was the only makeup her grandmother had used. Ari had startled Yiayiá awake when she had fallen into her bosom crying.

"*Endáxi**, Areté," Yiayiá said soothingly. Yiayiá was the only one who called her by her given name, which they shared. Yiayiá held Ari's face in her soft hands, the palms and fingertips worn smooth by decades of lovingly caring for her family. "Tell me what happened."

"That mean boy Kosmas, you know Kosmas Constandinopoulos, he takes the bus too... and on the way home from school he... he threw my lunch bag outta the window! Ya' know the pretty blue jean one that Mamá made for me...so I *punched* him." She swung her fist in the air.

"Panayía mou," said Yiayiá crossing herself. "How you get this, *mátia mou***?" Yiayiá lifted the ice bag off Ari's black eye.

"Well, he punched me back, Yiayiá. A boy hit me! Mr. Wilson heard me crying so he stopped the bus and got my lunch bag for me."

---

*Endáxi- Greek for *okay.*

**Mátia mou- Greek for *my (pretty) eyes,* a term of endearment.

"*Kalá**. Mr. Wilson, he a good man, not so smart, but good. And Kosmas not a good boy. His babbá is not nice to his mamá. He don't let her to go to church."

Yiayiá smoothed Ari's golden brown hair out of her teary face and kissed her swollen eye. She took her antique 90-bead hematite prayer rope out of her old smock. She placed it in Ari's tiny palm. "Areté, you take this now."

The prayer rope vibrated a little. "Oh!"

"Hold like this." Yiayiá draped the rope around Ari's fingers. The rope quieted.

"Why me, Yiayiá? Daphne's bigger." Ari held the prayer rope in both hands, terrified she would drop it if it vibrated again. Everyone in the family knew how important Yiayiá's prayer rope was to her. Yiayiá never let anyone touch it and now she was giving it to Ari.

"Your cousin Daphne she older, yes, but you and I have same name. Areté. You know why? Because you a warrior like me, *mátia mou*. I too old to fight now. See, the prayer rope chooses you. It don't move for nobody else. Now I sure it is you, Areté, you must to continue the warrior legacy of the womans in our family."

"Okay, Yiayiá. I'll go. Where's the Lego-city?"

Yiayiá chucked her under the chin. "No Lego, *mátia mou*. My English no so good, but it is *legacy*. Is no a place. It mean you to follow my path and all the brave womans in our family for many years. God chooses you. When you a woman, He will to send a messenger to help you."

*Kalá- Greek for *good, fine*.

"You mean like the UPS guy who delivered my bicycle?"

Yiayiá laughed from her belly. "Ah, *mátia mou*. You will to know him when he comes." She folded her hands around the prayer rope in Ari's hands and kissed them.

Ari folded her hands around the precious prayer rope the same way. Even though she had always treasured it, it hadn't been useful for anything but a fidget. *I'm forty-seven years old and still no messenger has shown up to tell me anything about 'my family legacy.' Did I make the memory up like one of my stories?*

A gust of cold wind blew down Main Street. Ari felt a cinnamon warmth surround her and she stopped shivering. The prayer rope vibrated exuberantly in her palms. She made a fist so it wouldn't fall to the ground.

"Deirdre knows who you are now."

Ari was amazed to see a beautiful man sitting across the table from her. "Um, I'm sorry. What did you say?"

"Deirdre knows who you are now. Now that Deirdre knows you possess the prayer rope, you need to be told what it is, *and what you are*, Areté," the man said.

"Only Yiayiá called me—how do you know my name?"

"That prayer rope has chosen one woman in your family for generations to help her in the battle for the Kingdom. The silver crucifix tied at the end is hollow. Inside it are two slivers of the True Cross. That is why it vibrates, like it is right now, when spiritual beings such as angels or demons are near you."

Ari looked around the empty street. She didn't want to be alone with this wacko. "And what kind of spiritual being are *you* then?"

"I am your guardian angel." He beamed at her like a proud father. He had dark golden gentle curls which were slicked back with styling cream and he wore a cobalt blue suit, white dress shirt, and a matching tie. He looked like he'd stepped out of a men's cologne ad, but he smelled like a bakery.

"You're too good looking to be my guardian angel." She pointed west. "Hollywood is *that* way."

He broke eye contact. "I have always found your sarcasm tedious, Areté. I hope you will lose the need of it soon."

"Please don't call me that. OK, I'll play along. You know my name. What's yours?"

"I am Sansennoi."

"Sanse—what?"

"It's pronounced 'Sán-sen-noy.'"

He looks like Matthew McConaughey when he smiles...a bit younger...maybe forty? Ari repeated, "*San*sennoi. Your name sounds familiar. Frankly, you don't look like an angel, you look like a model and you smell like a pastry chef. All that cinnamon."

"I favor the scent of cinnamon spice, because it helps the human brain to be more alert and focused. As for my physical form, if I appeared to you as I truly am, you would tremble." He touched his fingertips together.

"Oh yeah? Try me. I'm pretty tough."

With a gleam in his eye, he stood and straightened his lapels.

She had to push her chair away from the table and lean her head back to take in his full height. "Wow, I didn't think you were that—"

Without warning, a starburst of light showed forth from him. Ari gasped and fell to her knees. She covered her head with her hands and peeked through her fingers.

He emerged from the light in full Roman battle gear—a cobalt blue breastplate, a tunic which ended above his knees, and gold and leather sandals laced around his muscular calves. He withdrew a fiery sword from under his heavy scarlet cape which was attached to his broad shoulders between a pair of magnificent wings the color of 24-karat-gold. He set the tip of the sword on the sidewalk. The pavement glowed in a seven-foot radius around him warming Ari's legs.

"I told you." Sansennoi had both hands balanced on the pommel as he leaned over Ari who was cringing on the ground. "I will not hurt you, Areté. Please sit in your chair."

She understood why Balaam had prostrated himself before the angel of the Lord in that narrow place where there was no room to turn to the right or to the left. A warm tongue licked her hand. A man and a dog stared at her.

"Are you alright, ma'am?" the man asked.

Ari motioned toward Sansennoi. *"Don't you see him?"* she whispered.

"See who?"

"The angel."

The man eyed her strangely. "I'm sorry, I don't see *an angel* anywhere." He glanced around the Pommes Frites patio. "All the tables are empty, ma'am."

His dog was barking at Sansennoi and wagging its tail. Sansennoi bent and patted its head.

"How can you not see him? He's right there. He's petting your dog." Ari pointed at Sansennoi who was scratching the dog behind the ears. If dogs could purr, this one would've been.

"Let's get you in this chair." The man humored her like she was his dotty aunt. He gently pulled her up by the elbow and she resisted, but he eased her into the chair. She pushed herself far back into the chair and covered her face with her arms, while peeking at the angel's radiant glory.

Sansennoi sheathed his sword, sat, and as imperceptibly as he had appeared as an angel, he transformed back into his men's cologne ad attire.

"Ma'am, would you like me to call—" the man saw Sansennoi.

"I will tend to my friend now. Thank you for your assistance," Sansennoi said.

"Well, I'll be dam—" The man rubbed his chin. "Okay. You folks have a nice afternoon." He gathered up the dog's lead.

"Thank you. You and Trixie have a nice walk," Sansennoi said to the man's back.

The man and his dog kept looking back at Ari and Sansennoi all the way to the next corner—Trixie pulled on the lead to go back and the man pulled on her to get as far away as he could.

"Now do you understand my need for a disguise when I walk among men?" Sansennoi asked.

All the previous cockiness in Ari's voice was gone. "I couldn't handle it. You were right."

"Do not despair. I showed you my full God-given glory. I wanted to make an impression on you. You need to believe I am who I say I am."

"Oh, I believe you're an angel now, don't worry." Ari had been captive of an adrenaline rush and pressed her palms to her cheeks and shivered. "Sansennoi—are you sure I can call you Sansennoi? I feel like I should address you as Saint Sansennoi or Mr. Archangel at least."

He chuckled. "I am not an Archangel or a saint like Michael is. In the hierarchy of angels I am of an order called the Powers. It is our duty to prevent demons from destroying the world. Please call me Sansennoi. I want you to feel at your ease with me."

"It's strange, but I feel like I already know you."

"You do. I have been with you every day since you were baptized as an infant."

"Are you the warm cinnamon blanket that's been following me around lately?"

"Yes, I am. I have never left your side since you were a baby. Do you recall the time you jammed your front bicycle tire in a crack in the sidewalk and flew over the handlebars onto your face? You would have been paralyzed from the neck down had I not caught you in my arms. I was also there when you were seventeen and so discouraged by your SAT score that you ran the railroad tracks. I held the oncoming train back long enough for you to barrel over the tracks. And remember when you were a freshmen in college and you let those two upperclassmen walk you home from the library? I slammed your dorm room door in their faces and saved your virt—"

"Okay...okay, I get the picture. I can still remember looking over my shoulder at that train realizing that I'd almost killed myself. My heart was racing...I hadn't heard the warning bells or seen the flashing lights at all, I was so upset. I thought it was a miracle."

"It was. It is by the Providence of the Lord you are still alive *and well* today. I have spent many years protecting you from yourself. It has not been easy." He clasped his hands and rested them in his lap.

"I don't know why God gave me to you in the first place. You'd think a Power-level guardian angel like you would be too important to babysit me."

"When you were born, *I* was given to *you*, not you to *me*. You have been my special assignment, Areté, because you are a warrior for the Kingdom."

"Call me Ari, *please*. Look, I'm a pretty good wife, mother...and I guess writer. But I haven't done anything even *remotely* warrior-like."

"Not yet. However, you will, and you will need my guidance. The path ahead is difficult. You will need all your strength and the Holy Spirit to do what the Lord wants you to do. I have come to tell you who you are. You come from a long line of strong women. Aret—, *Ari*, you are a spiritual warrior like your yiayiá was."

"So I didn't make it up." Ari leaned forward. "*You're* the messenger Yiayiá said God would send me?"

"I am. You were born into a special family. The females in your genealogical line have qualities which are ideally suited for this battle."

"Like our talent for sarcasm?"

"That comes from your sharp intellect which you have used to browbeat others most of your life. It is time you put it to good use like you did with Deirdre today."

"Deirdre is the second peculiar person I've encountered lately. That guy at the hardware store was creepy like her."

"Her name is Lilith, not Deirdre. The incidents occurring in your life are the Lord's way of getting your attention, of preparing you for what lies ahead."

"Well, He got my attention all right." Ari shifted in the iron chair. "I know I'll regret asking this, but what lies ahead?"

"Lilith."

"OK, who is this Lilith? *Deirdre's* the creepy one."

He looked toward the tavern. "The woman in there whom you know as Deirdre is not Deirdre anymore. The demoness Lilith has taken over Deirdre's body and is in control of it. Did you notice a sulfurous smell around her? That is the lingering stench of Hell. And the nervous tic in the corner of her mouth? That little bit of drool? An indwelling spirit puts tremendous pressure on the body of its host. She also has Antaean strength and knowledge of past events. These are the signs of demonic possession."

"I knew she was bad when I first met her, but do you expect me to believe she's a demon?"

"Yes. If you believe I am an angel, you must believe that other spiritual beings exist as well. As radiant as I am, she, Lilith, is dark."

"Believing in angels is easy. I don't want to believe demons exist."

"You must. It is time for you to be who you are. The Lord gave you the divine gift of the prayer rope to help you. He also gave you intelligence for a reason, and stubbornness too—"

"I'll make sure to tell Hector that *God* gave me that last one," Ari said.

"You must decide if you will use these gifts to fight for the Kingdom of God, or only for yourself."

"You make me sound like such a *jerk*."

"You *can be* and *have been* the former, Ari. I await your decision."

"I've gotta tell you right now? Can't I have a few days to think about it...I mean we're talking about life and death here, aren't we?"

"Christ said, 'For whoever would save his life will lose it; and—"

"Yes, yes, I've heard that one."

"You do not know the Word of the Lord or Him well."

Ari didn't say anything. She looked away. *He's right*. She was silent a few moments. Then quietly, "I've always felt my life was meant for more than this. So okay, I'm listening. What am I supposed to do?"

Sansennoi looked into her eyes without blinking. "For now, go back inside, but be careful in there, my little tigress. The entity who lies within Deirdre is ancient and evil. You will never be the same after you encounter Lilith in her fullness."

He pulled a parchment scroll sealed with red wax from his breast pocket and handed it to her. "Read this and we will discuss it afterward. I have translated it for you from the original Hebrew. Also, I know you read the printed news media every day.

Look for any upcoming events which involve Sundays, holidays, or snakes."

"Why should I focus on Sundays, holidays, and snakes?"

"Because Lilith will be. Read the parchment. It explains the lie Lilith believes about herself."

"I don't like your cryptic guidance, Sansennoi."

"Baby steps, my dear. I will only reveal to you as much as you can handle. Remember how you reacted to my true form earlier?"

"Yes, I made holes in the knees of my panty hose."

Sansennoi leaned over and kissed her on the forehead. "Go now. I will come to you later." His lips left her skin and he was gone.

Hector opened the front door of Pommes Frites and bumped into his wife. "Where've you been, Ari?" He put his arm around her in a half embrace and sniffed her hair. "Did you go to the bakery?"

Ari pulled away and peered into her husband's face. His concern seemed genuine. "No. I ran into Marion and you know how she goes on and on about Pom-tom."

"No wonder you went missing. Marion can out-yap her yappy Pomeranian."

They walked back to the table. Ari glanced at Deirdre. *You mean Lilith.*

Lilith curled her lips. "You left abruptly." She pushed her chair out and stood a foot away from Ari.

Ari stumbled backward.

Lilith clasped her hands together to tighten the leather between her fingers.

Laurie stood from the table. "Ari, you missed Deirdre's stories about her travels. She's been all over the world."

"I'm sure Deirdre's good at telling tales," Ari said.

Hector looked from his wife to Deirdre. "Well, it's time for my Sunday nap, folks. Let's go, koúkla." Dorothea followed her father.

"That's a good idea. Let's go nap like Greeks, darling." Lilith took Samuel by the arm. She kissed Laurie on both cheeks and whispered, *"Let's do lunch soon—alone."*

"Sure, uh, that'd be great." Laurie blushed a little.

Lilith said, "That's how they say farewell on the Continent, Laura-lee."

Ari pushed down her disgust. She said goodbye to Laurie with a simple hug—none of that kitsch Continental kissing.

CHAPTER 25

Ace Guns

Late Sunday Afternoon | November 8th

Lilith and Samael went back to the hotel. The bodies needed rest. They ordered room service.

A buff young man knocked on the door. When she opened it, he stepped away from the cart. He ran his hand through his sandy-colored hair, tousling it back. "Uh, I brought your dessert and *exp*resso, ma'am," he said in his dumb snowboarder way.

Lilith pulled him and the cart inside the room.

He glanced around the two-bedroom suite. "I'm not allowed to—"

"Don't speak." She kissed him hard.

Samael rolled over in his sleep in the bedroom to the right.

He jerked away from her. "Is that your old man over there?" He peered at Samael through the curtain of bangs which half covered his face.

"Never mind him, he's dead asleep," she said against his pink cheek. She breathed into his ear.

He groaned but pushed her away. "It's too raw with him right over—"

"I chose the time and place. You bear my seal on your body...Travis." Lilith removed his shirt. She traced the bulging veins underneath each eye of the screech owl tattoo on his muscular forearm. "Come." She led him to the adjoining bedroom and sat next to him on the bed.

"Will I remember anything?"

"Yes... but first you must say you are mine." She brushed the tips of his fingers with her lips.

"I am yours, Mistress." His simple mind succumbed to his more developed body.

She kissed him. Open mouth on open mouth, deep into the kiss, Lilith's spiritual essence invaded him. Perfect possession. Deirdre's body collapsed onto the bed.

Lilith positioned Deirdre's body in the middle of the bed. *Ah, to be in a man's body again.* She undid the uniform jacket and flung it to the floor. Now only in a white t-shirt, she lifted her arms over her head and stretched, admiring her biceps.

Lilith went to the kitchenette, poured a glass of Bushmills, and added one drop of water. She came back to the bedroom and stood at the end of the bed sipping her whiskey and eyeing Deirdre. The woman had curved herself around a pillow. The corners of Lilith's lips curled up.

Lilith went over to Samael. "Room service came."

Samael rubbed his eyes. "Are you ill? Your voice sounds a little rough." He opened his eyes and saw Travis. He peered into the young man's eyes. "Oh, it's you darling…"

"This body should prove enjoyable."

Samael sat up and slapped her veiny arm. "Ace guns."

CHAPTER 26

The Alphabet of ben Sira

Sunday Afternoon | November 8th

Ari held the parchment scroll Sansennoi had given her. "I'll be in a minute," she said when they pulled the car into the garage. Hector nodded. She'd been oddly silent on the ride home from Pommes Frites. He could wait. She always told him eventually. He took Dorothea into the house.

Ari slid her index finger under the dark red wax seal and broke it. She unrolled the single sheet of parchment paper to reveal words written with black ink in a fine hand. She read:

The Alphabet of ben Sira

Soon afterward the young son of the king took ill, said Nebuchadnezzar to ben Sira, "Heal my son. If you don't, I will kill you."

Ben Sira immediately sat down and wrote an amulet with the Holy Name, and he inscribed on it the angels in charge of medicine by their names, forms, and images, and by their wings, hands, and feet.

Nebuchadnezzar looked at the amulet. "Who are these?"

Ben Sira said, "The angels who are in charge of medicine: Sennoi, Sansennoi, and Samangaluf. I will tell you the story behind the amulet, my King:

After God created Adam, who was alone, He said, 'It is not good for man to be alone' (Genesis 2:18.) He then created a woman for Adam, from the earth, as He had created Adam himself, and called her Lilith. Adam and Lilith began to fight. She said, 'I will not lie below,' and Adam said, 'I will not lie beneath you, but only on top. For you are fit only to be in the bottom position, while I am to be in the superior one.'

Lilith responded, 'We are equal to each other inasmuch as we were both created from the earth.'

But they would not listen to one another.

When Lilith saw this, she pronounced the Ineffable Name of God and flew away into the air.

Adam stood in prayer before his Creator: 'Sovereign of the universe!' he said, 'the woman you gave me has run away.' At once, the Holy One, blessed be He, sent these three angels to bring her back. Said the Holy One to Adam, 'If she agrees to come back, fine. If not, she must permit one hundred of her children to die every day.'

The angels Sennoi, Sansennoi, and Samangaluf left God and pursued Lilith, whom they overtook in the midst of the sea, in the mighty waters wherein the Egyptians were destined to drown. They told her God's word, but she did not wish to return. The angels said, 'We shall drown you in the sea.'

'Leave me!' she said. 'I was created only to cause sickness to infants. If the infant is male, I have dominion over him for eight days after his birth, and if female, for twenty days.'

When the angels heard Lilith's words, they insisted she go back. But she swore to them by the name of the living and eternal God, 'Whenever I see you or your names or your forms in an amulet, I will have no power over that infant.' She also agreed to have one hundred of her children die every day.

Accordingly, every day one hundred demons perish, and for the same reason, we write the names of the angels Sennoi, Sansennoi, and Samangaluf on the amulets of young children. When Lilith sees their names, she remembers her oath, and the child recovers.

That was not at all what she had expected to read. It was a fairy tale, an ancient myth explaining sudden infant death syndrome. The story also said that Lilith had been Adam's first wife, not Eve. *Seriously?* Ari wanted to dismiss it. It was satirical. It seemed pieced together. But Sansennoi had given it to her; he hadn't said The Alphabet of ben Sira was true. What he had told her was the scroll 'explained the lie Lilith believes about herself.'

She lowered the parchment to her lap. *So I'm dealing with a delusional, child-killing ancient demoness.*

She got out of the car and shut the heavy door to the garage. When it came down with a slight bounce on the hard cement floor, she felt closed off and trapped in an impossible situation which Sansennoi had asked her to confront. She shook the scroll. *How am I supposed to take on this Lilith? Why did I agree to do this? I'm an idiot! I should've minded my own business.*

She walked into the house. "Hector!"

Ari sat at the kitchen table waiting for Hector to read the scroll. He handed it back to her. "OK, did you write this? It's weird."

"No. Is that all you have to say about it?"

"Well, what do you want me to say? It's a preposterous story."

"I know it is, but an ang— well... this is gonna sound crazy, but I met my guardian angel today outside Pommes Frites. I didn't run into Marion. I ran into him. He gave me that scroll." She crossed her arms.

"Yeah right."

"It's true. I got ... jealous when I saw Deirdre getting all cozy with you watching the race, so I went outside."

"So you must've left right before I got up and moved as far away from that woman as I could get and still see the TV." He brushed off his arms like he was wiping away dirt. "She gave me the creeps."

"Oh, *agápe mou*, I'm so sorry I doubted you. I couldn't even see I was so jealous. Ruined a brand new Badger lip balm too…"

"And I don't like her husband either. Samuel came onto you, and you were dumbstruck."

"They're both evil. She's got powerful energy in her hands. I think that's why she wears those gloves."

"Really? Her gloves are weird, but that doesn't make her a demon."

"Deirdre's not a demon, she has one inside her. This Lilith." Ari pointed to the scroll.

"OK, I'll play along. Tell me how you got that while I was avoiding Deirdre's evil eye." Hector danced his long fingers around in the air.

"Quit it. Listen to me. I got so freaked out by her that I went outside to calm down. I sat in front of the tavern and this beautiful man appeared out of nowhere. He said he was my guardian angel."

"More fairy tales." He went to the fridge to get a Coke.

"I didn't believe he was an angel either, so I challenged him. Then Sansennoi, that's his name, revealed his true form to me—flaming sword and golden wings—and I was blinded by his radiance. I fell on my knees and covered my face."

Hector took a swig of his Coke. "You said his name was 'Sansennoi'. So he's one of the angels in the scroll?"

"Yes."

"Why did Sansennoi make his grand appearance now? You're forty-seven years old. He's a little late, isn't he?"

"Please don't make light of this. It's too far-fetched even for me to make up. Sansennoi told me that he showed up now because Lilith knows who I truly am."

"And you truly are...?"

She glanced away. *I can't believe I have to say this out loud.* She deadpanned, "A spiritual warrior from a long line of women in my family who were also warriors."

Hector's eyebrows couldn't rise any higher.

Ari laid Yiayiá's prayer rope on the table. "This vibrates now when spiritual beings like angels or demons are near me. Deirdre, well Lilith, saw it at the tavern and when I put it in her hand, it burned her. You saw her holding ice cubes, didn't you?"

He picked the prayer rope and swung it back and forth. "So... this is a Greek spook detector."

"Look, Yiayiá was a spiritual warrior too. She told me when I was a little girl. A lot of my life made sense to me today. Sansennoi said the women in my genealogical line have the qualities of intelligence and stubbornness—"

"So now that's a positive quality?"

"I told Sansennoi I'd make sure I told you *God* gave me that *gift*... to fight Lilith."

"Let me get this straight: you met your guardian angel today, this Sansennoi character... who told you that God wants you to fight a demoness... who thinks she's Lilith, Adam's first wife turned baby killer, and whose demon children are going to take over Ashuelot Hollow?"

Ari furrowed her brow. "Don't you think I know it sounds farcical? But it doesn't matter what we think. Lilith believes what The Alphabet of ben Sira says about her. I still don't know what

I'm up against. What is this Deirdre/Lilith combination? Right now what I need from you, dear husband, is for you to believe me and support me in this lunacy. I'm... kinda... you know... scared." She got up from the table and paced back and forth.

"You're *serious*, aren't you?"

"Of course I'm serious. Why does God want *me*, a middle-aged mother, to become a demon hunter? My faith isn't strong enough! I told Sansennoi I'd do it, but I wish I didn't have to."

He saw the fear and sincerity in her eyes. He went to her and put his hands on her shoulders.

"Forgive me, *agápe mou*. I'll try and suspend my disbelief, as you writers say."

"It's okay. I didn't believe it at first either. Who would want to? It's weird stuff—angels and demons. It makes me look crazy. Geez..."

"What're you going to do now?" He stroked her forearms tenderly with his hands.

"Learn as much as I can about Lilith, angels, and The Alphabet of ben Sira. I have a lot of questions: what are demons? And why haven't I ever heard of Lilith?"

"I'd like to know why the Sovereign of the universe didn't ask Adam, 'Hey Man, what'd you do to her to make her leave Paradise?'" Hector said to the floor like he was God on high.

They laughed. It broke the tension in the room.

"And if Lilith, or whoever she is, thinks she was the first woman, and not Eve, then she took her revenge on Adam way too far and became a sort of demon queen mother. Makes me think of the monstrous slimy alien queen laying her eggs in the movie *Aliens*." Ari grimaced at the image which came into her mind from the movie. "Maybe Lilith's demon children are taking over the world like the alien queen's take over humans."

"That was a gross movie, ugh…" Hector shook his head and shoulders.

"It's among my favorites. Pfft, I wish you liked sci-fi as much as I do. Anyway, I'll see what I can learn. Can you be in charge of Dorothea for a while?"

"I was gonna to take my Sunday 'after dinner' nap…"

"Oof, how can you sleep now?"

"Hey, I'm not the newly-appointed demon hunter, Sigourney, you are." He saluted her.

"Cut it out. Fine, go set Dorothea up with a movie, then you can still have your nap. How's that sound?"

"Like bad parenting."

Ari playfully shoved him out of the kitchen then went to her office to begin the search.

CHAPTER 27

Metal Chick

Sunday Afternoon | November 8th

Ari got sucked down the rabbit hole the moment she entered the word 'Lilith' into the browser search window; she followed it wherever the turns led her. Lilith was either a heroine or a demon who was a seductress and a slayer of infants at the same time. Artists, poets, and writers had been fascinated with her for centuries. Lilith was mentioned by name once in the Bible in Isaiah 34:14, and there was an ongoing debate about the meaning of Genesis 1:27-28: "So God created man in his own image, in the image of God he created him; male and female he created *them.*" It was the 'them' which was troublesome.

Ari ordered two encyclopedias: one about angels, another about demons. *What suggestions are gonna pop up now on my 'Recommendations for You in Books' Amazon page?* She printed out Protestant, Orthodox, Muslim, and Jewish beliefs about demons. Many similarities existed.

Angel theories were more universal. She had a binder full of information by the time her eyes got tired. She checked on Dorothea and found her asleep on the couch. She turned off the TV and covered her up with a blanket. Ari took a cat nap next to her on the love seat to rest her brain.

The nap was unsatisfying because the word 'cockroach' scrolled across Ari's mind the whole time in a ticker symbol along the edge of her screen of consciousness. She pushed it away every time it rolled back around. *Why that word?*

She got up and distracted herself by clipping articles from the newspaper. She kept them in a plastic file box and used the information in her stories. In the file labeled 'Evil' was an article about a mother who had super-glued her two-year-old daughter's fingers to the wall. The 'Weird' file held the one about the study of Millennials who'd preferred to be electric shocked than be alone with their own thoughts for fifteen minutes. The article about a fancy dog brothel in Brazil was filed under 'Outrageous'. She filed an article about how to react when a crocodile bites and rolls you in the 'Survival' folder. Ari spread the Sunday paper out on the dining room table like a treasure map and bent over the pages with her fingers poised like a greedy pirate.

Sansennoi had said to be on the lookout for future events which involved Sundays, holidays, or snakes. "That's not much to go on, is it?" she asked out loud in case he was nearby.

She scanned the Police Log first, but found nothing odd. She turned the page to the Entertainment section where an ad caught her eye:

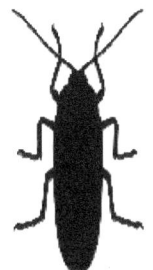

6th ANNUAL MIDNIGHT METAL MANIA
Sunday, November 8th at Bob's Pet Bungalow
A 1-year-old female soul sucker python (value $1,000) will be awarded to the contestant who eats the most discoid cockroaches, meal worms, & horn worms in 5 minutes. Registration starts at 11 PM. Entry fee $30, includes a Midnight Metal Mania t-shirt!
Hosted by 106.6 FM's DJ Sean

554 Park Avenue, Ashuelot Hollow, NH 03433
Tel. (603) 357-BOBS
Bob's Pet Bungalow
"The best yet for your pet"

That's it! Sunday and snakes. Lilith's bound to show up. Ari clipped the ad. "Sansennoi, if I'm right about this, please give me a sign."

A cinnamon breeze blew the ad to the floor.

She picked it up. "Got it. I'll meet you there tonight at 11:50."

Ari did her usual lengthy bedtime ritual with Dorothea: brush teeth, pee-pee, PJs, and read a picture book. Then she would sing her to sleep. It was her nightly benediction over her child.

"I'm gonna get ready now," Ari said to Hector closing Dorothea's door halfway behind her.

Hector frowned. "Please don't go, Ari. I have to stay with Dorothea. I don't want you to go by yourself."

"Sansennoi will help me."

"Look, I've never seen this Sansennoi, whoever he is. I do believe in guardian angels, but having a conversation with one outside a tavern in downtown Ashuelot Hollow is *apístefto*- just unbelievable."

"I have to go. You know that."

"When you're like this it's either 'lead, follow, or get out of the way,' isn't it?'"

"Come on *agápe mou*, it's not like that." She tried to put her hands on his forearms.

He shrugged her off. "I choose to get out of the way this time."

As she watched him walk down the hallway. She looked at the ceiling, "Why are You doing this to me? All I wanted was for my life to mean more. What kind of absurd purpose is this?"

"The kind you were born for," said a still small voice inside.

She shivered and shook off the tingling feeling as she walked to her bedroom.

Ari stripped out of her sweatpants and shirt. She put on her tightest push up bra and an old t-shirt. She cut the collar, ripping the t-shirt halfway down until the whole front of the black bra was exposed. She pinned the two sides of the t-shirt back together with several large safety pins over her cleavage. A black leather motorcycle jacket, skinny jeans, and the prayer rope were next. She tied her long platinum hair into a pony tail, balled it into a bun, and shoved it under a black leather baseball hat. She didn't want Lilith to recognize her, or anyone else for that matter. She turned sideways and looked in the full-length mirror. "Not bad for forty-seven."

It was 11:30 PM. Hector was lying on the couch watching some British guys racing mobile homes around a racetrack. He was shelling peanuts.

"Will you wait up for me?" She bent down to kiss him goodbye.

"Ari. You can't go out like that." He paused the show and stood to take a good look at her.

She tucked everything back in place. "I won't bend over, I promise. What do you think of my 'Metal Chick' disguise? I researched it online."

"What's that written on your neck?"

"It's a fake tattoo. Can't you read it?"

He shifted his glasses to the top of his head. "It says 'Ache Enemy'."

"Oh for Pete's sake. It's supposed to say 'Arch Enemy.' I had to write it backwards with a black Sharpie in the mirror."

He waved his hand up and down her profile. "You've taken it too far this time, Ari."

"I can't go to Midnight Metal Mania dressed like a mom."

He tapped his temple. "You know you become obsessed when you learn something new—remember that vegan food kick you made us all follow last summer? That ended with a binge at Wendy's."

"This is different." Her hands went to her hips.

"At least that was supposed to be healthy, so I went along with it, but this—I don't even know what to call it—this *demon chase* you're on now, it's dangerous—to you and our family...think about *Dorothea*. What would she think if she saw you like this?"

"That's not fair. You know she's not gonna see me like this."

"OK, what if you get hurt? Or worse? What would Dorothea do without her mother?" He put his warm hands on top of hers.

"You think I haven't agonized about that?" She took his hands in hers entwining their fingers together. "I don't like this whole demon battle either. I didn't choose it. I was chosen."

"You could've said no."

"I think our family would be in greater danger if I had. Why else would Sansennoi introduce himself to me today right after all this strange stuff that's been happening with the creep and Deirdre?"

"I dunno, Ari. He chose a *private* audience with you. Who knows who he truly is."

"You're jealous."

"Angels aren't always good. Some of them fell, you know." Hector wouldn't let go of her hands.

"Look, I gotta go. Will you wait up for me at least? Maybe say a prayer to the *Theotókos**?"

---

*Theotókos- Greek for *the God-bearer (The Virgin Mary.)*

"Praying to the Holy Mother of God definitely, because I know I won't be able to sleep." He crossed himself.

"Have your phone next to you in case I need you."

"Sansennoi's not tough enough?" He flapped his arms.

She caught his wrists. "You're a pain in the butt, Hector, but I still need *you*." She patted her pocket. "I also have Yiayiá's prayer rope. I'll be fine."

"Be careful, Ari. Power angel or not, wacky prayer rope or not, I don't like this at all."

"I know, but it's what I have to do." She kissed him on the mouth. A peanut butter kiss.

CHAPTER 28

The Onerous Path

Sunday Night | November 8th

Lilith was ravenous. She lifted the stainless steel domed lid on the cart and in silence she and Samael ate cheesecake. Their appetites were satiated for the moment.

Samael got up and stretched. "I'm going to bed. Are you coming, darling?"

"I want to explore what this male body can do." Lilith flexed her pecs. "I want to go out."

"Stay." Samael put his hand on her shoulder.

She grabbed the Sunday paper from the trolley. In the events section of the newspaper was an ad for 'Midnight Metal Mania'. Well, she'd see that they got what they asked for.

She went into the bedroom and told Samael about the snake.

"Love, why don't you simply pinch it?"

"There's no challenge in that."

"Must you always take the onerous path?"

"Come with me."

"This body is knackered, darling. Show me your prize when you return." He rolled over.

It was 11:30 PM. She left dressed in the young man's black trousers and white t-shirt.

Lilith picked up her Louis Vuitton purse then dropped it back in the chair. "Won't be needing this tonight." She dug out the key fob for the Jaguar and attached it to Travis's lanyard which was heavy-laden with keys. She walked out of Suite 254 swinging them on one finger.

CHAPTER 29

Power Metaller

Late Sunday Night | November 8th

It was a cool night, not a cold one, and there was no wind. Bob's Pet Bungalow was in the Ashuelot Hollow Mall—an ugly swath of commercialism built in the outskirts—skirting the town center to keep its hideousness far away from the quaint New England town square. The strip mall was only ten minutes from her house, but Ari wanted to be a little late to be able to slip inside the pet store unnoticed. At 11:50 PM the Mall's parking lot was empty except for several rows right in front of Bob's. A banner stretched across the front of the pet store which said 'Midnight Metal Mania' in black and red letters.

She scanned the lot for the ruby Jaguar with the Golden State plates. It took her a minute to find it—Lilith had parked in between two pickup trucks. *I was right, she's here. Now where's*

Sansennoi? Ari rolled the beads of the prayer rope, worn smooth by generations of women in her family, while she waited.

The prayer rope vibrated. "Oh!" she almost dropped it.

A whoosh of cinnamon displaced the air in the car. She blinked and Sansennoi was in the passenger seat. He looked the same way he had that morning with his hair slicked back wearing the cobalt blue suit.

"Why are you still dressed like *that*?"

"My wings and flaming sword would not fit with this setting."

"True, but you're not dressed for this crowd." She pointed at the pet store. "That's why I wore this."

He straightened his lapels. "That is inappropriate attire for a respectable woman."

"Really? Many 'respectable women' have dressed 'inappropriately' to fight for God's justice. I took Art History in college. That painting, the one about Judith, who put aside her widow's sackcloth, and spruced herself up to bravely enter the Assyrian camp and hack off their captain Holofernes' head? A woman's gotta use the tools given to her."

"Judith knew what her purpose was. I am not sure you do, Ari."

She crossed her arms.

He put his hand on her forearm. "What do you suggest I wear?"

"You could go as a 'Power Metaller.' I'll show you on my phone. See? You've got the hair for it."

"I understand." In the blink of an eye he was the mirror image of the power metaller on the screen.

Ari took in his flowing mane and simple t-shirt which stretched over muscular arms that ended in leather wrist cuffs. "That's...*better*." She forgot for a few seconds what she was doing there.

"The hour is midnight." Sansennoi got out of the car.

Ari and her guardian angel walked across the quiet parking lot.

"OK, so what's the game plan?" she asked.

"We are not here to play games."

"What I meant was, how should we approach the situation? Do we confront Deir—, I mean, Lilith?"

"We will stay in the background and observe. Do you know the Jesus Prayer?"

"Kinda. Yiayiá used to whisper it when she held her prayer rope. Something like, 'Jesus have mercy on me?'"

He gently shook his head. "It is this: Lord Jesus Christ, Son of God, have mercy on me, a sinner. The Jesus Prayer succinctly states what you need to say to God when you are under duress."

"Lord Jesus Christ, Son of God, have mercy on me, a sinner. Do I have to say the 'sinner' part? It's true, but it'd be kind of a downer to say it over and over again."

"You may shorten it, however, you must say it with your lips softly. If an evil alien thought tries to enter your mind, then you must push it away by saying the Jesus Prayer out loud. Otherwise, the demon might overtake you."

"Great. Can't you protect me from that? Be my wing-man?" She chuckled at the bad pun.

"I will never leave your side, but you must learn how to shield your soul through the power of the Holy Spirit. I cannot interfere until you have exhausted all other alternatives."

She looked toward the pet store and grimaced. "I hate roaches."

"All God's creatures exist for a reason, even cockroaches."

"What's the purpose of a cockroach?"

"They feed on decaying matter, then release nitrogen back into the ecosystem through their—"

"Oook-ay... but why did God have to make them so disgusting?"

"Roaches serve the same purpose as evil—to contrast the light, to highlight the beautiful creatures of this world."

CHAPTER 30

Midnight Metal Mania

Early Monday Morning | November 9th

Muffled cheers came from inside Bob's Pet Bungalow. Two young women stood next to the front door smoking. Ari got an eyeful but didn't meet their eyes. They were textbook representations of modern methods of mutilation. One had tattoos all around her neck and on the backs of her hands. You could tell she was a white girl only from her makeup-free face. *She's a coloring book.* The other one, a 'trophy metal girl,' had iron-straightened long black hair and would've been a pretty girl if she hadn't pierced every part which could be pierced on a body. Her ears were so full of holes and metal pins they drooped like those of a Scottish fold cat.

The coloring book one said, "Whoo-hoo! Jezebel, look what grandma's got." She elbowed the pretty pierced one who slowly raised her head. "Where'd you score that Matthew McConaughey look alike, Cougar?"

The pierced one, Jezebel, said, "Shut up, Jinx." She sized up Ari. "Cougar, don't mind my sister." She held out her hand to stop Ari. "Wait up—you *do not* wanna go in there. It's wicked brutal. Me and her had ta' split before we puked all over. Stay out here with me and Jinx. Let the eye candy go inside with the other guys."

"Thanks for the heads up—and the compliment, but I gotta risk it," Ari said. Her prejudice against the women was replaced with pity. *What kind of mother had named her daughters Jezebel and Jinx? They hadn't stood a chance of turning out well after being branded like that at birth. Names do matter.*

"Hey, it's your rodeo—but don't say I didn't warn ya'." Jezebel crushed the butt of her cigarette with the heel of her heavy black boot.

Sansennoi held the door open for Ari. It closed behind them and they were swallowed by the beast. The store smelled of cedar bedding, animal urine, and beer. All the ceiling lights were off and colored strobe lights had been set up behind DJ Sean's table. Black metal music banshee-howled from the four corners of the store. Young men in their twenties in biker jackets, spikes, and black leather boots bobbed in waves of straight dark hair and silver chains hooked on belt loops to the deafening music.

Ari prayed silently to center herself. She mouthed the words in 4/4 time to the rhythm of the music which throbbed in her brain. "Lord Je-sus Christ... Son of God have... mer-cy on me." She and Sansennoi stayed in the shadows.

A long row of tables was set up in the back in the eerie glow of the fish and reptile section. Terrariums shimmering with snakes, chameleons, turtles, frogs, and brightly-lit aquariums teeming with fish, surrounded the contestants in the shape of a Π. The water in the tanks rippled to the beat of the music.

Eight male contestants wore t-shirts which said 'Midnight Metal Maniac' with paper numbers pinned on them. Each stood behind a big white plastic bucket and two smaller ones on the long tables. The big buckets had 'DISCOID COCKROACHES' hastily written on them, the two smaller white buckets had 'HORN WORMS' on the one and 'MEAL WORMS' on the other. Cockroaches and horn worms crawled onto the rims of the buckets to escape being on the buffet.

A man in his sixties with Keith Richards hair and worse skin, had the soul sucker python draped on his shoulders. He stroked the snake, smiling at the large turnout. *That must be Bob.*

Ari searched the crowd for Deirdre.

"I can't find her," she said to Sansennoi.

"Lilith might be in another body now. You will not recognize the face, just her mannerisms."

"So it's true. A demon can hijack a person's body... like when a carjacker jumps into a running car, shoves the driver out, and takes off?"

"A powerful demon like this one can, but only if the driver leaves the keys in the ignition, either out of carelessness or intention. If people knew how vigorously demons coveted their human bodies, they would never let their guard down."

"How does she enter them?"

"The transfer is made through an orifice in the body. The person Lilith is in now is probably one of her many followers who has given the demon permission to take them over. Humans require rest, but demons never sleep. That is part of their torment. Lilith is here to amuse herself, to win the snake. She has an age-old affinity for them."

A buzzer sounded and Bob shouted into the mic, "Go! You have five minutes, Midnight Metal Maniacs!"

Ari surveyed the line of young men at the tables. They had several cans of domestic beer next to them to wash down the squirming bugs. The store employees were tallying each kind of insect they ate while the friends of the contestants shouted out the numbers after each swallow their buddies managed, "5... 6... 7," and so on.

She looked away shivering in disgust. The crunching sound the men made chewing was identical to the one she made when she cracked a roach with her leather sandal. She covered her mouth so she wouldn't vomit. She understood now why Jezebel and Jinx preferred to wait outside in the cold instead of enduring this Gehenna.

She made herself turn around again. The men behind the buckets stared at the ceiling and held their mouths shut with their hands to prevent themselves from retching.

A young man at the end of the table was getting the most cheers from the crowd. The guys in front of him yelled out his count, "47... 48... 49." Ari saw the corner of his mouth twitch oddly. The young man grabbed a handful of roaches out of the bucket with a flourish, held it up to the crowd, and stuffed the squirming mass into his mouth. The mob loved it. He crammed in a fistful of meal worms next. *That's gotta be her.* Ari whispered to Sansennoi, "Number 8." He nodded.

She fought hard against her gag reflex by silently saying the Prayer while shifting from one foot to the other, now in 2/4 time to the beat of her heart: "Lord Je-... sus Christ... have... mer-cy... on me."

The buzzer went off. *Thank God.*

The numbers were tallied; the arrogant young man at the end was the winner. Bob announced, "Contestant Number 8 is the new Midnight Metal Mania record holder with a total of 57 cockroaches, 17 horn worms, and 44 meal worms. That's *double* the old record!" The crowd clapped and booed at the same time in support of their friends who didn't win.

Bob kissed the python, placed it on the young man's shoulders, and handed him a can of beer. The young man gulped down the whole can and let out a loud burp. The crowd laughed. Contestant Number 8 was clearly enjoying his moment in the spotlight. Bob waited for the laughter to die down. He held the mic in front of the young man and said, "What's your name, son?"

The corner of the young man's mouth twitched and he looked confused for a moment. "Uh, Travis." His pink wind-burned cheeks now looked a little green.

"Congratulations, Travis!" Bob raised the young man's arm over his head in a show of victory and the crowd cheered anew. "Crank up the music, DJ Sean!"

Several men slapped Travis on the back as he left out the front door. Ari and Sansennoi followed him into the cool but purifying night air.

CHAPTER 31

Jinx & Jezebel

Early Monday Morning | November 9ᵗʰ

The prayer rope quaked in Ari's jeans pocket. She held it firmly and it stilled.

Travis passed the two young women standing outside the front door.

Jinx grabbed the back of his t-shirt. "Yo, Number 8, where're you runnin' off to so fast?"

"Yeah, don't leave gorgeous... we wanna find out what other records you hold." Jezebel stroked the snake's head with one hand and ran the other up the heavy silver chain holding his keys, then hooked her fingers into his belt loop.

"Yeah, me and my sister can help you double that one too," Jinx chimed in.

Travis turned around with a wicked smile on his face and took Jezebel's hand and said, "I'm always up for a new challenge. Come here."

"Oh!" He pulled Jezebel to him and shoved her against the store window. The thick glass vibrated to the bass of the music.

Travis kissed Jezebel on the mouth. When he pulled away she was bruised and breathless. He moved in to kiss her sister, but instead doubled over and retched. Jezebel and Jinx stood motionless as brown and yellow bile mixed with spiny roach legs and lime-colored hornworms gushed out of his mouth, splattering all over the pavement and them.

"Ughff—" Ari went over to the curb, and let the supper she'd been trying to keep down disgorge onto the blacktop.

Sansennoi said, "We need to attend to Travis now that the demon is weakened."

"Attend to him...how?" she asked, her throat hoarse.

Three burly men ran out of the pet store. Travis was choking and wheezing. They tried to steady him but backed off when they saw the live vomit. "Dude, *dude*, that's *vile* man." One yelled back into Bob's, "Call 911!"

Ari observed the crowd forming around Travis. A few were staring at him pointing and grimacing. Most of them were gleefully recording him on their cell phones. It was a modern-day crowd at the Colosseum—as bloodthirsty and merciless as the Romans had been. She was disgusted more by them than by the insect soup pouring out of Travis.

Jezebel and Jinx knelt beside Travis. "It's okay. Just get 'em out of you. The ambulance'll be here AS-AP."

Travis looked at them. "Don't leave me," he said as he fell to the pavement. He laid there convulsing on his side as insects crawled from his mouth and limped away through the vomit.

Ari could swear it was a look of human fear, not the hard black demon stare he'd had only a minute before. She stepped on a roach. *If Travis is still in there, I must help him.* She recited the Prayer quietly out loud. "Lord Jesus Christ, Son of God, have mercy on Travis, a sinner."

"What are you mumbling, Cougar?" Jinx looked at her. "Are you prayin'? Do you think that's gonna help? Look at him!"

Sansennoi took Ari aside. "Lilith has over-exerted the young man's body. He is dying, and she knows it. Keep the people back."

"Give him room to breathe." Ari tapped Jezebel on the shoulder.

"Get off me," Jezebel said.

"Yeah, back off, Cougar." Jinx stood and unfolded a switchblade in Ari's face.

Ari stood her ground and continued saying the Prayer. A power came over her which she had never experienced before. She was emancipated from fear. She spoke in her tender but firm mother's voice to the insecure, immature, and unloved child she perceived under all the ink. "Jinx, I'm trying to protect your sister."

Jinx's expression softened. She put her hand on Jezebel's arm. "Hey, Jez—do what she says."

"Back off, Jinx." Jezebel brushed her hand away.

"Really, get up now, Jez." Jinx shook her shoulder.

"Don't leave me here alone...kiss me one last time," Travis moaned and lifted his head to Jezebel.

"See, he needs me. I ain't goin' nowhere," Jezebel held his head. She moved in to kiss him.

"Stop!" Ari said. She spoke in Jezebel's ear. "Look, I know what's wrong with him. You need to move back and let my friend and me help him." She pointed at Sansennoi.

Jezebel looked over at the angel. When she saw the sincerity on his and on Ari's face, she stood. "OK, Cougar, but if you hurt him, I'll hurt you." She wiped her hands on her jeans.

Ari knelt next to Travis.

CHAPTER 32

CPR

Early Monday Morning | November 9th

Ari patted Travis's arm but kept her distance. "Hang in there, Travis."

"They said it…it was gonna be the ultimate VR game. So I got the owl tat—" His voice was ragged and weak.

"Yes, its eyes are quite realistic."

"She lied to me…she said it'd be like *Works of Mercy*, ya' know…but this is too raw, man." He closed his eyes. "She lied to m—"

"Stay with me, Travis!" Ari slapped him on both cheeks. His neck gave no resistance, nor was he breathing. She put her ear to his chest. No beat there. *I have to give him CPR. Ughf.*

She swept two fingers into his mouth to clear it and wiped the bile and bugs from his lips with her t-shirt. She leaned over…her mouth was wide open…

Sansennoi yelled, "Ari no!"

Travis's body animated. His powerful hand grabbed the base of her neck. He smashed his mouth onto hers. The eyes were not his. *Lilith.* Lilith's spirit tried to cram its way into Ari's open mouth, but she was praying the Jesus Prayer. The evil essence screamed and burned, and was blocked from entering Ari's body. She fell backward and Sansennoi caught her in his open arms and drew her to him.

"*NO!*" Lilith shrieked. The crowd shuddered in unison then cried out in disbelief as they witnessed Lilith's black spirit surge out of Travis's dead mouth and swirl in the open air. Her dark essence had no option but to enter the python which was coiled behind the young man. The snake's body writhed for a few seconds then lay still. Travis's body went limp and dropped to the pavement, a discarded wet towel.

Jezebel ran to Travis and put her ear near his mouth. "He's not breathing! Somebody do something!"

Ari pulled away from Sansennoi and went to Travis. She rolled him on his back and put her ear to his mouth. No breath. She took his pulse. "Does anyone here know CPR?" She looked into the crowd. They had their arms crossed and grimacing, shaking their heads. *Yeah, I agree. I don't want to put my mouth on his again either.*

She did anyway. She breathed into Travis's mouth and pushed on his chest to the beat of "Stayin' Alive" which she'd read in an article about CPR. For several minutes she sweated and prayed over him.

Sansennoi put his hand on Ari's shoulder. "He is gone."

"No, I can save him." She jammed her hands back on Travis's chest.

"Get off him." Jezebel jerked Ari to her feet. "Gimmee your blade, Jinx."

"*They're too many people here, Jez,*" Jinx whispered to her sister.

"Gimmee the blade *now*." Jezebel held out her palm to Jinx. Jinx gave her the knife.

Jezebel took a step toward Ari unfolding the switchblade. "I told ya'… that if you hurt *him*…I'd hurt *you*."

Ari took a step backward and ran into Sansennoi. "Pray for her," he said.

Ari said, "Lord Jesus Christ, Son of God, have mercy on you, Jezebel."

Jezebel took another step forward and growled in her face, "Shut up."

Ari didn't. "Lord Jesus Christ, Son of God, have mercy on Jezebel."

"I'll cut your tongue out, Cougar. God forgot about me a long time ago." She pushed Ari hard on the chest back into Sansennoi and put the blade against Ari's cheek.

"No, He didn't," Sansennoi said and moved his hand in front of Jezebel's face. Her eyes closed and she slumped to the ground. Jinx caught her right before she hit the cement. Ari helped Jinx lean Jezebel against the pet store. Jinx cried and cradled her sister's head in her arms. Ari knelt next to her.

"What'd your man do to her, Cougar?" Jinx's eyes held true love and fear for her sister.

Ari looked over her shoulder at Sansennoi with a 'Well, what did you do to her?' expression on her face.

The angel put his hand on Jinx's shoulder. "Your sister will regain consciousness in a few minutes. Do not be afraid." Jinx's face relaxed and she stopped crying.

Ari remembered the python. It was gone. "Where's the snake?"

CHAPTER 33

Iggy

Early Monday Morning | November 9th

"Opportunity knocks once," said a man aptly named "Iggy" for the two-inch mohawk shaved onto his head to look like an iguana was holding on with four hairy clawed feet. While everyone else was looking at the cat fight between the cougar and the trophy metal girl, Iggy put the snake around his shoulders and unhooked Travis's lanyard. He saw the Jaguar key among the others. His eyes widened.

An ambulance siren wailed in the distance. He sprinted to the Jag, almost falling down he was so high, and got in. The snake's forked tongue flitted in and out of its mouth and tickled the little hair tail which curled around Iggy's neck.

The python said, "Take me to the Ashuelot Hollow Inn, Son of Adam."

"Whoa. Cool, a talking snake. That must've been some good stuff. Sure, I'll take ya' wherever ya' wanna go, since I getta drive this baby." Iggy patted the dashboard as he drove out of the parking lot unnoticed. "BTW, my dad's name is Eric, not Adam."

CHAPTER 34

The Serpent in the Garden

Early Monday Morning | November 9th

Ambulance lights flashed in the distance. Police sirens wailed their way to Bob's Pet Bungalow. Midnight Metal Mania was over. The throng dispersed, scurried to their vehicles, then squealed out of the parking lot. Ari and Sansennoi helped Jinx drag a lethargic Jezebel to their truck. They searched for the snake. It wasn't anywhere. Sansennoi took Ari by the elbow. "We should leave. The demon must be in the python."

"Can she do that?" Ari asked. "Jump into an animal?"

"Yes, she can. A demon can take over any living thing. Even a bird or a fish if it desires."

They drove out of the mall just as the ambulance arrived. "I thought demons only inhabited humans because we have a soul."

"Are you sure other creatures do not?"

"No."

"They do. The difference between them and you is that humans can be filled with the Holy Spirit; other life forms cannot. Only you were made in the image and likeness of God. We angels were not. It is one of the reasons demons are jealous of you."

"For millennia many people have thought Lilith was the serpent in the Garden of Eden from what I gathered about her online. She's depicted tempting Eve in paintings, poems, stories, amulets, and statues."

"Lilith has propagated her ancient fallacy well. To stop her we must find the python."

"Maybe Bob picked it up, happy to recoup his prize," she said. "I'll stop by the pet store in the morning and snoop around."

"That is a good place to start. Listen to the Holy Spirit in you. You will acquire more wisdom from Him than from anywhere else. He will help you defeat Lilith." He kissed her on the cheek. "I love you, my little tigress. I will be in touch."

She was alone. She shuddered and rubbed her forearms, hugging herself.

Ari drove home mulling over all that had happened over the past week. It no longer mattered how or why she had gotten involved in this whole demonic mess. It was a struggle she couldn't ignore any longer and a battle she couldn't let the other side win. A veil had been lifted and she'd been made privy to knowledge of the spiritual realm. Sansennoi was right. She'd have to start listening to the Holy Spirit and stop reacting to her feelings.

The silver BMW's brights cut the blackness of the night. The trees did not move. Nature was still, and reverent. *How fitting*.

The headlights caught four yellow retinas of deer standing by the right side of the road ready to jump across. She braked hard. A doe and her fawn stared at her. "Come on across, girl." The doe nosed her fawn which waited beside her, then tiptoed across the road. The fawn bounded ahead of her. *Dorothea*. Ari's heart quickened into a ball of feathers behind her sternum. She pressed on the gas pedal and raced home.

CHAPTER 35

Room Service

Early Monday Morning | November 9th

The man with the iguana mohawk drove Lilith's Jaguar to the Ashuelot Hollow Inn.

Iggy knocked on Suite 254.

Samael opened the door.

Iggy held up the snake's head. "This your snake, man?"

"No. Shove off, mate."

Iggy stopped the door with his foot. "Look, *mate*, she told me to drive here in the Jag."

Samael opened the door and peered at the python. "Darling?" he said.

The python hissed in Latin, *"Ex hoc stulto nunc, cape me, Samael*."*

"Whoa, what'd it say?"

"I'll take her." Samael reached for the snake.

Iggy took a step back. "Dude. I'm high, not stupid. This python's a soul sucker morph and worth a thousand bucks."

Samael opened his wallet and thrust five one hundred dollar bills at him.

Iggy fingered the bills. "Dude. That'll do...that'll do just fine." He lifted the snake from his shoulders and handed her to Samael.

"Do not speak of this to anyone—or you will regret it," Samael said.

"Okay, dude, chill out. I won't say anything, I promise." Iggy turned to leave.

"The keys." Samael held out his palm.

"Oh yeah." He hung the lanyard on Samael's wrist. "Hey, how'm I gonna get back—"

Samael shut the door on him.

The snake turned her smooth head toward Samael. "Why didn't you kill him?"

"Why didn't you?" Samael locked the door.

"He's one of ours."

---

*Ex hoc stulto nunc, cape me, Samael- Latin for *Get me off this imbecile now, Samael.*

CHAPTER 36

Snake Kiss

Monday Morning | November 9th

Deedee had dozed off again. The sound of water running brought her back to consciousness. She opened her eyes. *Where am I?* The room was dark. The only light came from the bathroom. The happy reality of her dream... with Andrew and Justin reading books all cozy together in bed—the one she'd just woken from, receded into the nightmare of the bedroom she was still in. She tried to lift her hands—in slow motion—in dreamy fuzziness... but it felt heavier than that... like a synthetic lethargy, like waking up in a recovery room. It took her a few moments... *oh*—the man had shoved a pill down her throat. *I'm so thirsty.* She coughed and tried to swallow. Her terry cloth tongue was bound between her bottom teeth by a robe sash. *I have been discarded by God like a dirty towel.*

Magnetic metal flakes of memory struggled to pull themselves together into information her mind could comprehend. Something was holding them back. Deedee did not want to remember. Her will was focused on one goal—to save her son and unborn child from Lilith. What if that crazed demon woman is in my house right now, stalking my son? Justin would be hiding behind the heavy living room curtains, holding his T. rex pillow. God, you've forgotten about me, but please watch over my son until I can, please. Tears welled in her eyes. A still small voice whispered in her mind, **"Use your talents."** A surge of hope filled her. *They've bound my body, but they can't bind my mind. Use logic...for Justin's sake.*

The water stopped running. The bathroom door was ajar. Her heart pounded so loudly that she was sure whoever it was could hear it. She lifted her bound wrist. Her arms glistened with sandalwood-scented oil. She was dressed in a scarlet negligee. Her body had been washed and oiled. Prepared. She shifted her weight, stifling a groan. *Must try... for Justin... maybe the oil will help my hands slip out of the ties... push through the pain...* she tried to wiggle free—

The door swung open, illuminating the bedroom. Deedee saw blood red pictographs drawn in neat lines on the ceiling above her. *I've seen these before.* Long-buried memories of her mother and the rites she and her friends performed late at night in the basement shot to the surface.

A man walked toward her, his face hidden in the shadows. He was carrying something... a snake! Her leg muscles tightened, her body was ready to run. She struggled to free her wrists and ankles, but the knots in the red scarves binding them to the bed tightened the harder she pulled. She clenched her teeth. *Don't black out again... don't lose control to this... to this... animal.* He laid the snake on the bed next to her. It glided toward her. Deedee shook her head. "No!"

"Daughter of Eve, you were born to serve us." *The man held the sides of her head firmly in his smooth hands. She looked up at him, finally recognizing who he was.*

Deedee's will weakened for a moment and a few of the metal memory flakes rushed back together. Her body trembled uncontrollably. *Don't black out... they control you when you do. Stay in control for Justin... don't... black... out... stay... here... for Jus... tin.* The python coiled slowly under and around her neck, then squeezed. The man slipped off the gag. Deedee opened her mouth, gasping for air. The snake unhinged its jaws, slid its head beside her ear, and struck down. The python sealed her mouth with its own. *Get it off me!*

A blast of fiery hatred tunneled into her throat. *No, not you again... leave me alone.* Lilith's spiritual essence forced its way into Deedee's body. Deedee fought against it and grappled with Lilith as they both landed in the blackness of Deedee's mind.

"Back in your cage." Lilith shoved Deedee and she fell backward into the white bone cage. Lilith slammed the door shut. Her voice was a low leopard growl. "You no longer exist. To fight me is futile. If you do, I will dispose of your body after it gives birth to my daughter. If you do not obey me in the meantime, I will slay your son."

Deedee's memory fragments assembled into that dreadful moment her will had been trying to hide from her. *What have I done? I can't lose my son. Or my unborn daughter.* Deedee curled into *a ball, rocking herself back and forth. Spare my children... I'll be good... she said over and over.*

Lilith strode to the front of Deedee's mind. She put on Deedee's eyes, the windows of her soul, easily like a pair of glasses.

The snake unclamped itself from Deedee's face and was a dumb reptile again.

Deedee's eyes had changed. "Free me." Lilith lifted her bound limbs. Samael untied the red scarves and she touched her wrists. The wounds healed instantly. "My legs, Samael."

"Forgive me, darling." He looked at her, hopeful.

"I will rest this body now. Fetch breakfast in the morning for my new baby; she's hungry after all this activity." Lilith kissed the python and pressed it against her cheek.

He frowned. *His* hunger would have to wait.

CHAPTER 37

Ache Enemy

3 AM Monday Morning | November 9th

On the way home from the pet store, Ari had not 'seen' the road ahead of her. She was focused on Dorothea. That deep mother fear, which all mothers know well, crinkled into an electric ball of aluminum foil in her intestines.

Home at last. She tore into the garage and raced up the stairs to Dorothea's bedroom. She flipped on the hallway light and stopped in the doorway, hand on the frame. Her body shivered involuntarily. She shrugged off the stiff leather jacket, shedding the ugly alien skin.

Her daughter was in bed. Ari sagged against the wall and caught her breath. She listened for the usual sounds: the cute little snoring gurgles and the full sentences the child said in her sleep. The only breathing sounds Ari heard were her own. Dorothea was as still as a stone. The aluminum ball of fear unfolded itself and re-animated, scraping the lining of her stomach. She bent to feel her daughter's soft breath on her cheek. Ari brushed a curl from Dorothea's perfect forehead and traced the girl's eyebrows with her finger. "*Moró mou?* Mamá's home."

The child stirred and spoke, "Mamá."

"Oh, sweetness." She kissed her daughter's forehead. *I almost left you motherless. Forgive me.* Ari crossed herself looking heavenward. "Thank you." She pressed Dorothea's small hand to her cheek. She kissed it and tucked Dorothea's blankie in her hand and the girl immediately popped her thumb in her mouth. Ari gently ran her fingers across the embroidered name on the blanket, Δωροθέα, which the child shared with Hector's mother. Along the border, frolicking lambs wore either tiny bells or wildflower wreaths. Dorothea soothed herself by rubbing their nubby whorls of wool between her left thumb and finger. Dorothea's *yiayiá* had lovingly labored on it for years waiting for her son and his wife to conceive a child.

Ari curled her arms over her head. She directed a pained stare upward. "Doesn't she need me more than You do? You better protect her from this mess I'm in."

She made herself leave the room. The exhaustion increased with every step she took down the stairs. She walked past the living room and heard Hector snoring on the couch. She'd forgotten all about him. Wife guilt set in, Ari shoved it away—she was a mother first. She was grateful that he, an early-rising lark, had at least tried to wait up for her. She covered his shoulders with an afghan his mother had knitted.

Hector sat up knocking foreheads with her. "Ow! What time is it? You okay, Ari?"

"I'm fine," she said rubbing her forehead.

"Man, it's like you're wearing a steel helmet. Thank God you're okay." He crossed himself three times and pulled her tightly to him. "Tell me what happened."

"Hector, I can't breathe," she said into his chest. His heart was beating fast. He loosened his embrace a little. "I'll tell you in the morning. It's after 3. Let's go to bed. I really need you to hold me."

Ari woke from a dream where she was being dragged underwater in an aquarium. A weight was pulling the covers tautly behind her back. It took her a few moments to comprehend that Dorothea had climbed onto the bed and was sitting in the middle of it. She opened her eyes and looked at the clock. 7:07 AM. She rolled onto her back. Dorothea was holding her blankie and sucking her thumb.

"Mamá, what's that black stuff on your face?"

"Oh, I forgot to wash it off. It's eyeliner." She caught Dorothea's foot. She knew how to distract her daughter. "This little piggy went to market, this little piggy stayed home, this little piggy had roast beef..."

"Mamá, my tummy's hungry. Can you make me *loukoumádes**?"

"... this little piggy had none, and this little piggy went wee, wee, wee all the way home!" Ari tickled her daughter all the way up to her ear.

Dorothea's tinkling laughter filled the bedroom.

---

*Loukoumádes- Greek for *honey doughnut balls.*

"Maybe we can make loukoumádes after school today, *moró mou*." She hugged her and set her on the floor.

7:15 AM. Ari willed her feet to the floor.

Hector was in the kitchen. "Good morning, *agápe mou!*" Her husband was an infernally cheery morning person. Ari was not. He kissed her on the cheek which she turned aside for him to avoid mutual morning breath.

She grumbled, "Good morning," into his ear.

"What time'd you come home last night? I didn't look."

"Four hours ago."

"I didn't sleep much either, you kept kicking me." He walked past her to the fridge. "You awake enough to tell me what happened last night?"

"Wait until someone is—" she glanced at Dorothea and made a teething brushing motion.

"Right."

"Thanks for making me espresso." She tipped the cup to her lips. It was the elixir of life.

"I thought it would help bring back the woman I love—" Hector ran his finger across the misspelled fake Sharpie 'tattoo' she'd drawn on her neck. "—and not my Ache Enemy…"

Ari laughed in spite of herself.

CHAPTER 38

Tail

Monday Morning | November 9th

Ari dropped Dorothea off at school then drove to the Ashuelot Hollow Mall. The Mall looked innocuous and commonplace at 9 AM. When she'd told Hector the whole story that morning, saying it out loud in the light of day made her feel stupid. He doubted her recollection of what she had seen, so did she. She drove slowly by the pet store.

The spot where Travis had died was cordoned off with yellow caution tape. A corner of the 'Midnight Metal Mania' banner had unfastened. It now read 'Midnight Metal Ma—'.

Bug parts littered the pavement. *So I didn't make it up.*

A black Porsche drove up and parked in front of the pet store. Yiayiá's prayer rope shuddered in Ari's pocket. *Oh no...* She grasped it in her palm and it instantly quieted. She looked up and did a double take. *Samuel?* She stared at him through the windshield. It hurt to look at him; he was *a nail-bitingly beautiful man. No! A demon remember!* Samuel hadn't seen her. He went into Bob's.

When Samuel came out a few minutes later with a small box, she tailed him. Ari followed him to the Ashuelot Hollow Inn. She parked beside a laundry service truck. Samuel got out, but didn't look around, so she guessed he didn't suspect she was stalking him, or maybe he didn't care. He strode to the glass doors of the hotel and went inside. Ari followed.

Samuel pushed the button for the second floor.

Ari took the stairs. She ran to the second floor and quietly panting, opened the door to the stairwell a crack and peeked out.

The elevator dinged and Samuel walked down the hallway. Ari made a mental count of how many doors he passed. 1...2...3...4. Four. He opened a door on the left side and went in.

She kept her eyes fixed on the spot where Samuel had disappeared, right next to the fire alarm. She caught her breath then trod lightly down the hallway. She counted the doors 1...2...3...4 until she stood in front of Suite 254. Lilith was in Suite 254. That's all she needed to know for now, she was bone tired. She took the back stairs and left out the rear entrance, then drove home to take a nap.

CHAPTER 39

Gethsemane

Monday Afternoon | November 9th

After her nap, Ari needed to take a walk to clear her head. North Chapel Burying Ground where she often went was four centuries old and had great swaths of pavement throughout. Reading the gravestones humbled her.

It was a gorgeous late fall afternoon. The lungs of autumn exhaled their salutations across her body. Ari paused on a little wooden bridge. The cattails along the brook were corn dogs exploding, spreading fluffy seeds across the water. Her soul lifted with them. She released her pony tail, loosening it with her fingers. The platinum ends danced on her shoulders. *It feels good to be alive. I don't want to die.*

The breeze warmed her face like taking cinnamon rolls out of the oven. Yiayiá's prayer rope jiggled in her jeans…and Sansennoi appeared at her side—in full battle gear.

"Goodness!" Ari jumped back from the railing.

"You have always startled easily." Sansennoi clasped his strong hands near the abdomen section of his cobalt blue breast plate, right below the indentation of his navel. Only the hilt of his sheathed sword was visible under the scarlet robe which hung heavily from his powerful shoulders. It was unmoved by the wind, but the feathers of his golden wings ruffled delicately around the edges.

"I know, but look at you, all angelic glory and those..." She pointed to his twelve-foot wing span. "What if someone sees you?"

"I need no disguise among the dead. They have already seen angels."

Ari hitchhiked her thumb up and down. "Either lifting souls up or dragging them down there...eh?"

"You oversimplify the journey."

"Well, in case someone living shows up, can you at least put those away? If Hector saw you now, he'd believe me."

Sansennoi folded his wings neatly under his robe. "Your husband is a good man of deep faith. He will come around. You should treat him better."

"You heard us this morning." She looked out across the brook.

"I hear you every morning."

Ari turned and walked over the bridge onto the broad pavement which wound around the graves. Sansennoi followed her. "Look, I found where Lilith is staying. She and Samuel are at the Ashuelot Hollow Inn, Suite 254. I followed him there this morning."

He nodded.

"You said you'd answer my questions as we went along, so I want to know who Lilith really is."

"Then I must first tell you about Lucifer, the Father of Lies. Lucifer was not created by God as *ha-satan*, whom you know as Satan, the 'adversary.' He was created 'Lucifer,' the 'bearer of light', a great angel, the greatest of the seraphim—the angels of light, love, and fire—the highest order of my kind. Lucifer's high rank was distinguished by his twelve wings, he was unlike any angel in heaven."

"You admire Lucifer."

"I did. We angels were in awe of him. He transcended all of us in knowledge and beauty. But he became proud, thinking himself better than the Most High. Many angels followed Lucifer. When they did not repent, God cast Lucifer and his fallen angels out of heaven into the depths of the Pit. Their angelic light burned black. Lucifer and his followers embrace darkness, evil, hatred, and all that is the antithesis of the Almighty. Evil was born in the utter perfection of my brother, Lucifer, who chose by his own free will to become Satan, the adversary of Man."

"It's fascinating to learn about this from an eye witness, but how does it tie in with Lilith?"

"When not in a human body, Lilith lives, in a cave by the Reed Sea. She is *not* as she claims, the first woman created by God. Instead, she is a *second* class of evil spirits called the *mazziqin*, evil spirits who injure. Lilith and her hoards are in a subclass of mazziqin called night terrors: half-spirit, half-human hybrids who are the results of the defilement of women by Satan's fallen angels. Fallen angels are of the *first* class of mazziqin."

"Lilith is a second-class citizen in the evil spirit world? Is that why she deludes herself thinking she pre-dates Eve?"

"Do not dismiss her power. Satan has trained her well. They will fight side by side in the battle of the end times."

"You must be tired waiting for that."

"I am patient because time is not linear for me. This helps me endure you, my little tigress." He playfully tickled her under the chin.

Her angel was a bit of a rascal. In that moment Ari knew he loved her. She wanted to love him back, to trust him, but it was hard to relinquish control of her life. What would happen if she did? *Terrifying thought. Stall. Ask more questions.* "I failed at the Midnight Metal Mania contest and Travis died."

"That was not your fault. Travis had already succumbed to evil. Did you see Lilith's mark of the screech owl on his arm? Few can resist her once she sets her sights on them. There was no way he could have survived her severe usage of him. I know Lilith well. I have been warring against her since the Flood. Her body was drowned, and over the millennia she has become a powerful spirit. She is the second part of your two-fold task."

"What's the first part?"

"First, you must protect the Locke family. They are in great danger. Lilith has made solid progress with her oppression of Laurie, Randy, and their daughter Amy. Little Elijah has been spared so far."

"And the second part is?"

"Lilith must be exorcised from the body of Deirdre."

"Great. You want me to be a Ghostbuster. Do I get a plasma gun?"

He stalked away.

She ran to catch up. "Hey, I'm sorry."

He stopped and looked at her unblinking. "Your glib remarks offend me. This is real. More children will die if you are careless. Deirdre Morrigan's body is fully possessed by Lilith. Deirdre goes by 'Deedee'. You must free her."

"How am I supposed to do that?"

"You need a priest. You will work together."

"Why me?"

"Deedee suffers greatly, trapped within her own mind, while the female demon does what she pleases with her body. You have angered Lilith and she will use Deedee to hurt Dorothea."

"Over my dead body. How did Lilith possess her in the first place?"

"Deedee is the child of a sorceress who gave her to Lilith at birth. Lilith recently called in her debt. She used Deedee's vulnerability against her. Deedee and her husband were desperate for another child. Deedee *and* Laurie need your help. Lilith's next target is Laurie."

"Look, I feel for Deedee. I know how infertility can make you willing to try anything. And Laurie's okay. But neither of them are my friends! I don't think I can or want to save them. I have my own child to worry about."

"Deedee does too. Her little boy Justin doesn't know where his mother is. She dropped him off at kindergarten and never came back. She has been missing for over a month. Lilith lifted Deedee's hand against her own son to kill him when Lilith had a moment of control over her body. Deedee ran away to protect her son from herself. Lilith will kill Laurie's children when she has used up Deedee's body and moves on to Laurie's."

"Why would she do that?"

"That is what she does. She is a child slayer. Lilith constantly seeks revenge for her demon children whom I must find and kill. That part of The Alphabet of ben Sira is true: Sennoi, Samangaluf, and I have been culling her progeny for ages. The world would be overrun with demon-human hybrids like a plague of locusts if we did not."

"I need to sit down a minute." Ari sat on a bench. "I didn't know there was a person trapped inside the body Lilith is in. Why didn't you tell me this before?"

"It was not time yet. You were not ready to take up this cross."

"Huh, believe me, I'm not sure I am now either. You said Deedee is married. What's her husband's name?"

"Andrew. They live in San Francisco."

"How'd she end up in Ashuelot Hollow of all places?"

"The demon was drawn to the name, Ashuelot because of the name of her birthplace. 'Mesopotamia' means 'a place between two rivers.'"

"Ashuelot Hollow lies between the Connecticut and Ashuelot Rivers."

"Lilith has wreaked havoc across the country in Deedee's body. You know of her atrocities from the newspaper articles you clip."

"The ones about prolicide. I began collecting those articles because I couldn't wrap my head around what would drive a mother to kill her own child."

"Demonic oppression is one reason. Lilith is the worst reason."

Ari picked up a stick and drew infinity shapes in the soft dirt. "That makes sense. Lilith uses different women's bodies here, and in other countries, to kill their own children seemingly out of the blue, with no provocation, right?"

He moved his hand in an arc. "There is an invisible spirit world all around you. You have been given all the charismata necessary to vanquish the demon: courage, wisdom, tenacity, discernment. If you are willing, my dear."

"I can't do battle with a child killer! Dorothea might get hurt. I couldn't bear to lose her. I would die *with her*. I know I would." She stabbed at the ground with the stick.

Sansennoi stepped in front of her and quieted the stick in her hand. His voice was low and gentle. "Dorothea might die if you do not fight Lilith. She has threatened to slay your daughter too, merely for her amusement."

Ari let the stick fall to the ground. She grabbed his wrists. Her eyes were feverish and over bright. "I don't want to do this! You're an angel, why do you need me?"

"That is the problem—angels are forbidden certain interactions with human beings. If I disobey, I would be an abomination like Lilith. So even though I can navigate both the spiritual and the physical realms, your spirit resides in this world in the flesh of a woman. Therefore you have power in a way I do not to fight Lilith while she is in the flesh. Together, with God's help, we will subdue the demon."

"Dorothea could die because my faith in God isn't strong enough." She pounded her fists on her lap to hold in the tears.

"No, you are of the order of Deborah, the prophetess, a judge of Israel. She was a formidable warrior, firm in her faith in the Lord. You will prevail, by the grace of God."

"You're wrong. I'm not like Deborah. You don't know what's in my heart." A tear escaped. Ari hastily wiped it away.

"Yes, I do. You trusted God would give you a baby even when it seemed hopeless. You had the faith of Hannah. I was there with you in that doctor's office. I saw your tears, your determination, and your surrender to His will. That took enormous courage and faith."

"Yeah right," she scoffed.

"Why do you think I call you my little tigress? You jumped through flaming rings of fire to have Dorothea! You persevered through the pain of the injections, through the doubt that the IVF would not work, through the fear of remaining childless. What I see in you is the heart of a heroine."

"Do you honestly mean that?" Ari was crying in earnest now.

"My child, it is why you were born. God has been preparing you for this your entire life. Think back and you will see the journey that has led you to this moment: standing with an angel in *your own* garden of Gethsemane, with *your own* cup of affliction before you. You must decide to take it up or not."

She rose from the bench wiping her face with her sleeves. Sansennoi followed. They walked in silence for several minutes. His words resonated to her in perfect pitch. *I have always felt like a heroine, but I have rarely acted like one.* She knew this was one of those defining choices she'd make and remember years later. Her life would never be the same again.

A leaf fell from a denuding maple and tumbled across their path, pushed to animation by the wind. *I need to let go and freefall into God's hands like that leaf.* She picked up the leaf and turned her face to the sky. The wind gently flowed over her, in and around, clearing her fear away. She was filled with resolve.

If God thinks my tiny bit of faith is enough to do this, then who am I to question Him? She looked over at her angel. *Isn't he proof that God exists? If I do nothing, Lilith might kill all our children.* At that realization, a mental stake shoved in the ground and anchored her. She had to take a stand against such evil. She stopped and looked at Sansennoi. "OK, I'll do it."

His smile to her was the sun. "You always make the right choice in the end." He enfolded her in his golden wings.

Ari had never felt so loved and protected. "Okay, tell me what I have to do. I'm new to this spiritual warrior stuff."

A white dove flew over their heads and landed on a low branch of an oak tree a few feet away. It fluffed its feathers. Ari looked into its intelligent gold-rimmed eyes. It bobbed its head at her and flew away.

CHAPTER 40

Runes

12 PM Tuesday | November 10th

Laurie got to Panera Bread on time. Deirdre sat in a corner booth. "I'm not late am I?"

Deirdre stood and kissed Laurie on both cheeks nearly touching her lips as she moved from one cheek to the other.

Laurie blushed. *That was weird.*

"No, you're on time. I got here early to secure us a booth."

"I'm *so glad* you called me yesterday... I haven't done this since I left Ohio."

Deirdre held up the pager. "Come sit. I ordered for us. I'm treating you to tomato soup and a turkey and Swiss sandwich on wheat to start you on your new diet. It's time you took better care of yourself."

"You're the boss. I love turkey and Swiss."

"Wonderful."

The pager buzzed.

Laurie watched Deirdre eat. She had never seen anyone down a bowl of soup with such voraciousness and not spill a drop. *It looks like a bowl of blood.* She pushed her half-eaten bowl aside.

"Satiated?" Deirdre looked up at last. The corner of her mouth twitched and she wiped it with a napkin leaving a dark red stain.

"Yeah, that sandwich was enough." Laurie laid her napkin on the tray. "Let me buy coffee and dessert."

"No dessert. Fetch us both a double espresso."

When Laurie returned with the coffee, Deirdre had laid out several brochures in a fan shape facing Laurie's side. 'New York City Getaway Weekend' was written across one. Laurie scooted into the booth. "What's all this?"

"I need to check on my new condominium. Why don't you accompany me to New York this weekend? They have great food, shopping, Broadway plays... we could do it all."

Laurie pressed her hands together. "That sounds wonderful! I've always wanted to go there." She frowned. "I don't know if Randy can get the weekend off to watch the kids at such short notice." She picked up the Getaway brochure but didn't open it.

"You deserve to be treated well, Laurie."

Laurie put the brochure back on the table. She pulled her necklace through her fingers. The pearls ran cold across the back of her neck. She spread the brochure open. Her eyes lit up. She sat back in the seat. "Oh... I don't know..."

Deirdre pulled a black chamois bag out of her purse. "These will help you decide. Hold out your hands." She placed the bag in Laurie's open palms.

Laurie felt the weight of the bag and jounced it from one hand to the other. "What's in here? It sounds like Scrabble tiles."

Deirdre grabbed the sides of Laurie's hands and held them still. "Be gentle with them."

Laurie's mouth sprang open. Deirdre's hands radiated an animal presence.

As did her eyes. They locked on Laurie as she spoke. "These are my runes. Hold the bag for a few moments and let the runes feel your vibration. Then ask a question."

Laurie wanted to look away but couldn't. "What should I ask?"

"Whatever is on your mind. Close your eyes and listen to your inner Self, the divine goddess within you. She knows what you need." She loosened the drawstring. "Ask when you are ready."

Laurie closed her eyes and tried to focus on a question... it was hard with the sounds of eating all around... the firmness of the bench... and the collage of New York images which ebbed in and out on the palette of her mind...then, right when she wanted to put the bag down—the question came to her. "OK, I know what I want to ask them."

"Go ahead."

"Okay... uh... How do I find joy?"

Deirdre laid out a white silk handkerchief. "Now put your hand in the bag, choose a rune, and place it on this cloth."

Laurie reached into the bag. Her fingers waded among the smooth flat tiles until one seemed to 'stick' to her. She placed the white irregularly-shaped little rectangle on top of the cloth. It looked like an ill-made Scrabble tile. An 'R' was etched in dark red on one side.

"Oh, that's splendid. Raido has chosen you. Raido is the rune that indicates any kind of journey. Your inner goddess is saying to you, capital Y-E-S, that a trip to New York will help you find joy."

"That little thing told you all that?"

"Yes, it did. The rune gives you its blessing to come with me."

Laurie sat back. "It's comforting to have such clear spiritual guidance. These are much more specific than reading my daily horoscope. Hey, we're both Libras, remember?"

"Yes, astrology is a helpful guide, but this is more personal. A rune casting like this is an ancient art of divination; a tried and true way to ask your inner goddess for guidance. Who is better than she at knowing how you should live?"

"Oh, I like the sound of that. My 'inner goddess.'" Laurie picked up the rune. "What's this made of? It's so light and smooth."

"Bone."

Laurie grimaced and put it back on the cloth. "I didn't need to know that."

"Bone is best for conducting the vibration of the Divine in this realm." Deirdre waved her hand in the air.

"Okay, Deirdre. I'll leave the voodoo to you. My inner goddess says I should go to New York with you this weekend, so I'll ask Randy."

"I'll make all the arrangements. The condo is ready—my new Spanish bed arrived... we can drive my car, it's so comfortable, you will never notice the distance. The City is only four hours from here. And we can go shopping on Saturday afternoon at

Saks, eat at my favorite restaurant, and *Top Girls* opens this weekend. I have box seats."

"Count me in. I'll talk to Randy tonight."

"Call me if he gives any resistance."

What could you do about it? Laurie pushed the thought from her mind. She spread the brochure out with both hands.

"A girls-only weekend away is what I need, Laura-lee." Deirdre sipped her espresso.

"You mean just what *I need*, right?"

"Yes, of course."

CHAPTER 41

Laurie Waffles

8 AM Friday | November 13th

L ilith and Samael were having a leisurely breakfast in bed. Lilith texted Laurie at 8 AM:

Girls only getaway in 24 hours

Two hours went by with no reply. Lilith texted again:

Pick you up at 8 sharp tomorrow morning laurie lee

Finally Laurie replied:

Sorry but randy not cool about me going to nyc

Lilith texted Randy:

Let laurie go to nyc this weekend, lover boy. Otherwise I'll overnight your trooper hat to her along with a handwritten synopsis of our evening together

Samael looked over her shoulder. "That ought to nick him in the bits."

Laurie called eight minutes later. "Randy just texted me."

"And..." Lilith laid her hand on the newspaper on her lap.

"He's okay with me going with you!" She paused. "It kinda surprised me because he's been so against the idea all week."

"The runes never lie. This is your inner goddess at work. She knows going to the City with me will lead you to your joy."

"You're always so right about everything."

"I'm psychic, remember?" Lilith smoothed a crease in the newspaper and hung up.

Ari didn't hear from Laurie all week. *Fine. I'll go see her tomorrow morning under the guise of a playdate.*

CHAPTER 42

The Rhodium Rule

Saturday Morning | November 14th

Deirdre picked Laurie up at exactly eight. "That's your caramel latte in the holder."

"Hey, thanks! You're always so thoughtful," Laurie said.

"It's my 'Rhodium Rule: Treat others better than they would treat themselves.' The Golden Rule pales in comparison."

Laurie lifted her latte, "To the Rhodium Rule!"

All the way to New York the Jaguar sped past state police who remained stationary in their cruisers. When Deirdre parked in front of her condominium on Fifth Avenue, Laurie's latte was still warm.

A uniformed doorman opened Deirdre's door. "Mistress." He bowed his head as he took her hand. A younger man in a matching uniform extended his to Laurie. "Miss?"

The men attended them closely. The young man carried their overnight bags not letting them touch the ground. He pushed the elevator buttons. Deirdre stood aloofly in the elevator as if accustomed to it.

I could get used to this too. Laurie was envious and exhilarated at the same time. She'd never been in such elite company before. She hadn't seen this side of Deirdre in Ashuelot Hollow.

The young man opened the door to Unit 16B to a palatial room of neutral grays and whites with windows all around. The condominium overlooked Central Park. The young man led Laurie to her bedroom and placed her overnight bag on the white duvet on the four-poster bed. The room was proper and elegant. She pulled back the duvet and ran her hand on the white satin sheets. "Like a cool stream of water..."

"Laurie, come," Deirdre called.

She went back into the foyer.

"Do you need anything?" Deirdre asked.

The young man winked at Laurie.

"No, I'm good, thanks." Laurie behaved out of character and winked back. *He's scary handsome.*

"Go." Deirdre handed the young man a list and several hundred dollar bills.

"Thank you, Mistress," he said.

No wonder he treats her so well.

"And Jesse, we'll need the limo in fifteen minutes."

Jesse left the room—a crown equerry off to fetch the queen's wheels.

"Jesse." His name in her mouth was a piece of gourmet chocolate. "The limo?"

"It's hard to find parking in the City, and I never take taxis. Too much human filth inside—"

"I've never been in one. I've never been in a limo either."

"Always the best for my friends, it's my Rhodium Rule."

"I like your rules."

"Let's freshen up then go to Bad Bass. Have you ever had baby eel?"

"Uh, no. I didn't think you could eat them. What time's our reservation?" Laurie looked at her watch.

"I never need a reservation." Deirdre's tone showed no sign of snobbery, only truth.

Laurie went back to her room. *Who is this woman?* Deirdre exuded an innate supremacy. It strangely attracted her.

As she brushed her long golden hair in the mirror, she reminded herself she had been a cheerleader, and president of her ΦBK sorority in college. *I was POPULAR.* Randy's patrol buddies always said, "You're lucky to have a woman like that waiting at home for you, Locke." Randy'd hold up her left hand, point at her wedding ring and say, "Yeah, and I got her all 'Locked' up, bro."

She looked at her plain ½ carat diamond bridal set. She knew she'd married beneath herself—her mother never let her forget it. It could've been worse. Randy was average-looking but clean cut, over six feet tall and he wore a uniform. That uniform had been her undoing, the reason she'd let him take her that night Amy was conceived in his cruiser. Fortunately he had turned out to be a good provider and they'd had a decent marriage for twelve years.

Until his father had died in the car accident and Randy drank every evening instead of only on the weekend. The beer cans piled up in the recycling bin. Then he'd gotten into a chest-shoving contest with his sergeant over his backlog of paperwork. After that, he was recommended for counseling and a transfer to another state—New Hampshire, a tiny cold sliver in the hinterland.

She deserved a weekend away from the life she'd settled for. To experience what she could have had. *So this is how the one percent lives?* She washed her hands with the hand-milled bar soap, then smelled her fingers. *Roses.* She left the bathroom determined to wallow in the luxury offered her and enjoy every second of her stay in the Big Apple. She met Deirdre in the living room humming 'I Love New York.'

Lunch at Bad Bass was excellently delicious. Laurie loved the baby eel. Halfway through Ari had texted her:

I know you're in NYC with Deirdre, I'm at your house. Came over because you haven't answered me. Very concerned about you. Be careful!

Laurie didn't text back.

Over lunch Deirdre and Laurie downed a whole bottle of Red Burgundy. They left the restaurant arm in arm, all happy chatty. The limo waited for them in front of the restaurant. Laurie giggled, "I feel like a VIP."

"You are. *Voluptuous Insipid Prey...*" Deirdre said under her breath.

They slid into the back and Deirdre told Jesse, "Saks."

At Saks Fifth Avenue Deirdre said, "Shoes."

Laurie wasn't sure if it was the opulence of the store or the wine, but she felt dizzy among the designer shoes. She tucked in her white blouse and adjusted her skinny jeans. At least she had on her pearls and tailored black trench coat. She felt out of place among thousand dollar shoes she'd only seen in magazines and never on a real person.

Deirdre beckoned her over to the Christian Louboutin display. She held up a pink patent leather four-inch heel with a black bow on the toe. "Gorgeous, yes?" She handed it to Laurie.

Laurie hesitated. It was a masterpiece. It belonged on a pedestal, not on a foot.

The salesclerk glided over to them, then simply stood with his hands clasped.

"Fetch her size," Deirdre gave him the pump.

"Deirdre, I can't!" Laurie blushed and knew she was, making her cheeks redden even deeper.

"Try them on for fun."

"No, I couldn't."

"Then try them on for me." Deirdre sat and patted the empty chair beside her.

Laurie sat. "Okay, if you insist. You didn't tell him I'm a 7 ½."

"He knows."

The clerk came back with a white shoebox. *If he had a velvet pillow he'd be the grand duke carrying Cinderella's glass slipper.* He alighted on a stool in front of Laurie and set the white box on the table beside her. His hands paused on his knees. "May I massage your foot, my lady?"

"Um... okay," was all she could manage.

The salesclerk took off her brown loafer and laid it aside. He lifted her right foot from behind the ankle and set it on his thigh. He slowly pulled on the toe of her trouser sock exposing her bare foot. Her toes were cold. He took her foot in both hands and rubbed.

The clerk was in his twenties, meticulously clean, and he smelled like the ocean. And his hands. Exquisite. They knew what to do. When he switched to her left foot, he rested her right one on his lap. Laurie stifled a groan. She had thoughts which embarrassed her, but not her body. He stopped and she opened her eyes. She fidgeted with her necklace.

Deirdre leaned over and whispered, *"Enjoy,"* into her hair.

The clerk pulled out a nylon footy from his shirt pocket and rolled it onto Laurie's foot. The footy was warm. He took a cloth bag out of the shoe box and slipped out the right pump. He gently slid the shoe on and buckled the strap. The heel fit, the leather was firm, but soft on the inside. He set her foot on the carpet. He got out the left pump and guided her foot in it with the same deliberateness. Then he set it next to her right foot and stood. He extended his hand to help her stand on the four-inch heels.

Indeed, she was Cinderella. Laurie took his hand and let him lead her to a full-length mirror. She felt the shoes had been custom made for her as she walked over to the three-sided mirror. She turned her feet this way and that, viewing the pumps from every angle. She was in love.

The salesclerk evaporated. *She was trusted with such expensive shoes?* Laurie sighed as she settled back into the chair next to

Deirdre. "I can't afford these no matter how much they're on sale."

"I can." Deirdre nudged Laurie with her elbow. "Let them be my treat."

"You already bought me lunch."

"They can be a late birthday present. One Libra to another."

"It's too much."

"Nonsense. Remember my Rhodium Rule?" Deirdre tapped the toe of the black pumps. "I can see you love them. Let me treat you better than you treat yourself."

"I do love them... but I really can't accept such an expensive gift, Deirdre."

"I insist. You want them, they're yours. A beautiful woman *deserves* beauty, Laurie." Deirdre had her gloved hand on Laurie's arm. She waited.

Laurie felt her resistance wane. "Where would I wear them? I never go anywhere nice."

"Tonight you will. You're hitting the town with me in style." Deirdre hooked one finger into the loafer and held it up. "A goddess can't dance in these, can she?"

Laurie twirled her foot around admiring the sparkly pump. The desire to own the beautiful shoes swelled in her chest. "Maybe you're right. What's wrong with enjoying life a little? Friend, I accept your gift. Thank you. Thank you very much."

Deirdre patted her arm. "Let's go back to the condo, rest a little, then dress for the show." She stood to go.

"Uh, can we just leave?" Laurie looked around for the clerk.

"Yes, of course. Why don't you wear them out?" Deirdre put Laurie's loafers in the Christian Louboutin box and handed it to her.

"Oh, okay." Laurie walked out of Saks holding the box to her chest. She was a teenage girl whose mother had bought her her first pair of high heels. She looked at herself in the full-length mirror in the elevator on the way down. Her heart beat a bit too fast; she was being carried along on a rapidly-flowing river. Who was that woman looking back at her in those big girl shoes?

CHAPTER 43

Four Olives on a Sword

Saturday Night | November 14th

Laurie adored *Top Girls*. After the play Deirdre suggested they go dancing. The nightclub was five blocks from the theater, so they walked, arm-in-arm down Broadway.

The pink pumps with the black bow, which went great by-the-way with Laurie's black leather skirt, were the first pair of high heels which had not destroyed her feet on the first wearing. "I can't tell you how grateful I am that you bought me these shoes! Thank you so much again."

"You're entitled to the best, my friend."

Deirdre stopped in front of a nightclub called Hard Drive. The long line outside testified to its popularity.

"Oh, we'll never get in," Laurie said.

"Shall we?" Deirdre led her by the elbow.

Deirdre and Laurie walked past the bouncer standing guard at the entrance. He bowed his great bulldog head, and held the door open for them.

Laurie walked through another door and stopped short. The club was a wild animal in a cage. Large clusters of colored lights raided down on the club cutting across the bodies of hundreds of people on the pulsating dance floor. Scantily-dressed women and men danced on raised platforms. Laurie did not recognize the style of music. It was a giant heart pumping to a beat which the instruments disregarded.

"This is how they dance in Hell," Deirdre shouted over the music.

The air was sweaty and fruity. "What's that smell?" Laurie yelled back.

"E-cigarettes."

Now Laurie noticed the occasional flickers in the dark corners of the room. "It looks like the twinkling fireflies we have back home."

"This place has little in common with Ohio. Come." Deirdre waved over a multiracial man stripped to the waist carrying a vintage cigarette shelf in front of him. He came and showed the women his wares. She pointed at two and he handed one to Laurie.

"I don't want—"

"Here, you do it like this." Deirdre took a drag from the e-cig, it lit up, and she blew the vapor into Laurie's face. "Guess which flavor this is."

"Uh, strawberry?"

"That's right. Now you try it."

"I'd better not. I smoked in college...I had to get hypnotized to quit..." Laurie turned the e-cigarette around her fingers like she used to back then. *How it all comes back so easily...*

"These taste better and there's no second-hand smoke."

"I...I can't." She handed it to Deirdre who pushed her hand away.

"Put it in your purse for now. Let's go to my table." Deirdre walked to a secluded table off to the side.

A young man emerged from the shadows, plucked the 'reserved' sign off the table, and said, "May I?" He helped Laurie out of her coat, then rolled back a velvet club chair for her. The young man repeated this for Deirdre, "Mistress," then disappeared with their coats.

"What's your pleasure, Miss?" Another waiter clad in black leather chaps appeared behind Laurie. He was right near her ear, his hard, oiled pecs at eye level. He smelled of patchouli. She was a sorority girl again.

"Uhmm...what do I want? Okay, I want a martini, with—"

Deirdre touched the young man with her gloved fingers. "Bring us two perfect martinis, Bombay Sapphire gin, shaken with four olives please."

"Four olives?" Laurie asked.

"Four is better. Three is an unlucky number," the waiter said wagging his finger.

Laurie watched his glutes alternate as he walked away.

"He's yours if you want him," Deirdre said.

"I'm married, remember."

"Enjoy life. You only get one."

I need a drink. The drinks arrived as if on cue. Laurie held the stem of the glass in her fist and stirred with the real crystal sword loaded with four olives. The gin in her mouth, throat, then stomach soothed and centered her. It was familiar. A high she trusted.

"Do you go out *there*?" Laurie pointed toward the undulating dance floor.

"Yes, of course. That's why we're here." Deirdre raised two fingers in the air. "Let's have another drink first." The waiter appeared with two martinis.

"I haven't finished this one yet."

"Well, drink up and try this one. It's Hard Drive's infamous 'dirty' martini. It effects everyone differently. Let's see your version." Deirdre chinked their glasses together.

Laurie watched how Deirdre held her glass by the bowl and did the same. She took a deep sip. Warm fingers tickled from her pelvis to the back of her head...numbing every part in between...sliding up her brain stem...cupping either side of her skull—and pressing hard. It let go. She smiled, stupidly, she thought, at her new friend. "You were right. I should enjoy life."

Deirdre vaped and offered it to her. Laurie didn't feel like her old self anymore. *My inner goddess wants to have fun.* She took the e-cig in her mouth, still wet from Deirdre's saliva, and sucked. Her mouth filled with the sweet vapors. She swallowed, burning her lungs. The buzz brought on a calm acceptance. She eased back into the plush velvet chair.

Deirdre watched her.

Laurie turned her head slowly and looked at her, knowing her eyes had that glazed-over look potheads have. She leaned her head on the back of the chair and closed her eyes. The beat of the music thumped in her chest. "This is awesome..."

Deirdre cocked her ear. "Do you hear that song? They always play it for me when I'm here. Let's go." Deirdre pulled Laurie up by the arm and dragged her into the throng.

Laurie used to go dancing in college. She was a good dancer, but Randy wasn't, so they never went to clubs. Her younger self emerged, her fun younger self, the one who had no fear or inhibitions. The old moves came easily to her. She swayed to the beat waving her arms in the air feeling free and beautiful. *I haven't done this in years...*She was sweating, so she unbuttoned her blouse halfway revealing the top of her red bra.

Deirdre yelled to Laurie, "Red's my favorite color." They danced in rhythm facing each other.

They attracted the attention of a man in a backward-facing baseball cap. Laurie couldn't read the saying on his T-shirt because a camera with a heavy lens hung around his neck, but it started with "You'll be famous..."

"Can I take your picture?" he shouted at Laurie over the music.

"Sure." Laurie yelled back, flattered she'd been selected over the younger girls on the dance floor. *See, I'm still hot.* She posed for the camera.

"Ditch the shirt," the man said into her ear. His breath smelled of beer. She stopped dancing. He took a step back, smiling impishly at her like a boy who'd just asked his girl cousin to show him her underwear behind the bushes at a family picnic.

Laurie looked at Deirdre and mouthed, "What should I do?"

Deirdre shouted over the music, "Go ahead, I've done it. He's famous in the clubs. It's an honor to be chosen."

"Only if you do it with me," Laurie yelled back.

"Glad you asked." Deirdre unbuttoned her blouse and it fell away to the sides of her body. The man shot pictures, greedy for the openness of her body.

Laurie remembered what she'd done in her youth. *How it all comes back so easily.* She pushed her shirt off her shoulders. Unfamiliar hands freed her from it. She didn't bother to turn around to see who it was. She stood next to Deirdre in front of the man's camera mimicking her pose.

After the man with the camera was done shooting, he pulled a white card from his back pocket and pushed it into the top of Laurie's leather skirt, then disappeared into the crowd. On the card was: www.killjoywashere.com.

"Oh dammit, Deirdre! He's going to post those. What if—"

"*Don't worry*, he doesn't know your name. Even if he did, Randy will see how hot you are."

"Yeah, but it kinda freaks me out." Laurie placed the card in her back pocket. She crossed her arms across her chest and looked around for her shirt. A young man behind her danced with it around his neck. She tried to pull it off him. He wouldn't give it to her. "I wanna kiss first." And before she could protest, he pulled her in and kissed her. She kissed him back.

Flashes from a camera lit them up. Laurie saw Deirdre whispering in Killjoy's ear. *What is she saying to—ooh...* Hot shots of flame stoked her passion. The young man moved to her neck. *Ahh, this is so good.* He devoured her right there on the dance floor. She didn't care.

Deirdre grabbed the young man. "I will crush your seed. Let her go." He broke away mid-kiss and winced. Deirdre held out her other hand and he hung the shirt over her open palm. She said, "Go," and released him.

He backed away holding himself.

Deirdre handed Laurie her shirt.

"Whadda ya' stop him for?" Laurie asked.

"He is unworthy of you."

They danced the next two songs, then Deirdre said, "Let's go back to the condo."

"Aw, do we have to? I'm just getting into the beat." Laurie was now in the center of a concentric ripple in the fiery lake of dancers.

"The goddess awaits."

Laurie and Deirdre hopped into the limo while flashes from phone cameras went off from the line of people still waiting outside. Laurie giggled. "They think we're famous." Her phone vibrated in her purse. She fumbled around for it.

"Who is that?" Deirdre demanded.

"I dunno. Oh, it's Ari again."

"Let me see." Deirdre brought Laurie's hand closer:

Laurie, are you okay? PICK UP YOUR PHONE. You don't know Deirdre like I do. She's dangerous!!!

"Do not reply to her."

"She's just being nice."

"Laurie, listen. Ari is not a 'nice' person. She's been most unpleasant to me."

"Seriously? When?"

"Do you recall how snide she was at Pommes Frites? Honestly, I think she's jealous that you're with me while she's stuck at home."

"But she's my friend."

"Please. I'm your friend. I'm trying to revive your inner goddess, not squelch her like Ari is."

Laurie put her phone back in her purse. She secretly typed with her right thumb,

Leaveme alobe im havung the tine of ny kife

CHAPTER 44

Anniversary

Saturday Night | November 14th

Ari told the man on the phone the numbers of the entrees she wanted, hoping he had written down the right things. It didn't matter. She wasn't very hungry. Chinese takeout wasn't Ari and Hector's first choice of how to celebrate their twentieth wedding anniversary, but there was no way either of them would leave Dorothea with a babysitter now.

Hector went to pick up the food. Dorothea was in bed, so Ari poured herself a shot of Hector's Metaxa 7 Stars. The brandy might hush her mind a little. To keep her hands busy, she scrolled through Laurie's text thread and re-read the messages from that morning.

> **thank you for all your phone calls. Btw, i'm going out of town. talk when we get back**

We? Ari noticed Laurie's slip, so she'd written back:

Where are you (plural) going?

She'd known by then that Laurie was in New York City with Lilith, but she wanted to see if Laurie would tell her.
Laurie had answered:

Just me. I needed a break! will visit my aunt in nyc. kids staying home with randy

When she'd stopped by Laurie's house at 10 AM that morning, Laurie was long gone. Randy had lied to her in the beginning until Ari had told him she knew his wife was with Deirdre.
Then Ari had texted Laurie:

I know you're in NYC with Deirdre, I'm at your house. Came over because you haven't answered me. Very concerned about you. Be careful!

Laurie hadn't answered back all day. Ari texted her again:

Laurie, are you okay? PICK UP YOUR PHONE. You don't know Deirdre like I do. She's dangerous!!!

The doorbell rang.
It startled her. She wasn't expecting anyone.

She looked out of the peephole in the front door. Hector stood there with a big smile on his face. She opened the door. "Did your garage door opener run out—"

"Is this 72 Chestnut Circle?" Hector had the long fingers of his right hand wrapped around the neck of a bottle of champagne and in the other a paper bag.

Ari knew what this was—one way they kept the spice in their marriage. "Agápe mou, I don't think I can do this tonight."

He leaned to the side and said in a low voice, "Ari, you said you needed a break from all the weird stuff happening lately. Tonight is our anniversary. Don't let Lilith spoil it." He set the champagne and food on the dining room table that Ari had decorated with their best china, crystal, and white tapered candles. "Sweet."

Ari's phone chimed in a text. "Sorry agápe mou, gimme a second." It was Laurie. *Finally.*

Leaveme alobe im havung the tine of ny kife

"What? Oh. 'Leave me...alone I'm having...the time...of my life.' So Lilith got to you, didn't she, Laurie?" Ari said to the phone.

"I thought we weren't going to let Lilith screw up our evening." Hector briefly clenched his hands.

She put her glass down. "It wasn't from Lilith. It's Laurie."

He whispered an expletive under his breath.

Ari clasped her hands in front of her. "Okay. I need to go to New York City to help Laurie."

"I was hoping we could have dinner and *dessert*." He tenderly took the phone out of her hand.

"I can't, agápe mou. After dinner I have to drive to New York and help her. She's there with Lilith right now, doing God knows what."

CHAPTER 45

Un-Locked

Saturday Night | November 14th

The night air invigorated Laurie. By the time they had driven halfway to the condo, she was ravenous.

"We need sustenance, Jesse," Deirdre said to the driver.

The limo pulled up in front of a bodega. When Laurie saw the red and yellow awning and the resident cat yawning outside, she cooed, "Oh, this is so New York." Once inside, she went for the food she never let herself eat: Cheetos, black licorice, and regular Dr. Pepper, not diet.

Deirdre wiped the dust off three Lindt bars and two bottles of Cabernet Sauvignon.

Laurie insisted she pay. "The simple stuff's on me."

The clerk winked at her and did not put her change into her open hand. He placed it on the counter. When Laurie picked it up, he placed his hand on hers and said, "You the most beauutifullest women in New York." Laurie pulled her hand back, "Uh, *thanks*." She heard him kiss the air at them as they left.

"Did you hear what he said?" Laurie asked Deirdre.

Deirdre mimicked the man, "We the most beauutifullest women in New York," and they burst out laughing in the back seat of the limo.

Jesse got out and carried their shopping bags when they arrived at the condo. He escorted the women to Unit 16B. He put the bags on the kitchen island.

Laurie whispered to Deirdre, *"Can he stay?"*

Deirdre motioned for Jesse to leave and locked the door behind him. "Be patient."

"I really gotta pee." Laurie kicked off her pumps and went to the bathroom.

She looked at herself in the big lighted mirror as she washed her hands. She was hot, wild, and free. Her younger self again, before marriage, before Randy, before the kids. She gave herself permission to be just Laurie tonight; not a wife and mother. "You deserve the night off, Mrs. Locke." She pulled the brush through her hair, flipped it over her shoulder, and strode to the living room.

"Deirdre?" Deirdre was at the kitchen island leaning over a mirror. She sniffed and wiped her nose. Even though Laurie had never seen coke before, she knew what it was. Deirdre handed her the rolled hundred dollar bill and motioned toward the white lines.

I'm in a safe place. Why not? It's my night off. Laurie took the rolled bill from Deirdre. "Like this?"

Deirdre nodded. Laurie inhaled the powder into her right nostril. She jumped backward from the pain. "Ow. That burns." She wiped her nose with her hand expecting to see blood on it.

"Do the next line fast and the pain will cease."

Laurie snuffed the second line quickly into her left nostril. *Yes, that was easier...yeah...* The coke hit her brain. A warm euphoria permeated her body. She wiped the powder from her wet nostrils and licked the back of her hand. The coke had an acrid but not unpleasant taste. She hopped onto the barstool across from Deirdre. "I feel awesome!"

"My friends deserve the best." Deirdre took the wrapper off a Lindt bar.

"Ooo, where are my Cheetos?" Laurie leaned forward and pulled the Cheetos out of the shopping bag. She ripped the foil bag open and the orange puffed batons blew all over the island. "Whoa...sorry." She scooped up a handful and shoved them into her mouth. And another. "Oh, these are sooo good. I love how the cheetle gets stuck to your fingers," she said licking it off.

"I hope a red goes with those." Deirdre poured herself a glass of the Cabernet. "Or would you prefer a beer?"

"A cold beer'd be great." Laurie bounded for the fridge.

"Let's go watch a movie in my bedroom. My feet are tired." Deirdre stood and stretched. "We'll have a slumber party and stay up all night."

Laurie came back with a bottle of beer. "I don't mind staying up. I'm not the least bit tired anymore....I don't know how you can sit still. I'm flyin'."

Deirdre turned on the TV.

Laurie flopped onto the queen-sized bed. She popped right back up again. "Do you want some licorice?"

"No thanks. I'll have another Lindt bar."

"I don't know how you eat like you do and stay so fit." Laurie pinched her belly roll.

"I have a high metabolism. I can fire yours up too if you like. The weight will fall right off."

"That'd be nice, but when I'm around you, I feel prettier already…and those guys at the club didn't notice my stretch marks or baby fat. And oh my God, that photographer took my picture! I hope nobody I know sees it."

"To hell with them if they do."

"Yeah, to hell with them. Wait, is this the bed you had special ordered from Spain?"

"Yes, it is. You remembered."

"It's beautiful." Laurie ran her hand along the hand-carved posts at the foot of the four-poster bed. "Wow, these carvings look like babies."

"They are my lost dream children. I had this made in honor of them." Deirdre caressed the bed post.

"I don't understand what you mean."

"I don't want to discuss it now; we're supposed to be having fun. *Parlez-vous français*?" Deirdre turned the channel to a French film.

"*Please* speak English. I've never watched a movie in a foreign language before. Randy hates subtitles. Hey, I'm sorry I asked about the, you know…" She tapped the bed post.

"Never you mind." Deirdre patted the bed. "*Venez ici* and *acquérir* a little culture."

"Whatever you say." Laurie plopped on the bed and leaned back on the plush pillows. She gnawed on the black licorice twist. She turned around, fluffed the pillows, and leaned back again. The coke charged through her veins. She wanted to be kinetic.

"Watch the movie," Deirdre said calmly from her cushy side of the vast bed.

Laurie tried to harness her racing horse mind and concentrate on the TV. The screen now showed two women holding hands. She stopped chewing and shifted uneasily on the pillows. She took a big gulp of beer to wash down the licorice which had gotten stuck in her throat. "I have to go to the bathroom."

"Again?"

"Yeah, I've been drinkin' like a fish all night. Back in a minute." Laurie swung her feet off the bed and stood. She fell backward and had to steady herself to stand up again. "Oh wow..."

"Are you all right?" Deidre asked.

"I don't know...my head's all fuzzy. Maybe if I...if I splash a little water on my face...I'll feel better."

"Call me if you need me."

Laurie staggered to the bathroom, hitting her shoulder on the doorframe. "Dammit." She closed the door. Inside the exhilaration she was riding, a sliver of dread was cutting its way into her happy groove. She held both sides of her head and looked at herself in the large lighted mirror. All of a sudden she felt vulnerable in that vast shiny white bathroom, high above Manhattan surrounded by Deirdre's opulence. Hours and miles separated her from her family. She was all alone...and she didn't feel so good anymore. She lifted the lid of the toilet just in case, and sat on the bidet next to it. Her stomach whirled in her gut. She put her head in her hands, elbows on her knees, and blacked out.

CHAPTER 46

Deedee the Watcher

Sunday Morning | November 15th | The Nativity Fast Begins

Deedee could not set down the dainty cup of espresso in her hand, or the newspaper in the other, nor could she make her own legs swing off the ottoman they rested on to go see how Laurie was. Lilith was in control, and she was drinking a morning pot of espresso and reading the Sunday paper.

Deedee no longer wallowed in self-pity. Her determination had been building since she realized she still controlled her own mind—her greatest asset. For several days she'd been observing, gathering information, and preparing her escape.

I will stop you, Lilith. I cannot let you do this to anyone else.

Ari's onto you. If I can reach her, she can help me.

You isolate your prey—you made me drive across the entire United States, then you took me over when we reached the edge of it.

Now you've separated Laurie from the herd like the vicious wrathful miscreation you are.

I witnessed your lustful circling, plying Laurie with gifts. How charming you are when you want to be. I was bewitched by you too when you said you'd help Andrew and me conceive a second child. How stupid I was. I put my only child in mortal danger by saying those strange words that came with the Fumsup! charm you gave me.

My body is your slave, but my mind and soul are not. By the grace of God, I will find your weakness. I must. For Justin's sake and my unborn little girl's. For Amy and Elijah. For Dorothea. They all need their mothers.

CHAPTER 47

Hair of the Dog

Sunday Morning | November 15th

Laurie was the mortar in a mortar and pestle set when she woke up. She didn't have exact memories from the night before, only disconnected moments which clicked across her consciousness like stills on a View-Master toy: a white snake. Cheetos. Jesse?

She slowly sat up. Her hands went to her pulsing head to hold it together and she cried out.

Deirdre came into the bedroom. "You're awake! Good morning." She sipped coffee.

"Don't talk so loud…"

"Shower later, we need to talk first." Deirdre picked up a long red silk scarf off the bed, trailing it behind her as she walked into the living room.

Laurie eased her legs over the edge of the bed. As she moved, her brain throbbed in her skull. She fell to her knees on the floor and crawled to the bathroom.

She made it to the toilet, grabbed the sides of the bowl with both hands and vomited. The sight and smell of what she'd thrown up made her retch again even harder. She flushed and pulled herself up onto the seat. *What happened last night?*

She looked at herself in the large lighted mirror. Laurie did not recognize her own face. The heavy eyeliner and mascara she'd put on the night before had smudged and she had a bite mark on her bottom lip, but her skin glowed, her eyes were shiny and bright—she was the ravished rutilant beauty in a love story. *Hello goddess! Nice to meet you.*

Laurie passed the war-torn bed stepping over the pillows on the floor, and saw the headboard had been freshly carved with symbols. She could not decipher them.

She hobbled to the kitchen wearing a white terrycloth robe she'd found in the bathroom. She got a glass of water from the tap, then lifted herself carefully onto a barstool. "Have you got any aspirin?"

"Here. You don't need them, but I knew you'd ask. Wash them down with this beer." Deirdre slid the bottle over to Laurie.

"God, Deirdre, I can't drink anymore. Can't you see I'm having the worst hangover of my life?"

"'If this dog do you bite, soon as out of your bed, take a hair of the tail the next day instead.' Hair of the dog, my friend."

Laurie groaned and shook four aspirins into her palm.

"I can make you feel better without those." Deirdre came around the island. She slipped her gloves off and cupped Laurie's face in her hands. A tingling warmth spread from Deirdre's hands to the crown of Laurie's head. "There. Instant hangover remedy."

"Oh, wow... it's gone." Laurie stretched her neck from side to side. "How'd you do that?"

"I retained the powers I had before, but now I use them for my own purposes, not the Tyrant's."

"What were you before?"

"You are 100% healed, inside and out now."

"Inside?"

"You're fine. I've ordered us breakfast. You need to eat to regain your strength for later. We have an appointment." Deirdre looked at her watch.

"With who?"

"My friends. We're meeting them today so you may be formally introduced to the group."

"I told Randy I'd be home in time to tuck the kids in tonight."

"This is our girls-only *weekend*... that includes Sunday."

"Don't get me wrong, I don't want to go home yet. And I appreciate everything you've done for me this weekend, I just..."

There was a knock on the door. "Room service." Jesse came in carrying two paper bags.

"Good morning, ladies." He set the bags on the kitchen island. "Remember me?" He did an Elvis Presley hip swing in front of Laurie.

Laurie tugged her robe tighter and averted her eyes downward.

"Go," Deirdre said.

"Yes, Mistress." He cast his eyes to the floor and showed himself out.

Laurie lashed out. "What happened last night, Deirdre?"

"You must be famished." She opened the bags and took out several plastic containers. A pancake-scrambled-egg-bacon-sausage-hot-buttered-toast-oatmeal-fresh-fruit buffet opened on the table. "I didn't know what you liked, so I ordered it all. Only the best for you, Laurie-lee."

"Why won't you tell me?" Laurie's chin trembled.

"You've done nothing wrong. Human bodies should be enjoyed without guilt."

"It's never been easy for me because... um, when I was in middle school... I was sexually abused by my... a close relative."

"I knew you had a degenerate in your past too."

"How could you tell?"

"I noticed your reaction when I told you about my ex-husband."

"Yes, at Pommes Frites. I felt a connection that day too. I've never felt comfortable talking about what Uncle—"

"It does no good to discuss it. You are a new creature now. Let the old Laurie go."

"I do feel different. Maybe you're right." *I've finally found the spiritual guide I've been looking for.*

"Do you like the present I gave you yesterday?"

"Yes, I love the pumps."

"No, not the shoes. Your inner goddess. Now you and I are sister goddesses."

"It's funny, I do feel like a goddess." Laurie piled her plate high. "A starving goddess." Her phone rang in her purse. "Oh leave me alone... it's been binging non-stop all morning."

"Answer it, it might be Randy."

Laurie held the phone. "No, it's Ari again."

Deirdre held out her hand. "Let me take care of her." Laurie gave her the phone.

Deirdre pressed the 'decline' button and opened the text window and wrote:

She's mine now

She pushed 'send' and dropped the phone into Laurie's purse. "She's not your friend, Laurie. Ari is jealous of my favor of you. Now go take a shower. We'll take the subway in an hour to meet your real friends. You'll like the subway."

"Okay." Laurie picked up her purse.

"What do you need that for?"

"I've got all my toiletries in here and I always listen to music in the shower."

"I've got Pandora wired throughout the condo. I'll play a song I know will have special meaning to you."

Laurie went into the bathroom and locked the door. She was curious to see what Ari's problem was. She scrolled through all Ari's messages that morning. In the last one Ari had answered Deirdre's text:

I'm coming for her

Laurie texted back:

It's laurie. Why are you bugging me ari? I'm having a great time!

Laurie took off the robe and the phone binged.
Ari texted back:

Are you okay? I'm here in Manhattan looking for you! Drove all night. What is the address of Deirdre's condo?

Laurie scoffed. Deirdre was right. *Ari's so jealous, she's driven all the way to New York to mess up my weekend.*

OMG what are you doing here

Ari: **I've come to save you from Deirdre**

Laurie: **I dont need saving**

Ari: **I've come to save you from yourself**

Laurie: **LEAVE ME ALONE**

Ari: **No, tell me where you are or I'll call the state police right now and tell them a trooper's wife has been abducted**

"You're bluffing, Ari." *But maybe not. If you're crazy enough to come all the way here to 'save' me, then you're crazy enough to do that.* "Fine, you win. We'll be long gone before you get here." Laurie texted the address, off by a few numbers:

1048 5th ave unit 42b

Ari: **See you in ½ hour**

Good luck. Laurie got in the shower. The built-in speakers played a song from her childhood; her parents hadn't been flower children back in the 60s, they'd been metal heads. Her dad's brothers had been metal heads too... and the youngest one in particular had liked this song... she froze. A song can bring back a memory in an instant and this one made her mind shoot back to when she was thirteen and the radio had blasted the same song in the background while her favorite uncle, the cutest one, the one who always brought her cool gifts from his Peace Corps travels abroad...the one she innocently flirted with as she hit puberty 'cause he was only ten years older... that trusted uncle, Uncle Gerry, was whispering in her ear... bad words... and his hands were doing... bad things. Laurie wanted to forget... tried to bury it like she'd done her whole life... so she turned the faucet all the way to the left... the scalding water burned and clawed at her skin... the physical pain muted the one in her chest... then a Voice slipped into her mind and she grinned at the revelation it brought: *You are a goddess now. Make Uncle Gerry finally pay for what he did to you.*

She screamed along with the Nazareth song, "Now you're messin' with a..." and for the first time, she meant herself, not him. Laurie closed her eyes and the Voice guided her as she reinvented the bad memory into one where she was no longer the victim. By the end of the song, she had re-written the past and unloaded the baggage she'd been lugging around for thirty years. She got out of the shower. In her mind, it was Uncle Gerry's body she stepped over, not the edge of the tub.

CHAPTER 48

Hunter College

Sunday Morning | November 15th

Ari was sorry she hadn't gone to New York right after Randy told her that Laurie was there with Deirdre. All day Saturday she'd made up a hundred excuses why she shouldn't go, but the truth was that she had cared more about herself than her friend.

Now Laurie was in trouble. Her last text had made Ari get in her car at 2 AM and leave her husband and only child behind.

Ari had never driven to Manhattan by herself. She was afraid of getting lost. Her sense of direction was terrible. Her family joked that she could get lost in an elevator. She had once as a kid.

Sansennoi hadn't appeared, in spite of her pleading, and that put her off balance too.

She parked the BMW in Hastings-on-Hudson at dawn, and got on a train. She got off at the 68th Street-Hunter College Station. She knew Lilith's condo was on 5th Avenue near Central Park. This stop put her close.

Her anxiety made her hungry. Ari found a deli with the provocative name of *'Wichcraft*. She ate a fried egg and bacon bagel with a double espresso while she texted Laurie. No response. She risked calling her. Got her voicemail. At last Laurie texted back:

She's mine now

Lilith. I hope I'm not too late.

CHAPTER 49

The 86th Street Station

Sunday Morning | November 15th

Laurie hummed after her shower. Ten minutes later she slid her feet into her shiny new heels and took long comfortable strides to the front door. "Let's go."

Deirdre smoked on the balcony overlooking Central Park. "What's your hurry?"

"Nothing... I'm just anxious to meet your friends."

"The right music can work wonders." Deirdre opened the door for Laurie. As she passed by, Deirdre eyed her from behind. *"I love your callipygian figure. I can't wait to try it on,"* she whispered.

Ari walked as fast as she could without attracting attention to herself. When she saw the sign on a building with the address 1048 5th Avenue, she hesitated. It was the Neue Galerie New

York. She stopped in front of the gated entrance. *This can't be right.*

She approached the museum guard. "May I ask you a question?"

He said, "Yes?"

"Are there any condos in this building?"

"This building houses German and Austrian art and design, not people. Search it." He glanced at the phone in her hand.

Her eyes narrowed. "You betcha." She walked to a tree a few feet away. She checked the text Laurie had sent her. 1048 5th ave unit 42b. *Cute, Laurie. You gave me the wrong address.* She looked at the sky in frustration. *I need a little help here!* Ari impatiently observed the base of the tree. *Every tree here is a canine public toilet.*

The prayer rope vibrated. Ari scanned the street. She heard a familiar laugh and turned in its direction. Laurie and Lilith emerged from a building half a block down the street. They headed for Central Park. Ari followed them.

Laurie was different now—she strode next to Lilith at an easy gait, oblivious to all else, her posture was straight, her nose in the air. They were aloof runway models walking arm-in-arm. They exited Central Park and headed down 86th Street. *Fancy walking shoes, Laurie.* Ari studied the women, her writer's eye picking up details in their body language. She formed an opinion with little difficulty: *Laurie trusts Lilith implicitly now. They're equals.* This last observation surprised her.

They passed through the entrance of the 86th Street Station House. Ari followed them. Lilith and Laurie walked toward the platform and stood on the yellow-marked edge talking with their heads close together. The next train was at 10:10. A large crowd amassed around them. The station clock read 10:05 in electronic orange numbers.

Ari had five minutes. "Hi Laurie."

Laurie turned around. "How did you find me?" Her voice was indignant even though her face was flushed pink. She looked radiant.

Lilith stood back from Laurie. "Yes, *how did she find you*, Laurie-lee?"

"Laura-lee texted me your address... a few numbers off," Ari said.

"Deirdre's taking great care of me. You're just jealous." Laurie stepped next to Deirdre and linked arms.

"Not hardly. You posted a link on your Facebook page last night to your shirtless pictures on Killjoy's party website."

"I did? How many likes did I get?"

"Laurie! Have you no shame?"

"Nope. I deserve to live life." Laurie linked her arm tighter with Lilith's.

"Go home, puritan." Lilith steered Laurie toward the platform again.

"I will. I'm taking Laurie home too." Ari pulled on Laurie's other arm.

"Stop it, Ari," Laurie said. She was a dog toy in a tug-of-war. *People are staring at us.* Ari let go.

Deedee saw Lilith and Ari fighting over Laurie. This was her chance! She tried the door of the white bone cage—it wasn't locked! Had it been open all this time? She crawled out, incredulous that she had. She paused for a moment to see if Lilith had noticed. She hadn't.

Ari let go of Laurie's arm... Do it now. *Deedee rose inside her mind and with all her strength focused on her palms, she made her hands* push *Laurie off the yellow edge of the platform and onto the subway tracks. Deedee ran back to the bone cage, pulled the door in, but did not close it, and peered through her eyes to see if her idea had worked.*

The waiting passengers let out a collective "Oh!" In a wave they moved to the edge of the platform with cell phones in hand to record and gawk at Laurie on the tracks.

Laurie was on all fours screaming, "Somebody help me!"

Lilith was the only one not looking at Laurie. She was staring at her gloved hands. She clenched her fists and looked around to see if anyone had seen her. Ari had. Lilith bared her teeth and rage-growled at her.

Ari did not sense Sansennoi's warm presence. She knew what she had to do. A surge of power welled in her body when she prayed, "Lord Jesus Christ, Son of God, have mercy on Laurie and me—both sinners." She jumped off the platform onto the rails.

A man in the crowd cried, "Oh my God! What is she doing?"

Laurie said to Ari, "I can't move! I think my ankle's broken." Then Laurie's expression changed and the fear in her eyes told Ari—the train was coming. The headlights coming at them from the tunnel illuminated Laurie's blonde hair.

Ari grabbed Laurie's arm. "Move," and pushed her toward the middle of the double tracks. Laurie stumbled over the 3rd rail and got zapped by the 600 Volts of electricity. She was thrown backward. A woman on the platform screamed.

"Get up." Ari dragged Laurie to the pillars which separated the north and south-bound trains. She helped Laurie up and told her to hug the pillar, then she pressed herself against Laurie's back. "Hold on. Here it comes."

An alarm sounded in the station. The train was upon them. It pulled into the 86th Street Station. The tunnel of air it created lifted their bodies away from the pillar. Ari's heart burst with fear. "Have mercy on us," she begged. Strong wings enveloped both her and Laurie, bracing them against the pillar. The rank subway air was displaced by an aura of warm cinnamon.

The train slowed and the conductor stuck her head out the window. "What the hell are you two doing there? Now I gotta shut this station down. Stay put."

"Okay! We heard you." Ari yelled back, thinking the conductor should've asked, "What the heaven?" *No one asks that, do they?* To Laurie she said, "You're safe now." Laurie whimpered.

"Hold on, Laurie."

"I can't... I'm... I'm..." Laurie fainted and started to collapse into the gap between the divider and the now stationary train. Ari pulled her back with a strength she didn't know she had. "I've got her now, Sansennoi. Thank you."

Warm air lifted her hair off her shoulders. He was gone.

Ari heard the shouts of the first responders on the platform. They had a bullhorn. "Can you hear me out on the divider?"

"Yes, I can." Ari yelled.

"We're going to ease the train back to get to you. Don't move."

The conductor glared at her, "Stay put, ladies."

"All right," Ari said.

The train whirred back to life. It ground in reverse. The crowd ahhed, clapping and whooping as the monstrous silver slug revealed that the two women were unharmed.

Paramedics swarmed onto the tracks. They lifted Laurie out of Ari's arms and placed her on a stretcher.

One of New York City's finest extended his hands to Ari, helped her off the divider, and led her to the short flight of stairs at the end of the platform. The crowd cheered again and she bowed her head, humbled by the unwanted praise and attention. Ari spotted Lilith. She brooded at the edge of the crowd, her arms crossed, tapping those damned gloved fingers on her forearm. Her cold eyes mocked Ari. Ari flashed her a cold smile back and did not break contact until a paramedic told her to sit on a bench. He shined a pen light in her eyes. When she looked back, Lilith was gone.

Laurie was carried up the station steps and put into a waiting ambulance. After Ari checked out fine, the paramedic said, "Can you walk?" She nodded and he helped her up the stairs. She got in the back of the ambulance and sat on a bench beside Laurie. It smelled of burned flesh. Laurie had second-degree burns on her leg. She murmured to herself. The doors closed.

"Which hospital are you taking her to?" Ari asked the paramedic.

"Mount Sinai West."

Bumping and swerving through the heavy downtown traffic made Ari sick. She asked for a barf bag and heaved into it. The drama on the subway tracks settled into her psyche. She trembled. The paramedic wrapped a thick blue blanket around her. Ari looked at Laurie and put her hand on her arm which was pierced with IVs and attached to machines. Laurie's heart beat rapidly.

"I'm right here, Laurie." She felt a tremor go through Laurie's body.

Laurie opened her eyes, blinking from the overhead lights. "Ari... thank you... I..." She turned her head away.

"You'll be okay," Ari said in her tender mother's voice. She brushed the matted hair off Laurie's brow. Her heart opened when she saw the shame and pain in Laurie's eyes behind the tears on her pale face. Laurie was a broken songbird wrapped in a white sheet.

"Deirdre pushed me onto the tracks... why'd she do that? I thought she was my friend." Laurie's little girl eyes searched Ari's.

"She is *not* your friend. Far from it."

"What'd you mean?"

"Now's not the time." Ari directed her eyes at the paramedic who watched them.

The ambulance stopped at the hospital. The doors flung open and two attendants stood ready to receive their patient.

Laurie panicked. "Don't leave me, Ari." She grabbed Ari's arm.

"I won't. Let me call Randy for you."

"*Nooo*... don't call him. I can't talk to him yet."

"Ma'am." An attendant helped Ari out of the ambulance. They wheeled Laurie through the sliding glass doors. Ari followed right behind.

CHAPTER 50

An Element of Grief

Sunday Morning | November 15th

Lilith was livid. She stood outside the 86th Street Station and watched all her hard work drive away amid sirens and flashing lights. *You will pay for this, Ari.* She was so in her head on the way back to the condo she didn't see the dog mess she stepped in.

The doorman rubbed his nose and politely stopped her as she walked by him. "Mistress, your shoe is soiled."

She slipped it off and thrust it at him.

Jesse rushed to her side and helped her into the elevator. He held her by the elbow and pushed the button to her floor in silence.

Samael heard Lilith cursing at Jesse in the hallway, so he held the door open for her. She brushed past, not acknowledging him.

"Where's your shoe, darling?" he asked.

"Lazy dog walkers."

"How unpleasant."

"Quite."

Lilith plopped down in a firm armchair and humphed when it did not give into her weight. She held out her hand.

He placed a glass of Bushmills in it.

She took a long swallow of the whiskey then laid her head back. Samael stood behind her and massaged her temples. For several minutes they were silent.

"Enough." She shrugged him off. "You didn't have to drive down here today. I'm going back to Ashuelot Hollow this evening."

"I know, love, but I saw Killjoy's pictures of you with the Locke woman online and was dying to know the details. Tell me."

"You are a silly gossip, aren't you." She brushed her hand on his chest.

"Eternal damnation is tedious and these humans are occasionally clever with their antics."

"True. Killjoy came when I summoned him. That will reflect well on him at his review. Last night went well. Laurie succumbed to my will. Watch the video on my phone."

"What's with the peevish mood then?"

"Ari showed up when Laurie and I waited for the train this morning. We struggled over Laurie, and I lost my focus. Deedee took control of her body, in that moment, and made me push Laurie onto the subway rails. Laurie looked up at me with puppy dog hurt in her eyes. Then Ari jumps onto the tracks and saves her from being julienned by the train."

"Bloody marvelous drama, love. I wish I'd been there. Where's the tart now?"

"In an ambulance on her way to Mount Sinai West."

"In Hell's Kitchen?"

"Yes, isn't that perfect? See to it her belongings are sent there right away."

"Done. At least the fruit of your labor is safe."

"For now, and I've added an element of grief to the mix."

CHAPTER 51

Hell's Kitchen

Sunday | November 15th

Ari passed through the metal detector of the emergency department of Mount Sinai West Hospital. The triage nurse directed her to sit outside the examination room they had wheeled Laurie into. Ari clutched Laurie's purse like a shield against the scores of eyes boring through her.

"Excuse me, is there another place I can wait?" Ari whispered to the nurse.

"Welcome to Hell's Kitchen, honey," she said sliding the exam room curtain shut in her face.

Ari sat on a brown vinyl chair. She wished she had something to read. There was a ragged pile of magazines on a table. A Reader's Digest was open in a permanent fan shape from all the grime it had absorbed from hundreds of hands. She picked at a hangnail and observed her strange surroundings like any curious writer would. Doctors and nurses whooshed in and out of Laurie's room.

An hour later the triage doctor came out and said, "You may see your friend now."

Ari peeked her head in through the curtain. Laurie was biting on the ends of her hair. She turned away when Ari slid the curtain closed. "What'd the doctor say?"

"Just leave me alone."

"Please let me help you."

"I'm beyond help," Laurie moaned.

"No one is while they're still alive. Please tell me what the doctor said."

Laurie faced Ari with angry tears in her eyes. "Fine. The doctor told me that I have a slight sprain and a second-degree burn on my ankle from falling on the 3rd rail. It's a miracle I'm still alive."

"Yes, it is."

"Well, I won't be for long. I asked them to give me a test for HIV, and because of that result, they gave me a pregnancy test too." Laurie sobbed a few breaths.

"Well?"

"They both came back positive."

"What? Say that again."

"I have HIV *and* I'm pregnant. Both tests came back positive."

"You're pregnant?"

"And I have AIDS." Laurie pulled on the ends of her hair.

"You have the HIV virus, not AIDS. You can take medication to control it. But the baby... I don't know— how many months are you?"

"I'm only a week or two." Laurie clutched her belly. "What have I done? What if the baby is infected too? Oh, my God."

"Lord have mercy." Ari made the sign of the cross for the first time outside of church.

CHAPTER 52

The Highway Home

Sunday | November 15th

Laurie's overnight bag and a bouquet of yellow roses were delivered via messenger a half hour before they checked out of the hospital.

"Looks like Deirdre wanted to unload any evidence of you in a hurry." Ari found a note:

> *Get well soon, Laura-lee.*
> *I will see you back home.*
> *Your sister,*
> *Deirdre*

"What's this 'your sister' business?"

Laurie was wheeled to a waiting taxi. "Please, Ari. I'm too tired and hungry to talk."

The taxi driver let the women off in the parking lot at Hastings-on-Hudson. Ari helped Laurie into the BMW. Laurie wanted McDonald's, of all things.

They went through the drive-through then on to I-684. They ate their chicken nuggets and fries in silence.

"Do you feel like telling me now about last night?"

"No."

"I want to help you."

"Can't you leave me be? This has nothing to do with you."

Seriously now? "Oh, yes it does. *My* child is in danger because of you. And Amy and Elijah are too." Ari shot her a look then turned her eyes back to the road.

"What are you talking about?"

"I know things about Deirdre that you don't. And I do care about you. I'd like to be your friend." Ari let a few miles pass in silence. "Please tell me what happened," she said softly.

"I don't even know where to begin. I guess it started with these shoes."

"Yes, I saw those."

"Yeah. Deirdre bought them for my belated birthday present. Look, they were on sale. She likes treating her friends better than they treat themselves. She calls it her Rhodium Rule."

"Of course she does. Anything else?"

"No."

"Are you sure? I need to know everything."

"We saw a play in the evening. I felt really good after the show, so Deirdre suggested we go to her favorite nightclub. She has her own table permanently reserved there."

"Not surprising."

"Well, that's when it got weird. I think there was more than vodka in my dirty martini. I felt free. When Deirdre asked me to dance, I really got into the music."

"That's when that Killjoy character showed up?"

"Yeah, I was flattered that he thought my forty-something body was good enough to take a picture of."

"Your pictures have been tagged by all your Facebook friends, and their friends' friends… and…"

"Okay, stop. I feel bad enough."

"You have *thousands* of likes, Laurie. I'm sure Randy's seen them already."

"Good. My husband hides in the basement watching women like that on his laptop. Now he can watch me."

"Anything else happen?"

Laurie shifted in her seat and was silent for a few moments.

"Deirdre is evil. I'll tell you what I know, but first I need to know what we're dealing with here."

"Fine. I'll tell you. But you're not going to like it. Don't judge."

"I'll do my best. Don't hold anything back."

"You asked for it. After the club, we went back to Deirdre's condo. Deirdre suggested we watch a French movie on her bed. I felt uncomfortable, so I left to use the bathroom."

Ari's knuckles were tight on the steering wheel.

"I blacked out in there. I woke up the next morning in my bed with a massive hangover. I guess it was the coke."

"*A Coke* or *the coke*?"

"*The coke*. Oh, yeah. I did two lines of cocaine."

"Laurie!" Ari looked at her and drove onto the berm.

"Keep your eyes on the road! Listen, all I wanted to do this weekend was to experience how the 1% lives. But I don't remember much about last night."

Ari's stomach clenched. The taste of raw kale came to her mouth.

"Think what you want, but Deirdre did free me from my past."

"It sounds to me like she took advantage of you."

"You don't understand, do you? Did anybody ever abuse you when you were a kid?"

"Thank God, no."

"Well, my Uncle Gerry did when I was thirteen. I killed him this morning."

"You killed him?"

"In my mind, but that was enough to free me from that bastard after all these years of being ashamed."

"I'm sorry. I didn't know."

"Deirdre figured it out. She understands. Remember when we were at Pommes Frites and she told us what her ex-husband did to her?"

"Yes, I remember that fairy tale."

"You're mean, Ari. Deirdre is a goddess. You'd better be careful."

"She claims to be a *goddess*?"

"She must be. Because this morning I had the most massive hangover of my life, and she placed her hands on me and healed me. Explain how she did that."

"She's a demon, Laurie. She has preternatural powers. Her real name is Lilith."

"What are you talking about? Demons don't exist."

"But goddesses do?"

"You got me. Okay, if she's not a goddess, then at least she's a psychic. She's predicted lots of things that came true in my life. And she's crazy rich, so she doesn't have to live by the same rules the rest of us do. That doesn't make her a demon, Ari."

"Do you honestly think, in your heart, in your gut, that that's all there is to it? Her money; her psychic power?"

Laurie looped her necklace around her fingers and looked out of the window at the trees which sped by. "I didn't think today would end like it did. I wanted to have a little fun for once. Deirdre pampered me the whole weekend."

"She was *grooming* you, not pampering you. Lilith wants to get her gloved hands on that innocent baby you're carrying. That's this particular demon's modus Vivendi."

"What? Speak English."

"Modus Vivendi: her way of life. Lilith is a baby slayer."

Laurie hugged her stomach. "That's ridiculous. Why would she want to kill my baby?"

"She wants to kill Amy and Elijah too. And my Dorothea. I told you that you needed my help. That's what I'm here to prevent. That and much more."

"What are you talking about, Ari?"

"Samuel is possessed by a demon like Deirdre is."

"You expect me to believe Deirdre and Samuel are possessed by demons? That's crazy."

"I didn't want to believe it either, but I do now. Demons are stuck here on earth tormenting mankind. They can inhabit humans and animals. The evil spirit in Deirdre is the oldest female demon. Her name is Lilith."

"You are completely insane."

"How do you explain her behavior then?"

"I dunno. I looked at Deirdre when I was down there on the tracks; her face was the same, but for a moment, her eyes were kind. She looked like a different person. Maybe she's schizophrenic. I doubt there's someone trapped inside her." Laurie looked at her hands and opened and closed them, then balled them into fists and hit herself on the thighs. "I don't know what to believe."

"Fascinating. It must have been Deedee, not Lilith who pushed you off the platform. Smart move."

"Smart? She almost killed me. Who's Deedee?"

"I'll bet Deedee thought that was the only way she could help you see through Lilith's deception. Am I right, Sansennoi?"

"Who are you talking to? Who's Deedee?"

"My guardian angel is here. I'll—"

"Ari, you're scaring me. *No one* is in the car with us." Laurie looked warily behind her at the empty back seat.

"Only I can see him. I'll paraphrase for you what he's saying: Deirdre, or 'Deedee' as she likes to be called, is fully possessed by Lilith. What that means is that Deedee is trapped in her own mind and the demon Lilith rules her body. Deedee is an unwilling participant. Sansennoi thinks Deedee's body is wearing out and that Lilith is preparing you to take over your body next."

"Sure, that's something to think about. Good, we're almost home."

"I'm not crazy. This is real. We should decide what to do next."

"I'm gonna hug my kids. I've been a crappy mother lately."

"Shh... cursing offends the angels. He might leave." Ari pointed her thumb at the back seat.

"Good, I'll curse some more. Your invisible friend creeps the crap out of me."

"Laurie."

"Oh, sorry Casper."

"Look, we need Sansennoi to help Deedee. She has a son and a husband back in California. She's been missing for over a month."

"I'm in no condition to help anybody. I can't even protect my own kids." Laurie cradled her belly in her arms.

Ari stopped in front of Laurie's house. It was late. She held Laurie's elbow as she hobbled to the front door. "I think you're safe now. Don't pick up your phone if Deirdre calls you—remember, she's the demon, Lilith."

"I have my own demons to worry about."

"Maybe I should stay with you tonight..."

"No, I'll be alright. Go home to your family. I'm fine, really. I'm going straight to bed."

"Are you sure?"

"*Yes.*" Laurie nodded. "Go home."

"Okay, I guess I'm being overprotective. I'll call you in the morning."

"You do that."

Ari leaned over to hug her, but Laurie turned and went into the house.

"Good night," Ari said to the closed door. *I've done all I can for now.*

Ari went home. It was after 9 PM, but Dorothea was still awake.

"Mamá! Mamá! You're back." Dorothea ran to her in footy pajamas. Joy and gratitude filled Ari to the brim. She embraced the innocence and pure love from her child. *I will protect you with my life. I'm certain of that now.*

CHAPTER 53

Home

Sunday Night | November 15th

Laurie closed the front door. *Ari's crazy.* She dumped her bags and coat at the bottom of the staircase to the second floor. Weak beams of light shone through the frosted windows in the door. She looked around at her house's shadowy insides. Familiar objects were now foreign, as if she'd walked into a stranger's house. Shoes were all over the floor. She idly kicked one out of the way. *My children will bury me. Amy and Elijah will be raised by someone else. She can teach them to pick up after themselves.*

The house was quiet, but not silent. The familiar sounds of her home asleep enveloped her—the loose furnace grate in the dining room buzzing, the water from the dishwasher gurgling down its pipe, Randy watching football on TV. *I'm home.* She shrugged off its welcoming embrace like a hug from a stranger.

I don't belong here anymore. She leaned against the wall and sagged into the pile of coat and bags. She looked up the staircase to the second floor where her children slept. *What have I done to you?*

Randy hollered at the Browns game in the living room. Her hand flew to her chest. She caught her breath and stared at the tree shadows playing on the opposite wall.

Her elbow vibrated. She hurriedly searched in the pile and dug her phone out before the ring tone could crescendo into its loudest setting. Deirdre's caller ID picture flashed on the display. She stuffed the phone under her coat hoping it would stop soon, but it vibrated until it reached its ring limit. It finally quieted.

She got a text. Curiosity, which kills both cats and humans, made her want to read it.

I'm in your driveway come talk to me

Why should I talk to you after what you did? She was glued to the floor. *What if Ari's right about you?*

A Voice entered Laurie's head. It was similar to a private thought but with a slight edge. **You don't believe in demons, do you? Ari is insane. Deirdre bought you pretty shoes...pampered you. She would never hurt you.**

Then another thought jumped in: *She left me on the subway tracks—she—*

Then the Voice—***treats you better than you treat yourself. Remember the Rhodium Rule? She sees the goddess in you. No one else does. They all try to make you feel ashamed. Like Uncle Gerry did. Well, she helped you get rid of him, didn't*** *she? Give Deirdre a chance to explain. In your pocket is proof you still believe in her.*

Laurie found the yellow rose from the bouquet Deirdre had sent her, in her trench coat. She'd hidden it there when Ari wasn't looking. The petals were fragrant and soft in her fingers.

Think about your kids.

The Voice: ***Deirdre can treat them to the Rhodium Rule if you let her.***

That's the demon talking... wait. These are my thoughts. In my *head. I don't believe in demons. No rational person would. I'm not crazy like Ari is.*

Laurie stood, the delicate rose cupped in her hand. She eased the door open, then stepped into the darkness.

CHAPTER 54

Cookie

Sunday Night | November 15th

There was no moon. No night sounds. No living creature stirred. Laurie limped on her bad foot to the ruby red Jaguar parked in the shadows. She groped for the door handle and got in. She didn't look at what's-her-name.

"Hi Laura-lee." Deirdre smiled at her like all was copacetic.

"Don't call me that. I sure don't know what to call you anymore."

"When did you get home?"

"Just got."

"You sound upset."

Silence.

Silence.

"You know why." Laurie looked at her.

"Let's take a drive." Deirdre let the Jag roll backward into the street, then down a block where she turned the ignition over. The powerful cat purred to life. They drove in silence for a few minutes.

"I thought we had a great weekend together," Deirdre said.

"Why'd you push me onto the tracks?" Laurie faced Deirdre.

"I didn't push you. Someone else did. Believe me, I'm as upset as you are."

"Huh, it happened so fast… but what about after I fell? You just stood there."

"I did help you, Laura-lee, by *not* helping you."

"I told you not to call me that," Laurie said through gritted teeth.

"It's a term of endearment. You are dear to me."

"I almost died and you didn't lift a finger to help me, Deirdre."

"You could've saved yourself."

Silence.

"Laurie, you're a goddess, remember?"

"If Ari hadn't jumped in to help me, I would've been cut in half. I sprained my ankle and couldn't move."

"I can fix that for you."

"You left me to die."

"You mistook my actions for heartlessness. And you have mistaken Ari's for selflessness. I knew you had the strength to save yourself. That woman enabled you to be weak. I'll never coddle you like that puritan wants to."

"That 'puritan' saved my life."

"Perhaps in that *moment*, yes. However, I tried to save it for your *lifetime*. My tutelage is not designed for everyone; it is for goddesses like us. Laurie, I chose you out of many."

"Lucky me."

"Maybe this will help you understand. A well-known Jewish story goes like this:

'A father was teaching his little son to be less afraid, to have more courage by having him jump down the stairs. So he put his son on the second stair and said, 'Jump, and I will catch you.' The little boy jumped. Then his father put him on the third stair and said, 'Jump, and I will catch you.' The little boy was afraid, but he trusted his father, and did what he was told and jumped into his father's arms. The father put him on the next step, then the next, each time telling him, 'Jump, and I will catch you.' Then the little boy jumped from a high step, but this time the father stepped back and his son fell flat on his face. The little boy picked himself up bleeding and crying and the father said to him, 'That'll teach you.'"

Silence.

"Do you see the parallel?"

"No, I don't, Deirdre. That's an awful story. How's that supposed to make me feel better?"

"Don't see you the moral?"

"All I see is a sadistic father."

"Let me explain. When the little boy's father caught him in his arms, he learned to trust others; when his father didn't catch him, the little boy learned to trust himself."

Laurie stroked the yellow rose secretly with her thumb. "I would never do that to Elijah or Amy, but I see what you mean."

"You must be strong and rely on no one."

"I thought the meek will inherit the earth."

"Humph. You must unlearn sappy tripe like that. The earth has already been inherited, and not by the meek—I assure you. Gods and goddesses like you and me rule the earth. We are free to do what we please."

"Our pastor says the only true freedom is in Christ."

"That's ridiculous. He wants you to be a sheep. A stupid beast who cannot think for itself. If you take the Christian manual literally—"

"You mean the Bible?"

"Yes, that. It was written by men, for men, to control us. Not one book was written by a woman. That's proof enough that those rules do not apply to us."

"I'm pregnant. They told me in the ER."

"You don't sound happy about it."

"Because they told me that I also tested positive for HIV."

"How did you contract that?"

"I don't know, Deirdre. You tell me. I can't remember a thing after I blacked out last night." Laurie gave Deirdre a flat look, her eyes narrowed.

Deirdre abruptly pulled off to the side of the road. She slipped her gloves off and looked Laurie straight in the eye, a typical liar's move. "HIV takes a few weeks to incubate to be detected in a test. You couldn't have gotten it last night."

"I haven't been with anybody but Randy."

"Maybe he has."

Laurie crushed the rose in her fist.

"I'll drive you home and you ask him point blank."

"If I got it from him, then I don't want to know."

"You already know. Laurie-lee. Randy has hurt your children by bringing this pestilence into your family. Hold him accountable for his actions."

"And who's accountable for mine?" The yellow rose bled onto her lap.

"You are. You are a formidable sister goddess now. Remember?" She squeezed Laurie's leg. Laurie tried to push her hand away, but Deirdre was unnaturally strong for a woman.

"That hurts," Laurie said, but Deirdre grabbed the back of her head and breathed into her face. Deirdre's signature scent of warm sulfur mixed with J'adore was intoxicating. The crushed rose fell from Laurie's hand to the floor.

The Voice was in her mind again, **Let me in, Laurie.** Laurie's jaw relaxed. A wisp icy breath wafted down her throat and landed in her belly where it pervaded her body. Lilith's essence traveled to the dyed roots of her blonde hair to her painted toes, lingered for a few seconds, then re-traced the route it had entered on.

Deirdre inhaled and let go of Laurie.

Laurie's back hit the door of the car. She held her throat, gasping for air. "Wh... at... did you... you do... to me?"

"I've left a little bit of myself in you; liken it to a harmless 'cookie' that a website server might leave on your computer." She put the gloves back on and wove her fingers together to tighten the leather between them. "You must confront Randy tonight." Deirdre did a U-turn and headed back to Laurie's house.

Laurie's eyes glistened. "I do feel different... but in a... in a good way."

Deirdre parked in front of the Locke house. Exeter Towne peered out his bedroom window expecting to see a BearCat truck idling in his neighbor's driveway.

"I'll come by tomorrow. Feel better?" Deirdre patted her on the cheek.

"Much." Laurie hopped out and noticed she wasn't limping anymore. She touched her ankle. It was as good as new. Huh.

CHAPTER 55

Randy—the Philandering, Pringle-Eating Warthog

Sunday Night | November 15th

Randy was where Laurie knew he'd be—in his armchair, watching the Browns vs. the Patriots game. The score was in the Browns' favor and her husband whooped, then burped just as loudly.

Siren, Randy's Irish Setter, loped over to her. "Finally noticed I was home, eh girl?" Laurie patted the dog's bony head.

A black ring binder, highlighters, a stack of papers, and a map of New York shared the surface of the coffee table with several empty beer bottles and a can of Pringles. "You've been busy."

Randy jumped at her comment. "Hon, I didn't hear you come in. Welcome home! I'll be with you in a minute, Cleveland's about to score again." He turned back to the TV.

"Pause it. I want to talk to you."

"It can wait. The Browns haven't beaten the Patriots since 2010. Only two minutes left on the clock."

"Pause it now or I'll turn off the mains."

He paused the screen and slapped the remote onto the couch between them. "What's up with you that's so important it can't wait two minutes?"

Laurie didn't flinch. "You always were a nasty drunk. What's up with me is wondering what's up with you."

"What the devil are you talking about? I've been right here all weekend." He took a swig from a sweaty bottle of beer and slammed it down next to eight others on the table—all empty.

You've left a water ring. You never listen to me. You will now. I am a goddess. You are a warthog. "I'm not talking about this weekend. I'm talking about where you've been all those late nights you were supposed to be on patrol. I have proof you were with other women."

He swiveled his chair around to face her. "Great, this again. I'm the new guy here, so they give me all the late shifts. You know that." He grabbed the can of Pringles and shook it into his mouth. Several of the chips bounced off his chest and fell onto the carpet. Siren scarfed them up.

You're a philandering, Pringle-eating warthog. "I discussed our relationship with Deirdre, and I—"

"What'd you tell that harpy about us?" He glanced at the coffee table.

"You know how girls talk about their men and—"

"I'll bet she's got a lot to say. Man, you're naïve." He shook his head and shoved more Pringles into his mouth. More fell to the floor. Siren crunched down those too.

"What do you mean? She's happily married to Samuel. He dotes on her."

"She don't act happily married." He faked his bad grammar.

"How would you know how Deirdre acts? You only met her once at Pommes Frites." She tried to engage his eyes to see the truth in him, but he wouldn't look at her.

Randy wobbled to his feet and wiped his salty greasy hands on the front of his sweatpants. "I need another beer. You want one? No? How about some Fireball?"

"Siren's gonna choke on those chips."

"She's my damn dog." Siren padded after Randy as he staggered into the kitchen and back again. She laid at his feet sweeping the floor with her feathery tail.

He was tipping the Pringles can to his mouth as he sat when she blurted out, "I tested positive for HIV and I haven't been with anyone else, so I got it from you." She stood there, arms akimbo.

He stopped in mid-motion of sitting and chewing. "When were ou tested fa ... ufhIV?" He stood.

"Yesterday in a hospital in New York City. And I almost got run over by a subway train too, by-the-way."

He took a swig of beer. "What the *hell* are you talking about, Laurie?" He started toward her still holding the beer bottle.

"No, don't touch—" He grabbed for her, but she stepped aside.

"Tell me what happened in New York."

"No. You tell me first why I have HIV. I have the right to know." She was in his face and for the first time, didn't back down.

"So who's the man of the house now? *You?* What happened in New York." He waved the open bottle around sloshing beer onto the carpet.

Laurie moved behind the couch. "Stay away from me, Randy."

He tried to grab her from over the couch, but she dodged him each time he lunged at her.

"You're too drunk to catch me."

He stopped and looked directly at her, probing her like she was a perp. He set his beer down, then hurdled over the couch. His unexpected agility caught Laurie off guard. He grabbed her arms and held her fast. "Too drunk, eh? I catch people all the time. It's my job. You're wrong about a lot of things. I've been investigating Deirdre on my own. She's not your friend."

"I'm not wrong about what a drunk bastard you are." She hissed spit in his face. *I am a goddess.*

"Mommy?" Elijah stood in the door archway. They hadn't heard him come down the stairs. The boy held his stuffed lion like a shield.

Randy let his wife's arms free.

Laurie shot her husband the most hateful mother's look, softened her face, and walked to her son. "Come here, 'Jah... it's all right." Elijah ran to her and hugged her around the waist tightly. She fiercely embraced him back, sad and glad at the same time. She knelt in front of her little boy and lied to him in that sweetest mother's voice which mothers reserve for their babies. "I just teased Daddy that I wanted the Patriots to win. We're ok." She tussled his disheveled hair and kissed him on both cheeks.

Elijah burrowed into her bosom. "I'm happy you're back Mommy. I missed you so much."

"Oh 'Jah, I missed you too."

The boy asked, "Are you sure you're okay, Mommy?" he pulled back a little and looked at his father then back at his mother.

"Yes, we're fine. You know how excited Daddy gets when the Browns play—"

Randy clapped him on the back. "Duke, our guys are first and goal. Two minutes left on the clock." He squeezed Laurie's shoulder. She endured his touch for her son's sake.

Laurie guided Elijah in the direction of the stairs. "Now you go back to bed and Mommy'll be up in a minute to tuck you in." The boy dragged his feet. He turned to look at his parents. They smiled at him.

"Good night, Duke." Randy had his arm around Laurie's shoulders.

The moment their son was out of sight she shoved his arm off. *"Don't touch me."*

Randy stepped away from her wiping her saliva off his face. "I've never seen you this angry." He stared at her in a way she had never seen him look at her before—like a stranger. He sat on the couch. He patted the space beside him. "Hon, let's discuss this, rationally."

"Why are you so nice all of a sudden?"

"Seeing our boy. Let's try and work this out—for him and Amy."

She went around the couch and faced her husband. "I prefer to stand. Tell me the truth."

He let out a long, slow sigh. "You know you haven't been taking care of me since we moved here—"

"You're not putting this on *me*, are you?" Her arms were akimbo again, her face flushed.

"I'm a man. I have needs."

"What about last week in the kitchen?"

"That was you throwing me a bone for the first time in over a year."

"You call that throwing you a bone? I thought it was beautiful." Laurie felt her cheeks flush.

"That was a joke. Lighten up a little."

"Who was she?" Laurie's voice cracked.

"Someone you know." He picked up a highlighter and clicked it with his thumb.

Laurie's heart collapsed in her chest. It sank to her belly, a burning coal. She stifled a wail. With each swallow the coal flared red in her gut. *Don't let this break you.* "Who was she?" She asked again.

"The woman I caught speeding two weeks ago. *She came onto me,* by-the-way." He scratched his knee. "It was only that one time. I don't remember any of it." He ran his fingers over his crew cut and leaned forward with his head in his hands. "I think I paid for it. Jesus, she tried to drown me in the river."

Laurie saw his guilty pose. "How many times?"

"Just that one time, hon. I swear."

"I don't believe you. You already lied to me about that night. You told me you got those gashes on your back from the broken window when you crawled out of your cruiser."

"I'm telling you the truth now."

"You have HIV."

"No, I don't. I had a full follow-up physical on Thursday and got a clean bill of health. I don't know where you got HIV from. It wasn't me."

Laurie's stomach fluttered. *If I didn't get HIV from Randy, then from where did I—* "Jesse."

"Who's Jesse?" He slapped his hands on his thighs and stood.

Laurie didn't like the look on his face. "What's her name? The woman from the gas station."

"Deirdre Morrigan."

"You're lying!"

"I have proof." He picked the binder off the coffee table. "It's all in here. I've been investigating Deirdre since I recognized her that day at Pommes Frites. I took her beer glass to headquarters the next day and ran her prints, but there weren't any on file. The night I was pushed into the river, there was a witness: a truck driver. Her car matches his description of a red Jaguar with California plates he saw speeding away from the gas station at the same time that night. She nearly ran him off the road. I've also talked with the owner of the station, I know the guy, and he let me see the surveillance tapes as a favor. Deirdre tipped my trooper hat to the camera. Here, see for yourself."

"It can't have been Deirdre." Laurie didn't take the binder from him. "If she's under investigation, why didn't you tell me?"

"She's not under official investigation. These are *my* notes. I haven't shared them with anyone. Deirdre threatened to tell you and the captain about that night. She said she'd FedEx my trooper hat to you along with a detailed account of how she got it. I wanted to tell you myself. You're moonstruck over her, so I knew you wouldn't believe me without proof."

"Deirdre would never do that to me. We're sisters."

"See for yourself." He held out the binder.

"No. She's never lied to me like you have." Laurie pushed it away and ran toward the stairs.

CHAPTER 56

randyRandy

Sunday Night | November 15th

Each carpeted stair step took more out of Laurie, and when she reached the top at last, she was no longer angry, just worn out.

"Mom?" Amy said as she walked by her bedroom.

She leaned into Amy's room. "I thought you were asleep, honey. I need to tuck your brother in. Give me a minute, okay?"

Elijah read a book in bed. "I waited for you, Mommy." He put the book down.

"I'm glad you did, 'Jah." She sat on the bed. She lifted his hair off his forehead and kissed him. His innocence comforted her. *At least my beautiful boy is okay.*

He looked back at her with the fullness of love that a child has for his mother. "Don't tell him Mommy, but I love you more than Daddy. He ignored us while you were gone."

"Why, 'Jah?" Her hand clenched the sheet, but her voice remained sweet for her son even as her hatred for his father roiled up again.

"Daddy said he was working on a surprise for you. He was on his laptop all day, printing stuff, and scribbling stuff in a notebook. And I got yelled at when I peeked at his notes. I was just curious. We ordered a pizza yesterday, 'cause Daddy told us to fend for ourselves. He said what he was doing was more important to us than cooking dinner. I'm still kinda hungry." He held his stomach and Laurie wanted to stab Randy in his.

"Did you bring me a present?"

"Yes, of course I did." *I forgot to buy the kids presents.* The back of her throat hurt.

"Oh, can I have it now? *Pleeease*, Mommy?" Elijah made his cutest face which always broke her resolve. Not tonight.

"You won't be able to go to sleep if I give it to you now. I'll make you a big breakfast and you can have your surprise after school." *It'll give me time to go buy something.*

"Aw...." He pouted toward the wall and she rubbed his back.

"I love you, Elijah." She kissed his hair and turned off the light.

"I know, Mommy," he yawned.

She left the door open a crack behind her.

The lamp next to Amy's bed threw flint gray shadows into the room. Amy sat on her bed, but she wasn't reading or even playing with her phone. She held the big Raggedy Ann doll her grandma had made and pulled on the strands of red yarn which were her hair. The sight worried Laurie the moment she entered the room.

"You okay, honey?" Laurie rolled the desk chair over to the side of the bed. She kissed her on the top of the head.

"Daddy was a real jerk while you were gone."

"Amy! Don't talk like that about your dad." Laurie put on the 'good mom' act even though she agreed with her daughter.

"You'd call him that too if you knew what he was up to, Mom." The girl pulled at the doll.

"Your brother told me your Dad didn't cook anything. That doesn't surprise me."

Amy pulled harder on Raggedy Ann's hair.

"Honey, stop doing that. You're destroying your favorite doll. Please tell me what's bothering you."

"You won't like it."

"Tell me anyway. I want to know what's upsetting my little girl so much."

"I'm not a little girl anymore, Mom."

"You're right."

Laurie let the silence do its work.

Amy didn't speak for over a minute.

It seemed like forever.

"I overheard Daddy talking to a woman on his cell phone."

"Okay. It was probably one of the female troopers at the headquarters."

"No, it wasn't."

"How do you know?"

"He was out in the garage whispering on his phone. I was curious, so I hid behind the door and eavesdropped on him. I wish I hadn't."

"Did you hear the woman's name?" Laurie had difficulty swallowing.

Silence. More hair pulling. *That poor doll. My poor daughter.* She put her hand over Amy's working fingers and said, "Please. You must tell me her name. You can't keep a secret like this all to yourself. See what it's doing to you?"

"It's your new friend, Deirdre, Mom."

"Are you sure that's the name you heard?"

"Yes. He said it several times and to make sure, I sneaked a look at his text messages. He has a long thread from her, with like over a hundred texts." Tears streamed down Amy's young face. "I'm so sorry, Mom."

"It's okay, baby." Laurie sat on the bed and hugged Amy while she cried. She held her until she quieted. Laurie's blouse was soaked with her daughter's tears and it clung to her chest which was caving into itself. *So, is it true? Did Deirdre sleep with my husband? Then try to kill him?*

"Don't tell Daddy I told you." Amy looked at her mother. The sadness had cried itself out and now fear showed through her wet red eyes. She wiped them with the bed sheet.

Laurie reached over the neat pile of books on the desk for the tissue box.

"How'd you read your father's text messages? His phone is locked with a password."

"He told me what it is in case he forgot. Remember he kept saying, 'This smart phone is smarter than I am?'"

"What is it?"

"You don't wanna read those messages, Mom."

"I have to. What's the password?"

"'randy'…with a small 'r' and then 'Randy'… with a capital 'R'. No space."

"randyRandy." *The cocky bastard. How true.*

"Mom, you're not going to divorce Daddy, are you?"

"No, honey. You're going to need him."

CHAPTER 57

The Damning Thread

Sunday Night | November 15th

Laurie went into the master bathroom and sat on the toilet. She sat there long after she'd gone. If what Amy said was true, then Randy was involved with Deirdre. Amy was young and could've made a mistake. *I sure hope so. How could Deirdre do this to me?*

She looked at herself in the mirror more out of habit than curiosity. Her 'goddess glow' had faded: her eyes were bloodshot and had black circles. She leaned into the mirror and touched her cheek. *Oh my God. I look awful. I look ten years older than I did on Friday.*

She put her hand on her soft belly. *Amy and Elijah are innocent victims of my ego; especially this one inside me.* She was exhausted. She turned off the bathroom light then trudged to the bedroom door to lock it. randyRandy could sleep on the couch.

She slumped to the floor, her back to the door. She raised her eyes to the ceiling. *I'm not going to pray to you anymore. I can't trust anyone. Not even You.*

The bedroom door knob rattled. Laurie startled awake.

"Hon, unlock the door." Randy knocked.

"Stop it! You'll wake up the kids." She whisper-hissed.

"Open the door, Laurie," he said in a low voice. "I need to sleep. Tomorrow's Monday."

"Go sleep with your dog. She won't care that you're a cheating pig."

"I told you, Deirdre threw herself at me... and when she didn't succeed in drowning me in the river, she drowned me in threats."

"I don't believe you." *I can't believe you. Please... doesn't anybody love me?*

There was silence on the other side for a few moments.

He slid his phone under the door with the thread from Deirdre open. "See for yourself."

Laurie heard his footsteps descending the stairs. She picked up Randy's phone and saw he'd scrolled to the beginning of the Deirdre Morrigan thread. It was true. Deirdre had begun the conversation, not Randy.

11/03/2015 Wed

Deirdre: I was displeased when I learned the river hadn't claimed you, sergeant #379. I met your lovely wife laurie tonight at church 11:15 PM

Randy: **STAY AWAY FROM MY WIFE 11:16 PM**

Deirdre: **Not a chance. We hit it off. The poor dear is so lonely 11:18 PM**

Randy: **LEAVE HER ALONE 11:20 PM**

Deirdre: **She's perfect for me 11:25 PM**

Randy: **I WILL FIND YOU & WHEN I DO 11:26 PM**

Deirdre: **I have your trooper hat, remember? 11:28 PM**

Laurie got up and laid on the bed in her clothes. She read and re-read through several days of daily texts between her husband and Deirdre. Deirdre had bombarded Randy with dozens of threatening messages every day. He stopped answering her after a few days.

So. Deirdre's not my friend after all. Just saying Deirdre's name in her brain revolted Laurie. *Ari was right. Your little stint into the world of the 1% was a complete disaster. All the nice stuff you thought you deserved, turned out to be curses instead of blessings. And the true blessings you did have—well, you turned your back on those, didn't you, dummy? Stop it. You don't deserve to cry. How could you have been so stupid?*

Laurie scrolled until her arms got heavy and fell asleep with Randy's phone in her hand.

CHAPTER 58

Man Plans, God Laughs

Monday Morning | November 16th

Randy dropped Amy and Elijah off at school and went straight back home. Laurie had woken up and was in the kitchen.

"You want some coffee? I made it really strong." She caught a yawn in her hand.

"I'm all set." He saw his ring binder was open on the table and his heart jumped.

She sat taking up as little space as possible. She took a tiny sip of coffee.

"How are you feeling this morning?" Randy tried to nonchalantly lean against the counter.

"Really stupid."

"You're not stupid, hon. Give yourself a break. Deirdre is a con artist."

She touched the binder. "I read your notes. You were right about her... Ari was right about her. I was dead wrong."

He folded his arms across his broad chest and saw her eyes go to his biceps. He was all shaved and squeaky clean in his sharply-pressed state trooper's uniform.

"No wonder she wanted you. I forgot how handsome you are."

"I only have one thing to say. I am sorry. I have no excuses for what I did."

"You could've said no to her."

"I did try. I fought it. I remember that much. But Deirdre's voice was like a corkscrew in my brain... I was drawn in by an invisible force. I can't recall much ... not anything about the act itself. All I remember is waking up with the river blasting in my face in the back of the cruiser. And the red-haired woman was gone. At the time, I couldn't even remember her name."

"Is that supposed to make me feel better?"

Randy knelt in front of her. "Laurie, I know I hurt you. Please believe me, I was only with Deirdre that one time. She's hounded me ever since. At least now that you know, she can't blackmail me anymore."

She looked him in the eyes. "You swear you were with Deirdre just that one time?"

"Yes."

"I'm still not over what you did with that brunette in Cincinnati. And now you go and do this."

"I was messed up bad after Dad's accident, you know that."

"Well, it must not have been that good with Deirdre, I mean she tried to kill you afterward."

"I honestly can't remember it at all."

"I'm supposed to believe that? That you can't remember having sex with a dynamo like Deirdre? What do you take me for, Randy?" She was a mongoose shaking the cobra of his infidelity at him.

He placed his big hands on her knees. "I'm telling you the truth. To this day, I can't believe it happened. If Deirdre didn't throw it in my face every day, I wouldn't have known. I didn't want to tell you because I wasn't gonna let it happen again, Laurie."

"You wouldn't have told me? Don't I have the right to know?" Her voice was shrill.

Randy remained calm, his voice tender. "I didn't want to burden you with that. It was my cross to bear. I didn't want to hurt you."

"Then you shouldn't have had sex with my friend!"

"She wasn't your friend then. You hadn't even met each other yet."

"Right. We hadn't."

"Can you please forgive me?"

They were silent for a few moments.

Laurie doodled with the strand of pearls he had bought her. *She does that when she's nervous. Or lying.* She said, "I think you're right about that 'it's my cross to bear' stuff. I'm not perfect either."

"What does that mean?" *More doodling. Do I want to know who he is?*

"What I meant to say was that it's not entirely your fault with Deirdre. Ari said that she's possessed by an evil spirit, a demon named Lilith, who wants to harm our family. She wants to kill Amy and Elijah and—"

"A demon? That's ludicrous," Randy scoffed.

"I know. I think Deirdre's schizophrenic. Ari talked about all kinds of weird stuff yesterday."

"How does she know that Deirdre wants to *kill* our children?"

"That's what her guardian angel told her. Yeah, I know how that sounds. Don't look at me like that."

"All your friends are wacko."

"I think Ari's crazy too, but her heart's in the right place. If it weren't for her, I would've lost the baby." Laurie slapped her hand to her mouth.

He grabbed her thighs. "You're pregnant?"

"Ow... don't squeeze so hard. I didn't want to tell you like that. Yeah, I found out yesterday in the ER."

"Hon, you have, uh HIV now. How will that affect the baby?"

She cupped his face in her hands. "I don't know. I'll have to go to my OB/GYN and ask. Are you okay with us having another baby? We didn't plan this."

"Man plans, God laughs. You know I always say that. The baby's a shake up, but maybe that's what we need right now." He stood and kissed the top of her head. "Don't you worry about Deirdre. Whatever she is, I'll take her out if she comes near my family." He patted the revolver holster on his belt.

CHAPTER 59

Father Leonidas

Monday Morning | November 16th

First thing Monday morning, Ari went to the Annunciation Greek Orthodox Church to find Father Leonidas. His seminarian student opened the side door for her. *"Kalimera sou."*

"Good morning to you too, Vasilli." He gazed at her with his big doe eyes. "I'd like to see Father Leonidas if he has a few minutes."

"Your husband called. Father is expecting you."

Ari grumbled under her breath about Hector's meddling as Vasillis led her to the priest's office behind the altar. Father Leonidas smiled and said, "Kalimera, Ari!" He slightly raised his right hand to her.

I'll submit to the 'entrance fee' since I'm here to ask for his help. She usually avoided it. She lightly kissed the back of his hand. "*Kalimera* to you too, Father."

"May the blessing of the Lord be upon you," he said and made a small sign of the cross over her head. "Have a seat." She had to step around his huge girth to get to the chair.

The church was cold with the heat turned down, but Father Leonidas's book-filled study was cozy. She'd only been in there once. Vasillis left the door open a few inches to keep the warmth in and the suspicion out.

Like I would ever allow him physically close enough to me to do anything inappropriate...Ari didn't like fat priests. They reminded her of the impious Monk in *The Canterbury Tales*. Clergy of any kind should be of a normal weight, skinny even, and live modestly. An overweight priest with a wry sense of humor made her suspicious of his faith. But Fr. Leonidas was all she had. Hector had reminded her that Greek priests performed exorcisms. "Why not ask Father Leonidas about it?"

Fr. Leonidas leaned back in his swivel chair. *It's a mushroom head about to break from its stem.* "So, Ari, what can I do for you? I haven't seen you since Pascha. I thought I'd have to wait till Christmas to see you again, like always."

"I know I don't come to Liturgy as often as Hector and Dorothea do."

"Well, maybe this Sunday, hmm? Then you won't be a 'ChristEaster' Orthodox anymore." He smiled and looked at his watch. "I have a few minutes. Presvytera Maria is making my favorite fasting treat, vegan loukoumádes, for breakfast. Now why'd you want to see me?"

"Your wife's an excellent cook. I'll be brief. Thanks for seeing me without an appointment." Her eyes settled for a moment on the deep gash he had from his hairline to his left eyebrow. *There's a story there. I've asked, but no one knows.* "I need to learn how to perform an exorcism," she said matter-of-factly.

The priest shifted his weight forward. She winced hearing the chair suffer under its burden.

"An exorcism?" He glanced behind her at the wall lined with old books for a few moments. "*Paidí mou**, you are not qualified to do an exorcism. Only priests are permitted to do them."

Ari crossed her legs at the knee. She knew it would displease him. The old grandmothers, the *yiayiáthes* at Annunciation Church tapped your knee if you crossed your legs during Divine Liturgy. "I have read that anyone can minister deliverance if they walk closely with Christ. You needn't be a priest. So I guess that means you don't have to be a man, either."

"Where did you read such nonsense?"

She looked at the floor knowing how lame her answer was going to sound. "On the Internet. On Christian websites."

"Well, then it must be true." He chuckled condescendingly, his fat hands clasped across his expansive belly. He was a salt and pepper-bearded Santa Claus. "Certainly the Internet is a far more reliable source on spiritual matters than the two thousand plus years of apostolic authority and the teachings of the Church fathers and mothers that I have behind me."

She had brought a photocopy of the page from the site with her. She unfolded it and read, "Anyone who pursues to deliver the afflicted from evil spirits must him/herself be right with God. One must be pure and protected by the whole armor of God to fight evil in spiritual warfare. The exorcist must be sure that the

---

*Paidí mou- Greek for *my child*.

devil has no hold on him or her. Exorcisms should not be entered into lightly."

"They should not be entered into *at all* by the laity, Ari." His voice was gentle now and he leaned forward, his palms open on his knees. "I would fear for anyone's soul who attempted one without the proper training. Yes, for approximately three hundred years after the death of our Lord, laymen did perform such rites. In 300 AD, this dangerous task was given to the priests. There was a good reason for that, my child. Don't try to do one by yourself. Let me help you."

Ari relaxed back. His voice was warm and comforting. She let her guard down a notch. "That's why I'm here."

"Why do you think the person in question is in need of deliverance?"

"I have proof and witnesses. My family and I have also been threatened by the demon."

Fr. Leonidas knitted his brow. "What kind of proof do you have?"

"Texts, eyewitnesses, and well, you're not going to believe me, but I have angelic guidance." She watched his face.

"Angelic guidance? I see. From whom?" His eyes were steady.

"My guardian angel, Sansennoi."

Now his mouth drew up like a bow in the most amused way. "Sansennoi? Not a name you hear every day. Sounds like the name of a Japanese luggage brand. Are you sure he's an angel?"

"Yes. He's an imposing figure, Father. His sword is a blinding flame. Before he appears to me, he sends a wave of warm cinnamon-scented air so he won't startle me." *I sound like a little kid trying to convince her dad that the boogeyman in the closet is real.*

She decided to push back. "Have you ever seen an angel yourself?" *There, that was more grown up.*

He looked at the watch. "No, I can't say that I have, my dear."

Ari was used to men his age being dismissive, after all she'd been born right in the middle of The Women's Liberation Movement. She had learned to stand up for herself. "Look, Father, if you don't believe me, meet the afflicted people in question yourself. We need to act fast. My family and my friend's family are in imminent danger."

"People? There's more than one demon-possessed person?"

"Well, yes. A woman and a man."

"You know this is a highly unusual request. Demonic possession is found to be the cause in less than one percent of suspected cases. I've only assisted in one exorcism, years ago."

"Was the exorcism successful, Father?" She leaned forward, hope in her voice.

"Yes, but Father Stephanos was an experienced exorcist and it was a lower-ranking demon inside the afflicted man, one that tormented him with gluttony. We exorcised it from him quickly." He looked away. "One must be careful that the evil spirit does not enter anyone attending an exorcism. I felt it try me. I resisted."

Ari's eyes went to the priest's huge stomach. "The demon spirit in the woman is ancient and powerful. Her name is Lilith."

The priest crossed himself vigorously three times. "*Christós kai Panayía**! How do you know this name?" He stared at her intently.

---

*Christós kai Panayía- Greek for *Christ and The Virgin Mary*.

"I've talked face-to-face with her. That's why I need your help."

At the mention of Lilith's name, Fr. Leonidas took Ari seriously. He agreed to meet her the following day at the Ashuelot Hollow Inn at 2 PM to see Lilith for himself.

CHAPTER 60

Do Not Disturb

2 PM Tuesday | November 17th

Father Leonidas was bent over his phone in his new burgundy Honda Pilot when Ari pulled alongside him. He didn't look up. She observed him. Three facts bothered her at once: his car was flashier than hers, he'd parked right in front of the Ashuelot Hollow Inn, and he hadn't acknowledged her presence. *He's into worldly luxuries, unaware of the danger he's in, and self-absorbed.*

Ari was already annoyed with him for picking such a late time in the day to meet—it had to be after his lunch *and nap*—because she had to pick Dorothea up from school in an hour. *It's hard to be a demon hunter and a mom with a little kid.* The thought took her aback. *Is that what I am now?*

She walked to the driver's side of the priest's car and tapped hard on the window. That mean little part of her heart hoped to unnerve him. Nope. Instead he raised his great lion's head and regarded her with his clear blue eyes. Ari crumpled under his scrutiny and stepped back.

Fr. Leonidas hoisted himself out of the car. Anyone could tell he was a priest by the large gold cross on a thick chain which hung predominately against the backdrop of his simple black cassock which he always wore even in public. But she thought Father Leonidas would be more comfortable in a Harley Davidson leather jacket. It was the long skinny man-braid which went halfway down his back that caused the incongruity. His ride should've been a hog not a Honda.

"*Kalispéra**, Ari." He walked spryly toward the front entrance, surprising for a big man.

She stopped him. "Kalis--Wait a minute, Father. What's your game plan?"

"For you to introduce me to the suspected demon-afflicted people."

"Are we just going to waltz up there and knock on the door?"

"Is there another way in?"

"Well no..." She followed him inside. In the elevator she said, "They're in Suite 254. You go first."

"Happy to."

The priest's unaffected manner, albeit a bit flippant, was probably meant to put her at ease, but it didn't. She jumped in her skin when the elevator chimed at the second floor. She had wanted to take the stairs and sneak down the hallway, but Fr. Leonidas had plowed straight to the open elevator when they'd entered the lobby.

*Kalispéra- Greek for *Good afternoon.*

She let him lead the way toward Suite 254. His large body might provide a buffer between her and any evil spirits. She made sure Yiayiá's prayer rope was in the front pocket of her jeans where she always kept it now. She curved her fingers around its familiar weight. *Pay attention.*

They stopped in front of Suite 254. The prayer rope went nuts.

"Close your phone." Fr. Leonidas glared at her.

She pulled out the prayer rope. "My yiayiá's *komboskíni** vibrates when beings from the spirit world are nearby."

"I see. Can it detect both demons and angels?"

"So far, yes."

"That's useful. Let me know if it goes off again."

Three 'Do Not Disturb' signs and one 'Do Not Make Up Room' sign were hanging on the door handle. "Well, all those signs can't be a good sign." Fr. Leonidas turned to see if she had appreciated his little joke, but Ari had her fist clasped around her car key, ready to stab at anything that moved. She motioned for him to go ahead. He knocked on the lime-colored door.

Ari stood on her tippy toes and peered over the priest's shoulder. Her heart was ramping her body up for an attack. Still, as afraid as she was, she felt a little safer with the priest there. Wasn't he a holy man, and wouldn't God help him? He seemed like a decent person, even though he was a little rough around the edges. And he wasn't afraid. His breathing flowed evenly from his wide chest.

The door did not open for Fr. Leonidas. He knocked again.

*Komboskíni- Greek *for prayer rope.*

From inside the room a low female voice said, "Leave *priest.*"

They both shuddered involuntarily. Fr. Leonidas spoke without hesitation, "Open the door."

"Be gone... priest."

"I will not."

There was no answer, but they heard movement from inside the room. Doors slamming, furniture being scraped along the floor, then a metallic boom. After a few moments of silence, the door opened a third of the way.

Ari stepped forward.

"Wait." The priest held her back. "Let me go first." His tone was fatherly and kind. He pushed open the door of Suite 254. Ari followed right behind him and shut the door. Her nose was assaulted by a wave of putrid, iron-laden air. She breathed in blood. There was no time to guard against it now. It was in her lungs. She stopped the urge to vomit.

Ari held her hand firmly over her mouth. Her eyes adjusted to the haze in the room. Something on the couch glowed white in the dim light and raised its triangular head, flicking its tongue at her. "Egh! It's the python."

"Let there be light." Fr. Leonidas flipped the switch. A mouse skittered into the shadows.

Ari froze. She felt vulnerable in the light. "Father! What if they're hiding in here?"

"Wouldn't it be best to see them then?" He put the end of his sleeve over his nose. "It smells like a rotten grave in here. Open a window."

Ari slid the glass doors all the way open and stepped out onto the balcony. She looked at the parking lot. The car parked under the balcony had a big dent in its roof. "Come look at this, Father. I'll bet they jumped from here onto that blue car down there." No answer. She poked her head inside. Fr. Leonidas was on the far side of the room. "Father? Did you hear me?"

She came back inside. The priest stood in front of a man sprawled in the corner, his head unnaturally bent to one side, his neck broken. It was the creepy demon guy from the hardware store. Penny's father. Ari's stomach lurched; she tried to stop it, but with the rank smell added to her visual disgust, she threw up the spaghetti she'd had for lunch. She wiped her mouth on an old tissue she found in her jacket. *I hope I don't find Penny in here.*

"Look up." Fr. Leonidas stared at the ceiling.

She grabbed his arm. Pictographs were drawn there with a dark fluid. *"Is it blood?"*

"I think so. Probably his." Penny's father sat in a semi-circle of blood. Symbols reflecting the ones on the ceiling were artfully carved onto his face and body. His chest undulated.

Ari fought her body's instinct to flee and found her inner resolve. "Is he still breathing?"

"No... no. It's the maggots moving around in there, eating his insides." Fr. Leonidas was markedly unfazed by the scene in the room.

She had to look away or she'd barf again, so she walked the length of the living room with her head cocked upward. "They look like phrases, similar to the way psalms are separated."

"These letters are Sumerian. It was the first written language, originating from southern Mesopotamia around 3,100 BC. I took extra courses in languages at the seminary. I'm a bit of a nerdy logophile."

"Me too, Father. I read that Mesopotamia means 'between two rivers' in Greek. Ashuelot means the same thing. Can you decipher any of it?"

"Well, these two pictographs here are repeated. The first word looks like 'baby' to me and that scary picture after it is a word you'd never want next to a baby. It probably means 'knife' or 'death', maybe 'kill.' See here," he pointed to the words, "and down here as well."

"You're right. They repeat in every other line." Ari followed the verses along the ceiling and found herself in the main bedroom. The one item in the room besides the hotel furnishings was a food trolley buzzing with flies. She walked into the bathroom, no one. *Thank God Penny's not here.* When she turned around, she shuffled back a step or two. Stapled to the opposite wall on either side and above the doorway in a wide Π shape, were baby blankets in blues, pinks, and pastels, stuffed animals, pacifiers—all the things which comfort babies were affixed to the wall. A nail gun lay on the TV stand.

"Father, you need to see this." Her voice rising in pitch.

He walked through the doorway and turned around to look where she was staring. He made the sign of the cross three times across his chest before the gruesome 3D display of baby loveys.

"It's a trophy wall," she said. "Sansennoi told me that infanticide is Lilith's obsession, her *joie de vie*... and a payback for the three angels slaying her demon progeny." She looked at her phone. "Father, I just realized it's 2:33 and Laurie's children, Amy and Elijah will be home from school soon. I've got a bad feeling that's where Lilith and Samuel went."

The bed behind them creaked. The prayer rope jumped in her pocket. She cradled it; it quieted. They turned around. Dorothea's blankie was neatly draped over the headboard.

CHAPTER 61

Blankie

2:33 PM Tuesday | November 17th

"That's Dorothea's blankie!" Ari grabbed Blankie. "See?" She showed Fr. Leonidas the Greek spelling of her daughter's name, Δωροθέα stitched on the blanket. An arctic ocean of fear rose around her. "I have to pick up Dorothea." Her eyes darted to the trophy wall.

"Paidí mou, calm yourself. Trust that your daughter is safe," said Father Leonidas.

"How can you say that? How did this get here then? It was on her bed this morning. I'm her *mother. I* have to protect her."

"Listen to me. Dorothea is protected by the Holy Spirit—she took communion two weeks ago, and she wears her baptismal cross."

"No, she doesn't. It's 22-karat gold. I don't want her to lose it at school." Ari sprinted to the suite door. "She's only got on a simple one I bought her. Hurry, Father."

"Well, that's better than nothing, but if she had her baptismal cross on now I wouldn't fear at all for her safety. I blessed that cross myself. After today, please make sure she wears it all the time. It will ward off evil spirits like Lilith," Fr. Leonidas said.

"You're not making me feel better. You're saying that spirits and doodads can protect my daughter more than I can. I love my daughter. I'm going to get her."

The priest grabbed Ari's arm. "I gave you 'doodads' to focus on because you are upset and afraid. The way I see it, Ari you have a choice to make."

"What choice?" Her face was ashen.

"To follow the Great Commandment, which right now would be you entrusting God to protect your daughter instead of trying to save her yourself. That would be loving the Lord your God with all your heart, soul, and mind. The second part of the Commandment will be harder for you: loving your neighbor as yourself. You must decide whom to help now: Laurie's children or your own child."

"You're asking me to choose between my Dorothea and Laurie's kids?" Ari's voice broke.

"I'm not asking. God is."

"I can't..."

"Your daughter is safe at school, and the demon is trying to throw you off its real target: Laurie's children. Amy and Elijah might be in the hands of Lilith as we speak. Trust that 'bad feeling' you had earlier. Didn't the blanket appear right after that? That's the Holy Spirit giving you discernment."

A calm place in her wildly racing heart knew he was right.

Fr. Leonidas recited a psalm,

> "Show me the way,
> O Lord wherein I should walk,
> for to Thee I lift up my soul.
> Rescue me, O Lord, from my enemies!
> I have fled to Thee for refuge!
> Teach me to do Thy will,
> for Thou art my God."

She hesitated a moment, hugging Blankie to her. "Okay, Father. Let's go to Laurie's. You drive."

CHAPTER 62

Demon Candy

3:30 PM Tuesday | November 17th

Ari called Dorothea's school from Fr. Leonidas's car on the way to Laurie's house. She got the voicemail. She called again. Again the voicemail picked up. "Father, the school's not answering. Drive over there, *please.*"

"No. The demons have thrown an obstacle in our path to deter us from the real threat they are most likely posing to Laurie and her children right now. Think of it like a fallen log across the road. We will drive around it and stay on course, by the grace of God. Call the school again."

"I've already tried *twice.*"

"Demons can manipulate elements in our physical realm. This is a clever decoy. The demon knows your vulnerability is your daughter. Don't fall for it. 'Love the Lord your God'…"

She dialed the school again.

The secretary picked up the phone. "Good afternoon, Ashuelot Hollow Elementary."

"Thank God you're there, Ceil. This is Ari Apostollis. I called twice and got the voicemail."

"That's strange. I didn't hear the phone ring. Ari, you sound upset. What's the matter?"

Ari pressed her hand to her heart. "Is Dorothea okay?"

"Yes, I just saw her class file in from recess a minute ago. Why do you ask?"

Ari let out a sigh of relief. "Oh, I got one of those paranoid 'mother feelings' and just wanted to make sure it wasn't anything. Thank God." She chuckled. "Hey Ceil, need a favor. I can't pick Dorothea up at 3:10. Could you please keep her in the aftercare program and tell Hector how much it is for the afternoon?"

"Ari, with all the volunteer work you do around this place, I think the school owes you one."

"Thanks, Ceil."

"Not a problem."

Ari hung up. "You were right, Father. Dorothea's okay."

"Glad to hear it."

She texted Hector, then dialed Laurie's home number. The machine picked up. *What am I gonna say? Geez...* Beep. "Hi Laurie, this is Ari. Uh, I'll try your cell now. Bye."

Fr. Leonidas frowned. "Maybe we're too late."

She feared the same. She called Laurie's cell. Again there was no answer. As a last resort she texted:

PICK UP YOUR KIDS AND GO TO A SAFE PUBLIC PLACE. I'LL MEET YOU THERE. DO NOT HAVE ANY CONTACT WITH LILITH/DEIRDRE!!! SHE'S A BABY KILLER

Father Leonidas slowed down when Ari said, "That's the Locke house there on the right, the one with the garage door open."

The ruby red Jaguar was parked in the garage next to Laurie's Jeep.

"That's Lilith's Jag and Laurie's home." Ari's voice quavered.

"Try to control your fear. It's like candy to demons, they gobble it up." He parked behind the Jaguar. "That'll deter them a bit."

She admired the priest's gumption.

He took an old-fashioned satchel out of the trunk. Ari pushed her glasses up.

"It's my bag of tricks," he winked. "Just in case."

She flipped her long ponytail over her shoulder and followed the priest into the garage. There was a Harley Davidson motorcycle parked on the side closest to the house. Fr. Leonidas brushed his fingertips along the handlebars of the massive, fully-loaded bike. "2004... FLHT Electra Glide Standard... fuel injected Twin Cam 88 engine... nice artwork too..." and abruptly turned away. He held open the door which led into the house for her. They found themselves in a quiet, messy kitchen. No dog greeted them like the last time she was there. *Where is*—

Ari saw a dark red furry body on the floor against the far wall. *Siren.* She knelt next to the dog. She stroked Siren's soft head. It moved easily under the pressure of her hand, without life's resistance, and the mouth lulled the tongue out. It looked like she'd been thrown across the room and had broken her back judging from the odd angle at which her legs were sprawled.

Ari stifled the sadness welling in her chest. She had to stay strong now for the children. "Poor Siren... you tried to help, didn't you, good girl?"

She laid her coat over the dog's body. "May your memory be eternal, Siren." She stood, hitting her chest several times with her fist and straightening her spine. The sorrow turned into anger, and there—there it was. What she needed now—that protective wrath which had served her well her entire life where tears had not.

She took in the disarray before her. A kitchen chair was overturned. Laurie's purse was spilled out on the tile floor next to her parka and one glove. Two book bags, two children's winter coats, and two sets of children's boots were in a pile next to the door leading out to the garage. It didn't look like an example of typical American sloth. It looked like an ambush.

"Father, they're here."

"It sure looks that way, doesn't it?" He had his bag of tricks open on the kitchen table.

"That's their Irish Setter over there dead. Her back's broken."

"Killed in the line of duty, you think?"

"I'm sure of it. Siren is—*was* a good d—" Ari grabbed his forearm. "Father... look at this." Next to the sink was a clump of blonde hair with a bit of scalp still attached.

"What?" He rummaged inside his bag.

She grabbed a kitchen towel and wrapped it around her wrist squeezing it in her fist. "Laurie has blonde hair."

Fr. Leonidas walked over holding a bottle of holy water. He saw the clump of hair. "We'd better find them fast."

They heard footsteps overhead.

Fr. Leonidas snapped his bag shut. "Let's go. Our friends are upstairs."

His round bearded face made Ari think, '*His droll little mouth was drawn up like a bow... And the beard of his chin was... salt and pepper you know.*' She chased her inner poet child down and made her sit in the corner. *Could Santa's twin beat this horrible evil?* Maybe she'd been wrong, all wrong about this, and him. "I wish you'd take this seriously."

His eyebrows pulled down in concentration. "You misunderstand my humor. Demons feed on the energy created by strong negative human emotions like anger and fear, which is why they try to scare us. To weaken them, we must starve them by remaining light and joyful in their presence. Do you think your anger helps you now?" He raised an eyebrow at the towel she clutched.

"It always has in the past."

"You should call on the power of the Holy Spirit, not your own."

"I don't know how to do that." She put the dish towel on the counter over the clump of hair.

"You pray." He put his big hand on the top of her head. "Lord Jesus Christ, have mercy on Ari. Expel the demons of anger and fear from her mind. Fill her with the peace of Your Holy Spirit and let Him guide and embolden her to fight Your enemies. Amen."

Oddly enough, the anger dissipated. "Wow, it worked."

"Why are you surprised? Now put a smile on your face and let's go."

CHAPTER 63

Jacuzzi

Tuesday Afternoon | November 17th

Ari let the priest lead the way. At the top of the stairs they listened. The only sound was her prayer rope vibrating gently in her front pocket.

A light was on in the bedroom at the end of the hallway. Father Leonidas walked toward the open door, the bottom of his black cassock brushing along the plush carpeting. They looked in Elijah's little boy bedroom at a shelf of neatly lined soccer trophies. No sign of the boy. Next was Amy's room with a large Raggedy Ann doll on the bed. No sign of the girl either. Ari felt her resolve to protect Laurie's children harden. *Where are they?*

Two paces from the master bedroom, the priest called out, "Hel-lo?" The door slammed in his face. "Whoa," he said smoothing his beard down. He tried the handle. It was locked. It was an old door, the type which needed a skeleton key to open it. Fr. Leonidas sniffed the air. "Do you smell cinnamon rolls?"

"Sansennoi's here." The air displaced behind her, and a weight settled in her back jean pocket. She pulled out a worn brass key. "Where are you?" she asked searching the empty hallway.

Sansennoi whispered, *"Close."*

"What am I supposed to do?" she asked, but the cinnamon scent evanesced.

"Is that your angel friend?" Fr. Leonidas asked.

"Yes, he just gave me this." She held out the key

Fr. Leonidas chuckled. "Well, apparently you do have divine assistance." He moved to the side. "Why don't you give it a whirl?"

She turned the key in the lock. When it clicked open, Lilith laughed from inside. The chilling sound was a cold steel blade running up Ari's spine, resting its point at her nape, poised there to sink in, and paralyze her limbs with fear. *Think happy thoughts.* The image of watching a movie with a bowl of hot buttered popcorn appeared in her mind. *That'll do.*

She threw the bedroom door wide open. The tigress inside her was rising. All thoughts of her own safety left her. *I must protect the children.*

The laughter stopped. She turned in its direction. Lilith was to her right in a chair with her gloved fingers steepled. Her black eyes glanced at Ari. Laurie sat at the end of her bed staring at the floor. In her hands she held the handle of an object, the rest of which was hidden in her lap. Samuel lounged in the window seat preening his fingernails. He didn't look up.

Lilith broke the silence. "Ari. How unpleasant to see you ag—" Fr. Leonidas walked into the room and stood beside Ari. "Ah, you brought the rotund priest too. You both can join us for our little event here this afternoon."

Ari said, "Laurie?"

Laurie lifted her gaze toward Ari. Her eyes were far away.

"Where are your kids?"

Laurie's eyes slid back to the floor. She twisted the hidden object between her knees. A dark, wet stain seeped into the cream carpet between her feet. Blood. That was a knife she held.

"Her mind is at peace now," Lilith said. "She will soon be a goddess in her own right."

"She's hurting herself. What have you done to her?"

Samuel admired his fingertips. "Darling, can we begin now? This is tedious." He tossed the nail file aside and stood.

Lilith glanced in Ari and Father Leonidas's direction. Samuel rushed at them with lightning speed. He grabbed Ari, threw her to the floor, and held her down with his foot on her back as he simultaneously pushed Fr. Leonidas against the wall. He had the strength of ten men. The priest got the wind knocked out of him. He crumpled to the floor gasping for air.

Lilith rose from the chair and lifted Laurie by the arm. "Let's make you a goddess, Laura-lee." They walked toward the master bathroom.

Ari's brain raced for a way to stop them. She calmed herself. A thought entered her mind. *Demons have humongous egos and therefore like to show off. Ask to watch.*

"Lilith! Wait. I want to watch. I'm curious. I promise I won't interfere." She tried to sound obsequious.

Lilith kept walking. "You're curious. Fine. Samuel, bind her hands, let her attend."

Samuel hauled Ari to her feet and dragged her to the window. He undid a curtain tieback rope and lashed her hands behind her back. He pulled it tight. She flinched. "There, that should keep you jolly," he said pushing her toward Lilith.

Ari stumbled hitting her leg on the corner of the bed. She looked for Fr. Leonidas. He was gone.

Samuel noticed his absence too. "I'll dispatch him, love."

Lilith steered Laurie into the bathroom by the elbow. Ari followed three steps behind them.

The bathroom was large, a newly-remodeled addition to the house. *Why are we in here?* She moved in closer. Amy and Elijah were in the Jacuzzi. They were twin fetuses curled around each other. She held back a cry.

Lilith positioned Laurie in front of the big corner tub.

Laurie pulled back slightly when she saw her children.

"First you will release these two burdens of your flesh which bind you to your old life. Then you will be free to be a goddess like me." Lilith patted Laurie's abdomen. "Together we will grow this little one to be a goddess by birth."

Laurie rocked on her feet.

Lilith rattled a prescription bottle in her ear. "They are asleep. I gave them Mommy's Valium."

Lilith looked over Laurie's shoulder at Ari. ***"I had Samuel stop the drain so as not to lose a drop."*** Lilith's lips did not move. She licked saliva from the corner of her mouth.

How did I hear that? Ari was a bound voyeur and could not tear her eyes away.

Lilith brushed Laurie's hair off her shoulder and whispered into her ear.

Ari could hear the demon's words as they corkscrewed into her brain and Laurie's as the Voice: ***"You and Randy are going to die from the pestilence of AIDS he brought into your family. Your children's bloodline is tainted... their suffering will be worse than death. If you love them—"***

"I do love them..." Laurie's voice quavered.

Get out of my head. Ari tried to free herself from the curtain tie, but the harder she pulled, the tighter it became. She tried to will the Voice out of her head. *Get behind me.*

Lilith positioned the knife in Laurie's trembling hands. ***"Then spare them the horror of seeing their mother die."***

It was a paring knife. Not a terrifying *Psycho* knife, but an innocuous tool everyone has in their kitchen. *Like I have in mine. The same kind I cut my thumb tip off with last year. The kind I'm terrified of.* Ari shuddered remembering the red blood spraying onto the yellow bunch of bananas she'd been separating. *Oh God. Why a knife?*

Laurie winced as if in pain. She raised the knife into the air.

The handset on the wall rang. "Call from ... Randy... (ring)... call from... Randy... (ring)... call from..." It echoed against the tiled walls piercing the tension in the room.

"Silence." Lilith tore the phone from the wall and threw it into the bedroom. The impact blew it to pieces. The ringing stopped. "Let's continue." The answering machine on the night table picked up.

"Hey hon—"

Laurie slowly lowered the knife. "Randy?"

Lilith yelled out the door, "Samuel."

Randy continued, "... I wanted to say I was sorry again. You and the kids mean the world to me... and now after what you told me yesterday, well, we've got a lot to look forward to..."

Laurie laid her hand on her belly. "Oh..."

"Samuel! Where are you?" Lilith screamed.

A metallic sound clanged from down the hallway.

"... I'll make dinner tonight so you can take it easy," Randy said.

"Samuel!"

"Lock up the Locke house tight, safe from the demons, haha! I love you, Laurie." He hung up.

"You do not love like I do, Trooper," Lilith said.

Laurie was a smiling Stepford wife.

Lilith's Voice was insistent, hypnotic. *"Randy lies. He feels trapped by you and your children. That's why he cheats."*

"Laurie, Lilith is lying. Don't harm your kids!" Ari said.

Lilith outstretched her hand and a force shoved Ari against the linen closet. "Be quiet or I will subdue you for good." She turned her attention back to Laurie.

Ari silenced her mouth but not her mind. *Maybe if I pray, the Voice will go away. Lord Jesus Christ, Son of God, have mercy on Laurie, Amy, Elijah, and me...* The Voice departed from her mind, but it expanded into the room.

The toothbrushes, the shower curtain rings—all the unfettered items in the bathroom, vibrated at the frequency of Lilith's Voice. *"Free them from future pain. I see Elijah at eleven being groomed by his soccer coach for abuse, not the big leagues. And I see, because of a legal loop hole, Uncle Gerry gains cus-*

tody of sweet Amy and does to her what he did to you. Both your children will grow up damaged and ashamed because you will die and no one will protect them. This is the only way to preserve their innocence."

Lilith reached into the bathtub and lifted Amy's arm off Elijah. The young girl was on her back with her chest exposed. As vulnerable as Isaac under Abraham's knife.

Laurie was a ventriloquist's doll speaking in the alien tongue, *"This is the only way to preserve their innocence."* Her arms hung at her sides, and the hand shook which held the knife.

Lilith came behind her and lifted her arms over her head, then let go. *"I cannot do it for you. Free yourself. Free your children. This is the only way."*

Sweat dripped from Laurie's temple.

It was hard to keep praying, but Ari did in her head. *Lord Jesus Christ, Son of God...*

Laurie spoke in unison with the Voice, *"We are sister goddesses. One flesh... forever... this is the only way to preserve their innocence."*

The short sharp blade was aimed at Amy's heart.

... have mercy on Laurie—A strong hand was on her forearm tugging on the curtain tie. The binding on her wrists fell away as Fr. Leonidas whispered in her ear, *"You get Laurie and I'll get the demon."* He placed a plastic bottle in her hands. *"Take this."*

Ari shoved it in her pocket.

Lilith had her back turned and hadn't seen the priest.

Laurie's hands swung down.

"Laurie, no!" Ari sprang at her. She grabbed the deadly pendulum and held Laurie's wrists. The knife waved above their heads.

Fr. Leonidas barreled into Lilith with all his weight. She hit the granite counter. He pushed her face into the mirror and held it there while he opened the bottle of holy water with his teeth. He splashed it in her hair. She threw him off screaming. The smell of sulfur and burning hair filled the bathroom. Lilith stuck her head under the faucet. She let the water wash over her, then turned around to face the priest. Her red seaweed hair hung from her heaving shoulders. She bared her teeth at him.

Laurie and Ari had stumbled to the side, the knife inching closer to Ari's face. Laurie's hands were white and throbbing from opposing Ari. Her eyes were fixed on the children.

Ari slammed her against the wall. "Let go of it, Laurie."

Laurie strained against Ari, pushing her back toward the Jacuzzi.

I need it to hurt. Ari dug her thumbnails into the soft skin between Laurie's wrist tendons. Laurie held onto the knife. *Can't she feel this? Press harder.* Ari drew blood. A thought shot into her mind. *You're not going to overcome her with your own strength.*

Laurie pushed Ari backward a step.

Ari prayed in Laurie's face. "Lord Jesus Christ, Son of God, have mercy on Laurie."

Laurie turned her head slowly toward Ari. Her eyes were cloudy. Ari prayed the Prayer again. Laurie blinked. The clouds cleared.

"Come back to us, Laurie. Let go of the knife. You don't want to hurt Amy and Elijah."

Laurie looked at the weapon in her hands. Her fingers were white. She let go of the knife like it was on fire. It skidded into the corner. Her knees buckled. Ari caught her.

"Ari?" Laurie grabbed onto her arm. "Oh my God... what have I done?" She turned away from the tub.

Ari sat her on the toilet seat.

Lilith's hard green eyes bored into the priest with an eternity of hatred in them. Fr. Leonidas held her off with his heavy gold cross. "Your trinkets hold little power over me." She grabbed the cross from his hand and yanked it off its thick gold chain. Fr. Leonidas cried out in pain and staggered backward holding the back of his neck.

"I am not of the lower-ranking shedim... this would deter them. I am the Queen of Hell and *this*... this grotesque symbol holds no power over me." She wove it through her fingers like a pencil.

"This one does." Ari held out the cross on Yiayiá's prayer rope. The cross with its two slivers of the True Cross hidden inside radiated light and swung back and forth.

Lilith stared at it. The priest's cross stilled in her hand. "Ah... we meet again. That on its own is merely cold impotent metal. Its power only comes through a true warrior. Therefore I do not fear it, and I do not fear you, Ari because you are weak. You know that, don't you? Your yiayiá rolls in her grave at your ineptitude." Her mouth twitched.

The demon was a liar. Ari held the cross unwavering between them. A physical energy welled in her, supercharging her body. The tigress she had called on her whole life had been the Holy Spirit all along. *Cool.* Her whole body went into warrior mode.

"You've heard this Prayer, Lilith. But has it ever been prayed for you?" She took a bold step toward the demoness. "Lord Jesus Christ, Son of God, have mercy on Lilith, a sinner."

Lilith's eyes pointed at the children in the tub. "Dorothea's next."

Ari steeled herself and took another step. "No, you have no power over us." The next step would bring her close enough to touch the Queen of Hell.

Lilith threw Father Leonidas's cross at Ari. The demon's hands were burned from where she had held it. Lilith ran into the bedroom.

Fr. Leonidas swept his hand over the room. "You got this?"

"Yep. Catch!" Ari tossed his cross to him.

"Thanks. Whew! That's warm." He pursued Lilith.

Laurie fell on her knees before the tub. "Are they... are they okay? Did I hurt them? They're not moving..." She looked at Ari. It was a pitiful look; one that Ari would learn to recognize: the 'I-am-so-bad-that-I-am-beyond-redemption' one.

"They're drugged from the Valium Lilith gave them."

Laurie bent to touch Amy, but pulled her hand away. Her shoulders heaved into a sob and she beat her fists on her thighs.

"Stop it, Laurie. Com' on, get up." Ari guided her out of the bathroom and helped her into bed. Laurie turned away weeping into her pillow.

Ari sat on the edge and softly recited the Jesus Prayer running the beads through her fingers for the first time in her life. A peace like gentle wings settled around the bed. "Try to rest now. I'll take care of your children."

Ari found them curled back around each other again. Their breathing was shallow. She lifted Elijah's eyelid to look at his pupil. It was normal. Then Amy's. Her pupils weren't dilated either. No drug overdose then. They were just deeply asleep. "Thank God."

Elijah whimpered when she picked him up, but she took that as a good sign. She placed him gently on his sister's bed. She brought Amy in and laid her next to her brother. They needed each other now. She pulled a soft flowered quilt over them. *Thank God they won't have the image of their mother with a knife poised above them to bury in their psyches later. I wonder if Isaac saw his father Abraham in that pose. How did his father justify it if he had? I hope that Abraham had enough compassion to lay him on his stomach on that rough altar on the mount.*

Ari left the room, but an inner guidance told her to go back. The bottle in her back pocket was heavy. She took it out. "Holy water. Well, it seems to work." She poured some into her palm and sprinkled a circle of it around Amy's bed and all over the door and window frame. Even on the central air vent. *I hope this acts like demon repellent.* She put it back in her pocket. Her fingers were wet, so she made the sign of the cross over the torsos of both children and across her own. It felt awkward, but strangely comforting at the same time.

She went back to the master bedroom. Laurie stared at the ceiling like her soul had left her. Ari brushed her hair out of her eyes. "Amy and Elijah are fine, they're asleep in Amy's bed."

"They're better off without me," Laurie said.

"No, they're not. Listen to me. Why would an angel tell me to help you if you weren't important? I didn't want to risk my life or my daughter's to save you and your children. But I am."

"I suppose I should thank you."

"Look, you don't need to thank me, what you need to do is *choose*. You can belong to God or you can belong to Lilith."

"God doesn't want me anymore."

"That's a lie. Everything Lilith told you was a lie. She wants you to be her slave. Masters lie to their slaves. The truth is that if you ask for God's forgiveness, you will no longer be a slave but a daughter, and His rightful heir. You will inherit the riches of God's grace. Not money and glory like Lilith promised you, but the true riches of love, the joy of salvation, peace of mind, and victory over death." Ari's chest tingled. It felt like someone else's words coming out of her mouth.

Laurie leaned on her arm. "Then why did God let Lilith hurt me?"

"He can use suffering and evil for His glory and for our greater good. You give Him a lemon, and He makes lemonade."

"Is that supposed to be funny?" Laurie roughly wiped her eyes on the duvet.

I'm starting to sound like Fr. Leonidas. "You're exhausted. We can discuss this later, okay?"

She still doesn't understand. Even I don't understand what I just said. She might try to kill herself... or maybe the kids again. Ari went into the bathroom and found the paring knife and the bottle of Valium. "Here. Take two of these and try to sleep. We can talk later. I have to help Father Leonidas now." She made sure Laurie swallowed the Valium with a whole glass of water. She grabbed a chair as she left the bedroom and locked the door with the skeleton key. She jammed the chair under the door knob.

Halfway down the stairs Ari discovered Samuel's crumpled body. A heavy pewter picture frame lay two steps below. She pressed against the wall to walk around him. His wrists were tied together, as were his ankles, and each bundle of limbs was secured to the banister. *Good job, Father.* Samuel strained against his bonds. They wouldn't hold him for long.

The Valium. Ari shook seven tablets into her hand. They looked like sweetheart candy with a 'V' hollowed out in the middle of the tablet. "Let's send you to the void." She smashed her cupped hand onto his mouth. He bit her. She kneed him in the back. He gasped and she crammed the pills in. She held his chin firmly while stroking his unwilling throat like you give an animal medicine. He swallowed. When he didn't stir, she let go. She walked quickly down the stairs, her platinum pony tail bobbing up and down.

CHAPTER 64

A Sepulcher for the Soul

Tuesday, Sunset 4:23 PM | November 17th

When Ari reached the first floor landing she stood and listened. The house was silent but unquiet. Where were Father Leonidas and Lilith?

She tiptoed to the kitchen. Fr. Leonidas's bag of tricks was not on the kitchen table anymore. An alien, fisher catlike-scream came from the garage. Ari felt a warm rush of wings behind her. Yiayiá's prayer rope vibrated gently in her jeans. She turned around. "I can't see you."

"I am here," Sansennoi whispered.

"Good, so you're sticking around?"

"I will be nearby. Do not allude to my presence. Center yourself by praying the Jesus Prayer softly. Lilith is in the garage."

"Oh goody." She opened the screen door, then shut the kitchen door behind her to keep whatever was going on in the garage from hurting Laurie and the kids; even though she doubted a pre-fab fire door could hold back Hell.

She stood on the concrete step. Her skin rippled like a horse tormented by black flies. The garage was freezing cold. She had stepped into a mortuary cold chamber. The prayer rope jumped violently in her pocket. She slapped her hand on it. *"Yes, I know the baddies are in here."* The prayer rope stopped moving. *Curious.*

Lord Jesus Christ, Son of God, have mercy on me. Ari's eyes adjusted to the caliginous cavern. The floor around the Jaguar was wet. Fr. Leonidas came around the back of the car pouring a ring of holy water around it. He saw her. "Don't just stand there. Close the garage door!"

She punched the console. The door ground shut. Holy Spirit in her or not, angel by her side or not, it was hard for her to resist the powerful urge to flee under the closing door. The heavy door came down sealing them in with the demon.

The driver's side window was rolled down. Lilith was in the driver's seat, her gloved hands on the steering wheel. ***"Ari. I need the keys."*** Ari felt the pull of the demon's Voice in her head and she moved forward a step.

Fr. Leonidas held her back with his hand. "Stop. Don't let her into your head. I can hear that evil Voice too. Do you know the Jesus Prayer?"

"Yes, I was saying it, then I got distracted."

"Well, don't. Recite it continuously in a low whisper and don't engage Lilith no matter what she says or does." Fr. Leonidas set the bottle of holy water on the workbench. He kissed a red and gold stole, hung it around his neck, and straightened it in front. "Did the man on the stairs give you any trouble?"

"He was conscious, so I drugged him. Did the holy water thing around the kids too."

"Good. You're learning."

"Give me the keys, priest."

Fr. Leonidas ignored the demon. "Ari, come over here, please." He was at the workbench. Randy's tools were neatly hanging in rows from a holed board on the wall.

"Do you have the keys?" She motioned toward the Jaguar.

He winked and patted his cassock pocket.

Those cassock pockets!

Fr. Leonidas handed her four eight-inch-tall, white vigil candles in red glass holders and a lighter. "Now go light these and place them in a diamond shape around the car. Turn on that work lamp and those hanging car ones too. I want no shadows in this room. We don't have time to take her to The Annunciation Church—I doubt she would or could enter it anyway. So we're bringing the church to her. His Eminence has given me his blessing to perform the exorcism here."

"Good. I think Lilith has a special connection to the Jaguar. Maybe that's her key to Deedee."

He lowered his voice, *"Her name is too, so while you're near the passenger side door, grab Deedee's purse from the front seat. Big fancy thing."*

"What do you want her purse for? What if she grabs me and pulls me into the car?"

"Make sure she doesn't. I need Deedee's driver's license, so I can say her full name during the rite. Names are essential to the success of an exorcism. I must know the given name of both the afflicted and the demon."

"Oh, for Pete's sake. Lilith told me Deedee's middle name once. I think it started with an 'e'."

"I need her whole name. Go, I'll create a diversion for you."

"Right." She cradled the four candles in her arms. "*Lord Jesus Christ...*" Lilith's terrible eyes followed her as she lit the first one and placed it on the floor in front of the Jaguar. Then on to the driver's side. *"Son of God..."*

"I know you're a baby killer too, Ari." Lilith's fetid breath invaded Ari's nostrils.

No, I'm not. She was as curious as Lot's wife, but she didn't look at Lilith. *"...have mercy on me...a sinner."*

"You had an abortion in your sophomore year."

Ari looked into those awful eyes. A slice of her soul separated and withered. "How do you know that?" She hissed. She had never spoken about it, not even to Hector, nor to her boyfriend at the time—who had gotten her pregnant.

"Ari! Do not talk to her. Continue with the task I gave you," Fr. Leonidas said.

She lit the second candle and set it on the floor. She hunched as she plodded to the back of the Jag. Her arms and legs were so heavy. She held on to the trunk to bend and light the third candle. *I am turning into salt.*

"God punished you for *twenty years* for killing that baby boy, didn't He, Ari?"

Was it a boy? She had always believed the baby had been a boy; that she had aborted *him*.

"You sinned a second time when you let that doctor dig into your womb, cut your son to pieces, then scrape him from your belly. Ah, I see no one waiting to drive you home...too risky...you left a stain on the seat you couldn't explain. My, my, the shame. Is that why it took you so long to have another child? All that heavy guilt impeded your creative flow."

Ari held her caving stomach as she dragged her feet to the passenger side of the car. Lilith's predator eyes followed her every move. The passenger window was rolled down and she spotted the purse in the front, its handle resting against the back of the seat. "I was forgiven that sin."

"Not if I still have access to it. It's been hanging on the meat hooks of Hell and rotting there, wriggling with maggots for twenty-eight years."

Ari told herself to focus on the handle of the purse. She lit the fourth candle and set it down.

Lilith continued. "You finally did conceive, albeit with considerable help from modern medicine. A-*dor*-able Dorothea."

Ari glared at Lilith. The malevolent eyes locked onto hers.

Lilith said, *"Know this. When I am free, the first child I kill will be yours—slowly."*

"You stay away from her!" Ari grabbed the frame of the door's open window.

Lilith put her fingertips to her lips. "I will run my fingers through her curly hair then—"

An object hit the shelves in front of the car. Lilith looked in the direction of the crash. Ari grabbed the handle of the purse and heaved it out the window.

The demon felt the rush of air. "That's mine!" Thick lounge chair cushions flew off a shelf in front of the Jaguar hitting Ari hard. She fell onto the hood of the car, then ran to Fr. Leonidas.

Lilith struggled with the door handle. "Release me, priest."

"Pipe down." Fr. Leonidas flicked holy water into the car and Lilith lurched sideways grimacing as the drops landed on her.

A baseball lost its kinesis next to the front wheel of the Harley. Ari picked it up. "Nice throw, Father." She set the ball on the workbench next to Deedee's purse.

"I can't keep the demon contained much longer. We must begin the rite. If you would find Deedee's license in there for me, we can begin. Women's purses are a mystery I'll never delve into."

"Here."

He held it up to the light. "Deirdre Ethane Morrigan. Boy, that's a strong Pagan name. Could be she was marked at birth for a witch's offering."

She watched him set up the exorcism.

Fr. Leonidas laid a twenty-four-inch square red table cloth with gold trim on the workbench. On this he placed several objects: the Holy Eucharist in a pyx, chrism, Q-tips, consecrated salt, a gilded Bible, a fifth vigil candle, a holy water sprinkler, a censor and incense, and a holy cross on a stand. His phone buzzed. "Vasillis'll be here in fifteen minutes. His Prius is slow. We might need his youthful strength to help restrain the demons."

"His Prius? The priesthood must pay well."

"You save a lot of money on the wardrobe." He pulled at his black cassock.

Ari smiled. "I suppose you would."

He handed her a burgundy hardcover book: *The Great Book of Needs, Volume III*[1]. His expression changed immediately as he pointed at the book. "This is not a 'Hollywood' exorcism. This is real. Proceed calmly and stay focused on the prayers. I must read them all. If I cannot finish them, Vasillis must take over. Ari, if Vasillis cannot, if he too succumbs to the demon's wiles, then *you* must finish them. The prayers must be completed once they are begun. If they don't work the first time, we must recite them again, and again. An exorcism is a war. One side will win and one will lose."

"I understand, Father. But how...how did Lilith know about the, the...you know the procedure I did in college? I've never told anyone. Not even Hector."

"Did you confess that sin to a priest?"

"Well...no. And back then, when I did it, I wasn't sorry. I was relieved. But after I had Dorothea, I understood the magnitude of what I had done, and I told God I was sorry. I've prayed for His forgiveness about it many times."

"Do you feel forgiven and at peace with what you did?"

"Not completely."

"That's because you must formally confess your sins out loud to a priest, otherwise they're still on the 'spiritual account books' so to say. Lilith is right. Unconfessed sins are known to demons. They are kept alive and well in an eternal directory in the spiritual realm. I liked her meat hook analogy. I think I'll use it in my next sermon."

---

[1] St. Tikhon's Monastery, *The Great Book of Needs, Volume III* (South Canaan, Pennsylvania: St. Tikhon's Seminary Press, 2002), 7-29.

"I'm not comfortable with the idea of confessing."

"Tough baloney. No one is comfortable confessing. However, a confessed sin, a truly repented one is forever erased from the spirit world's hard drive, if you will. The fire of God would fry it off that meat hook like Elias's sacrifice, erasing that sin forever, and the demons could never gain access to it again. Demons are soul hackers. You left yourself open to spiritual cyber-attack by not confessing your sin."

"I see what you're saying, but that's not what I've been taught. My parents rarely confessed."

"Ari, it doesn't matter what you've been taught to believe, it's how the invisible world, the eternal one outside our physical one works that matters. Never forget that you are a spirit first, then a body. What is permanent about you is your soul. And in that vein, I'll say it again: this is a spiritual battle. Either we will win through Christ, or Satan will win through the demon. We have the upper hand if we stick to the exorcism prayers. No matter what the demon says or does, *we must not engage* her in conversation."

"I'll try not to lose it again."

"Do you have any other whopper sins on your hard drive?"

"No, nothing like that."

"Good, still if Lilith brings up anything else you've done, ignore her this time, okay?"

"I understand."

"Remember, demons have knowledge of future events, they lie, and they conceal themselves and their true intentions to get what they want, so don't believe what Lilith says. We're banishing her back to Hell. Our job is to make Lilith suffer during the prayers—and she will because an exorcism is unbearable for them. Hell will look like a refuge."

Ari planted her feet on the driver's side of the Jaguar next to Fr. Leonidas. "I'm in."

"The demon will do anything she can to stay in Deedee's body. For her this human charade is fun. Let's spoil it for her, shall we?"

CHAPTER 65

The Exorcism of Deirdre Ethane Morrigan

Tuesday, Sunset 4:23 PM | November 17th

Even though he was in his late fifties, Father Leonidas was tech savvy like a teenager. Ari held *The Great Book of Needs, Volume III*. "Turn to page seven and follow along with me. I've got the same text in a PDF file here on my tablet."

She opened the four-hundred-plus-page book and read the heading on page seven: "A Supplicatory Office for Them That are Afflicted, Being Assailed and Oppressed by Unclean Spirits."

Fr. Leonidas nodded at Lilith. "If we do this wrongly, she wins. *Lepon**, until Vasillis arrives, you must say in a sure voice,

---

*Lepon- Greek for *well then*.

the 'Reader' and the 'Choir' parts which are marked in red. Obviously I'll say the 'Priest' sections. Pay attention to who says what. It's like we're having a spiritual conversation in the beginning, then it shifts to me alone going head to head with the evil spirit. Make sure I do not falter. If I do, God help us."

Fr. Leonidas took the large gold cross out of his pocket. "Can you help me put this back on?"

"Of course." Ari found a zip tie on the workbench and threaded it through the broken ends of the thick chain. She clasped it around his neck and pulled his long man braid out from under the gold chain.

He kissed the cross. He made the sign of the cross across his chest three times. He nodded at Ari to do the same.

She did a fair job of copying him.

Fr. Leonidas began the Office by chanting, "Blessed is our God, always, now and ever, and to the ages of ages."

"Amen," Ari said. "Heavenly King, ... uh, Father I don't know what the 'Trisagion' is." She pointed at the text.

Lilith mocked Ari. "You incompetent rib-sired woman! Do you think your botched rendition of those prayers is going to have any effect on me?"

Fr. Leonidas said, "The Trisagion is: ῞Αγιος ο Θεός, ῞Αγιος Ισχυρός, ῞Αγιος ῞Αθάνατος, ελέησον ἡμας."

Ari looked at him with a confused look. He held up three fingers. "Holy God, Holy Mighty, Holy Immortal, have mercy on us."

She joined him, "Holy God, Holy Mighty, Holy Immortal, have mercy on us. Holy God, Holy Mighty, Holy Immortal, have mercy on us." She crossed herself three times like he did. It was becoming easier.

"Now let's say, Our Father who art in heaven, hallowed be thy name..." After The Lord's Prayer, she was supposed to say «Κύριε ελέησον» 'Kyrie eleson' (Lord have mercy) twelve times, so she counted on her fingers, "Kyrie eleson, Kyrie eleson, Kyrie eleson, Kyrie eleson, Kyrie eleson, Kyrie eleson..."

Lilith counted on her fingers, "Kyrie eleson ... this little piggy went to market... Kyrie eleson ... this little piggy stayed home..."

Ari ignored Lilith, "... Kyrie eleson, Kyrie eleson, Kyrie eleson, Kyrie eleson, Kyrie eleson, Kyrie eleson."

She saw the Reader must now recite Psalm 142(3). She did a little jump. "Father, I know this one! My yiayiá made me memorize it when I was a little girl. She said I'd need it someday."

"She must've loved you dearly. Psalm 143 is the 'I love you' psalm."

"Yeah, she called it that too..." Ari counted on her fingers like she did when she was a child. "The 1 is for I, the 4 is for l-o-v-e, and the 3 is for y-o-u." She finally understood the full meaning of the psalm after all these years. Lilith stared at her, her face solid white marble except for the tic in the corner of her mouth.

Ari pressed the open book to her chest and recited in a strong voice,

"O Lord, hear my prayer.
In Thy truth, give ear to my supplications;"

Lilith gripped the steering wheel. The leather made a skin friction sound back and forth.

"In Thy righteousness, hear me,
And enter not into judgment with Thy servant;
for no one living is righteous before Thee.
For the *enemy* has persecuted my soul;
he—*she* has crushed my life to the ground;"

Lilith groaned, "Shut up, woman."
Ari spoke with even more authority and confidence,

"*She* has made me sit in darkness like those long dead.
and my spirit is overwhelmed within me;
my heart within me is troubled.
I remembered the days of old,
I meditated on all that Thou hast done;
I pondered on the work of Thy hands.
I stretched forth my hands unto Thee;
my soul thirsted after Thee like a waterless land. *Selah* ... "

Lilith swayed and held her hands to her ears.

"O Lord, make haste to answer me,
My spirit fails;
Turn not thy face from me,
lest I be like those who go down to the Pit.
Let me hear Thy mercy in the morning,
for in Thee I have put my trust."

The windows of the Jag rolled up, closing tightly. Ari's fortitude was shaken. "How'd she do that?"

The priest rolled his hand in a 'keep going' gesture. "Show me the way…"

Ari began quieter than before then gained her confidence back,

> "Show me the way,
> O Lord wherein I should walk,
> for to Thee I lift up my soul.
> Rescue me, O Lord, from my enemies,
> I have fled to Thee for refuge.
> Teach me to do Thy will,
> for Thou art my God.
> Let Thy good spirit lead me in the land of righteousness.
> O Lord, for Thy name's sake, preserve my life,
> In thy righteousness bring my soul out of tribulation,
> And in Thy steadfast love, cut off my enemies,
> and Thou shalt destroy all those who afflict my soul,
> for I am Thy servant."

Lilith was still.

Vasillis' red-haired head appeared in the side door window. "Father?" They hadn't heard his Prius pull up. He set a box on the workbench. He kissed Fr. Leonidas's hand and the priest blessed him with the sign of the cross.

"Son, bring me the St. Basil icon." Fr. Leonidas gave it to Ari. "Hold onto this for dear life, child. It was this saint who wrote these powerful prayers of exorcism."

The icon was made of wood and heavy. The face of Saint Basil with his balding head and long brown beard were hand-painted, but the rest of the icon was etched in sterling silver. It was the size of a large serving tray.

Ari asked Vasillis, "Have you ever been to an exorcism?"

He shook his curly 3-inch red goatee. "Nope. They teach the course on exorcisms in the final semester."

"I see."

Fr. Leonidas went to his black bag and pulled out a two-ounce plastic bottle. He took Vasillis aside. "Son, I need you to bring me Samuel. He's lying on the stairs tied to the banister. He's also in need of deliverance. Take this holy water and sprinkle it on the cords around his wrists and ankles then bring him to me. Be careful. God speed."

Vasillis turned to leave. "Wait a minute, Vasillis," Ari said.

Lilith raised her head, a serpent rising from the ground.

Ari looked into Vasillis' face. "Please check on Laurie and the children. They're all upstairs. *I barricaded Laurie in her bedroom. Here's the key.*" She handed him the skeleton key.

The seminarian smiled at her with his big doe eyes which belied his quiet courage. As he grabbed the screen door handle to leave, the Harley roared to life. Everyone except Father Leonidas covered their ears. He stared at the motorcycle like it was Old Yeller snarling at him from the corn crib.

Lilith screeched with glee. A ceramic gnome fell off the top shelf and exploded on the cement floor.

"Turn it off!" Ari hollered over the din.

Fr. Leonidas approached the Harley. He mounted the bike with the confidence of a bull rider in the chute. He hit the kill switch. "It won't die."

"Disconnect the spark plug wires!" He shouted to Vasillis.

Vasillis stuck his hand into the bike's left side but jerked it out. "It shocked me," he said shaking his fingers in the air.

Fr. Leonidas grabbed the holy chrism off the workbench and poured it into his palms, rubbed them together, then grabbed the handlebars. "Try now."

Vasillis pulled the two spark plugs out.

The bike's growl silenced to a low purr. It was quiet.

Lilith asked, "Remind you of the good old Red & White days, Father Domino?"

Ari watched as the priest dismounted and rubbed his arms absently, his eyes cast to the ground. They were wide at an amazement known only to him and to the demon.

"Can I open the side door, Father?" Ari coughed.

"Yes." Fr. Leonidas and the seminarian choked on exhaust fumes. The chill autumn air blew into the garage. He put his hand on Vasillis' back. "Go check on the Locke family now. Then bring Samuel down here."

Vasillis nodded and went into the house.

Ari read Psalms 22(3), 26(7), 67(8), 50(1)... they were the Septuagint Psalm numbers.

Fr. Leonidas read nine Odes. Ari's feet ached. It looked like Lilith had gone to sleep. The exorcism didn't seem to be working. Fr. Leonidas did not stop the prayers.

During the 9th Ode, the priest poured a teaspoon of holy chrism into his hand with his back turned to the Jaguar. He rubbed his palms together as he walked and stopped within a foot of the driver's side window. Lilith had left it open. "Ari, it's time to say The Exorcism Prayers of the *Xiropotamou* 98. Retrieve the copies from my bag."

The driver's window rolled up. Fr. Leonidas grabbed it with both hands and smeared the holy oil all across the top edge of the glass. It halted midway up. He flicked his fingertips at Lilith.

She whined and frantically wiped her face. Red splotches appeared where the drops of holy chrism had landed.

"Let us pray to the Lo... rd," Fr. Leonidas chanted while he used the holy oil on his hands to anoint Ari's forehead, both cheeks, chin, the backs and palms of her hands; then he did the same to himself.

"Lord have mer... cy," Ari intoned in response.

Fr. Leonidas spoke clearly and firmly, "I exorcise you, evil Devil, enemy of truth, by the awful and holy name of All-Powerful God the Father, the Son, and the Holy Spirit to tell me immediately how your name is called."

"Lilith."

"That is who you say you are, demon. Tell me your real name."

Lilith didn't look at him. She seemed oblivious to the new proximity of the priest. She rapped her fingertips on the steering wheel.

"I adjure you by the holy angels, thrones, dominions, principalities, powers, and authorities; by the many-eyed Cherubim and the six-winged Seraphim to tell me immediately how your name is called."

Lilith turned her head slowly like it was on a gear crank toward the two humans. She directed her direful gaze at Ari who stumbled backward like she'd been pushed. The Voice that came out of that milky white throat was unlike any vocalization Ari had ever heard. "*Names. I have many... in many tongues...*

I am Obyzouth, Onoskelis, I am the Scarlet Woman whom Aleister Crowley lusted and was damned for, the Queen of Sheba..."

Fr. Leonidas ignored the demon's rant. "I adjure you by the supremely pure Maria, Mother of God, by the twelve and seventy holy apostles; by the terrible and unimpeachable judgement and by the holy blood that flowed from the side of our Lord, Jesus Christ..."

Lilith's mouth was an open sepulchre. *"Helen of Troy, the dark aspect of the Mother Goddess..."*

"—by the twenty-four presbyters, forever presiding at the invisible throne of God and singing the unhalting song and by all the wondrous works of All-Powerful God that have occurred in heaven and on earth..."

Lilith's Voice rose with each name she spoke, *"—the Lady of the Beasts, Jezebel..."*

The priest kept his voice even, "—by the holy patriarchs, Abraham, Isaac, and Jacob and all the saints [who lived] before the Law..."

"—Naamah, female counterpart to Leviathan..."

"—by the holy fourteen thousand infants, those slaughtered under Herod..."

"—the screech owl, the princess of screeching..."

"—by all holy men and women, those who pleased holy God in their lifetime."

"—And the Queen of Zemargad... YES, I am the Queen of the Desert. I am all these ... and TOGETHER we are the LILITH... and..." Her chest heaved up and down.

"—I adjure all you evil spirits, by all the saints, that you tell me your names..." Fr. Leonidas showed Lilith the holy cross. "Behold the holy cross of our Lord, Jesus Christ. Depart evil Devil!"

"... we... are not going... anywhere!" Her Voice was a boxer's fist.

The punch of pure icy hatred nearly knocked Ari and Fr. Leonidas off their feet. Ari hugged her arms. "I'm gonna close the side door, Father."

"Go ahead, but that's not why it's cold in here. The demon is gathering every speck of energy she can to stay in Deedee's body. We're making progress." Fr. Leonidas winked.

CHAPTER 66

Pit Bull

Tuesday Evening | November 17th

The screen door banged into the wall of the garage. Ari startled and cried out. Vasillis pushed Samuel into the garage with his wrists tied behind his back. Samuel's head lolled on its stem like a drenched flower in a rainstorm; he stumbled down the stairs and fell to his knees hitting his forehead on the hard cement floor of the garage.

"Samuel," Lilith said. The Jag rocked on its tires.

The seminarian had a black woolen 300-knot prayer rope looped around Samuel's neck. He heaved Samuel to his feet and brought him to a hard stop in front of Fr. Leonidas. "He tried to bite me, so I had to be creative."

Fr. Leonidas said, "Lift up his head."

Vasillis grabbed a handful of lush black hair and held the handsome head steady.

"Ari, don't take your eyes off the other one."

Lilith was a crazed jaguar trapped in a cage. Chunks of metal, leather, and foam hurtled out the Jag's windows.

"Do you think I can?" Ari deflected the flying debris with the icon of St. Basil.

Vasillis' chin trembled.

Fr. Leonidas pressed the holy cross on Samuel's forehead. In the other hand he held the tablet. Samuel's body stiffened, his eyes rolled white into their sockets. He revived and writhed to pull himself away from the holy cross.

"Steady sir," Vasillis said.

Fr. Leonidas said, "I exorcise you, evil Devil, enemy of truth, by the awful and holy name of All-Powerful God the Father, the Son, and the Holy Spirit to tell me immediately how your name is called. I adjure you by the holy angels, thrones, dominions, principalities, powers, and authorities; by the many-eyed Cherubim and the six-winged Seraphim to tell me immediately how your name is called." The priest motioned for Vasillis to ease up a little on Samuel.

The moment Vasillis loosened his grip, Samuel came into himself and glared at Fr. Leonidas. He snarled, "You should be able to guess my name, priest. You've got my wife over there, you Harley hog—"

Vasillis jerked up the slack on the long prayer rope. Samuel gagged.

Fr. Leonidas said, "Take it easy, son."

Vasillis relaxed a tiny bit.

Fr. Leonidas continued. "Tell me your name, evil Devil, enemy of truth, by the awful and holy name of All-Powerful God the Father, the Son, and the Holy Spirit to tell me immediately how your name is called." He splashed holy water into Samuel's face. He screamed and fell to the floor shaking his head, but the priest held the holy cross firmly to his forehead.

Samuel lunged at Fr. Leonidas and bit his leg. He wouldn't let go. Vasillis strained hard to pull him back and tightened the slack on the rope, but Samuel held fast. "Like a pit bull, this one."

Ari didn't want to leave her post guarding Lilith, but she had to act. She stood over Samuel a few moments summoning the courage. *This'll sound worse than a cockroach.*

"Do it." Vasillis knew what she had in mind.

She cracked Samuel over the head with the heavy St. Basil icon. She winced at the bone to wood sound.

"Lord have mercy," Vasillis said.

Samuel slumped to the floor unconscious.

Fr. Leonidas stumbled backward grabbing his leg, grimacing from the pain.

"What do you want me to do with him, Father?" Vasillis asked.

Fr. Leonidas motioned roughly with his free hand toward the Jaguar. "Put him in the car with her. I'll do a 2 for 1 special on them."

Vasillis pulled Samuel to his feet and dragged him to the passenger side of the car. Lilith's eyes followed them like an owl's, her head turning on her neck the same Strigidaen way. Ari opened the door. He shoved the floppy rag doll Samuel into the Jaguar.

Lilith cradled Samael's head in her lap. "You'll pay for this, priestlette."

Vasillis slammed the door shut. He and Ari went to the workbench.

Fr. Leonidas had resumed the prayers.

Ari asked Vasillis, "Are Laurie and the children all right?"

"The kids are groggy but awake. I told them to stay in Amy's room no matter what they hear. Laurie's knocked out cold but breathing smoothly."

She turned her attention back to the rite. Vasillis carried a bowl of holy water and a fragrant bouquet of basil tied with twine to his mentor.

Fr. Leonidas dipped the basil into the bowl and flicked it around to purify the room. He was pulling out all the stops.

"Oh!" Ari was caught off guard having holy water sprinkled in her face as the priest said, "Lord Jesus Christ, Son of God, have mercy on Ari's soul." He repeated the blessing three more times inserting the names of all those present.

Lilith's eyes bored into Ari's unblinking.

Fr. Leonidas continued the prayer, "Let God arise and let his enemies be scattered and let them flee from his countenance. As smoke vanishes so may they disappear; as wax melts away from the face of fire, and snow from the burning heat of the sun."

Lilith exploded with laughter. It was a bottle bomb of painful shards of sound.

They covered their ears.

"Get St. Basil." Fr. Leonidas shouted over the laughter to Ari. She picked up the icon and stood next to him. She and Vasillis flanked the priest.

Fr. Leonidas began the prayer again. "Cursed Devil, why do you delay and not speak your name? Give glory to holy God;

take fright at these varied and many oaths. I adjure you by our Lord Jesus Christ. Speak your name."

Lilith stopped laughing and snarled, "Are you deaf? I've already told you my *names*. And I know yours too, priest. Dom... min... no... hahahaha."

Fr. Leonidas choked. He cleared his throat. "Jesus Christ conquers. The lion; he of Judah's race; he of the root of David; the Emmanuel. Christ reigns, Christ holds power, Christ slays, Christ grants life; holy, holy, holy Lord Sabaoth, heaven and earth are filled with his glory, Hosannah in the highest, and who is blessed through the ages."

Lilith ignored him, "Uh hem. Let's discuss you, Leonida. Or should I call you by your road name, Domino? You forgot to put the kickstand down on your Harley, then it fell onto the row of your gang's bikes... bang... bang... bang."

Fr. Leonidas's hands trembled along with his voice. "Cursed Devil, why do you delay and not speak your name? Give glory to holy God; take fright at these varied and many exorcisms. I adjure you by our Lord Jesus Christ. Speak your name."

"Domino Leo—that's got a nice ring to it," Lilith said.

"Let's read the Second Prayer of St. Basil...," Fr. Leonidas said.

"We haven't finished the Xiropatomou 98 yet," Vasillis said.

"Can't you see it's not working?" Fr. Leonidas smacked the book in his protégé's hands.

"Maybe it is, Father, that's why she's goading you now," Ari whispered.

"I am the priest here, not you two. We're switching to the Second Prayer of St. Basil, page 24." He cleared his throat. "Let us pray to the Lord."

"Lord, have mercy," Vasillis and Ari chanted, their shoulders dropping.

"I adjure thee, the blasphemous originator of evil, leader of the revolt of the adversaries, and the author of wickedness. I adjure thee and all the powers following thy will that fell with thee! I adjure thee—"

Ari observed the priest. *This feels wrong. Lord Jesus Christ, have mercy on Father Leonidas. Switching the prayers is probably what the demon wants us to do. Yes, I'm right. Look at her over there gloating.*

Lilith had a wide smile on her face. "You cannot adjure me. You're not fit to be a priest."

Fr. Leonidas stopped praying.

Vasillis stared at his mentor in disbelief. "Father, were you in a *motorcycle* gang?"

Fr. Leonidas's head hung, his beard swept his chest. He spoke in a low voice. "They were my first family. My mom skipped the hospital the night I was born. She didn't even stick around long enough to name me. Nobody wanted to adopt a preemie crack baby who cried all the time, so I was put in foster care. I ran away from the last home when I was sixteen. I got tired of owing people, so I was on the street for a while. The Hells Angels took me in when I bested the sergeant-at-arms of the local club. Foster kids know how to fight. The dude gave me his old bike. I finally belonged somewhere."

"I don't believe it," Vasillis said.

"You know this scar, don't you?" Fr. Leonidas pointed to the deep gash he had from his hairline to his left eyebrow.

"Yes, Father. You said you got it in a bike accident."

"You haven't seen these." Fr. Leonidas pulled back his sleeves showing them the burned mottled skin on his arms. Ari flinched. The priest's forearms were hunks of ground beef stuck on with shellac.

"When I was twenty, I crashed my Harley and it exploded. I had third-degree burns on the upper part of my body."

Vasillis was stricken with revelation. "It was a *motor*bike accident."

"The high collar helps." Fr. Leonidas stuck his finger inside his black collar and pulled it out revealing more pink lumpy skin.

"How devastating for you, Father," Ari said.

"No, it wasn't. You see, I had a visitor in the hospital burn unit: an Orthodox priest. He befriended me, told me to hang on, that I wasn't going to die because God wasn't done with me yet. I wanted to become a priest like him. He told me a man with tattoos couldn't enter the seminary. I was despondent because I had tattooed sleeves on both arms. But when the doctor took off the bandages, my arms were ugly but free from ink! God used my suffering for my own good."

They heard clapping and turned their attention to Lilith. "Most inspiring, Domino. You ought to submit your story to *Guideposts*." She slammed her palms on the horn.

"How is she doing that without the key?" Ari shouted.

Fr. Leonidas was talking to himself. "Nostalgia, no. Pride. That's the real reason I kept it." He went to the workbench and laid down his tablet. He picked up a handsaw.

"Domino... your sins are unconfessed." Lilith yelled and honked.

"Not anymore, demon. You have brought them to light and made me confess them. Lord forgive me my many personal transgressions." Fr. Leonidas flipped the scraggly salt and pepper braid over his shoulder and held it in his hand for a few moments. He pulled it taut and sawed the braid off. He cast it to the floor by the Harley. "My wife will be pleased." He shook his great head and the newly-cut strands of hair flared out onto his collar. He faced Lilith, "Let's continue with your removal from this child of God, shall we?"

Vasillis stared at his spiritual father utterly astounded.

Fr. Leonidas tapped on the burgundy book he held. "Where in the Xiropotamou 98 did I stop?"

Vasillis pointed at the line. "Uh... um, right here, Father."

Fr. Leonidas began with renewed vigor. "Cursed Devil, why do you delay and not speak your name? Give glory to holy God; take fright at these varied and many oaths. I adjure you by our Lord Jesus Christ. Speak your name. Fear thou, flee, flee begone, O demon unclean and defiled, infernal, abysmal, false, ugly, visible because of thy shamelessness, invisible because of thy hypocrisy—"

"Hypocrisy?" Lilith swiveled her head toward the priest. "You want to discuss hypocrisy? I am... an... expert. Hun... hun... hun."

Fr. Leonidas talked over her. Ari and Vasillis stood on either side of him.

The priest spoke in a firm voice, "I adjure you by him for whom every knee bends in heaven and on earth and in the underworld, that you tell your name."

The words came huskily out of Lilith's open grave mouth. "I am a victim of hypocrisy, not a doer of it... it was Adam... the first misogynist. I am who I am... because of him."

"I adjure you by him for whom every knee bends in heaven and on earth and in the underworld, that you tell your name."

"A mound of rendered fat is unworthy to engage me."

"I adjure you by him for whom every knee bends in heaven and on earth and in the underworld, that you tell your name." He repeated the phrase which seemed to be working.

"My beautiful body... was drowned... but this one is mine now..." She pounded her chest with her fist. "... this one was promised to me... by her mother... the Celtic witch... on the day she broke through her mother's womb... she was baptized in swine's blood ... and christened Deirdre Ethane. The Morrigan's daughter is *mine*."

Fr. Leonidas stopped the prayer. His voice was stern. "Deirdre, little Deedee, was not her mother's possession to give to anyone. She belongs to God, not you. She never did." He went on his knees.

Ari and Vasillis hesitated a moment, then awkwardly knelt alongside him on the cold floor.

The priest continued to twist the verbal knife, "I adjure you by him for whom every knee bends in heaven and on earth and in the underworld, that you tell your name."

At the sound of her name, *inside Deedee's mind, a lifetime of memories whirled in the air then funneled down...fitting themselves into a horizontal Jenga tower of comprehension...and stilling. Deedee raged at her mother—and forgave her. Deedee analyzed everything—and understood. Deedee repented—and prayed to God in heaven. She pulled herself together and fought back: kicking, thrashing, straining, and beating against the rib bone cage. Get out of my car and out of my body! ON... YOUR... KNEES.*

The driver's side door of the Jaguar slowly swung open. Lilith fell onto the hard cement. Samuel crawled out after her and crumpled to his knees. Lilith and he knelt side-by-side bowing their heads.

"I don't believe it," Ari said to Vasillis.

Fr. Leonidas repeated the prayer. "I adjure you by the name of Jesus Christ, he for whom *every knee* bends in heaven and on earth and in the *underworld*, that you tell your names."

Lilith's eyes rolled white into her head.

"Write down what she says."

Vasillis jumped up and found a piece of yellow sidewalk chalk.

Ari whipped her cell phone out of her back pocket.

They waited.

Lilith's white throat was bent in a hard crescent arc, her mouth open to the ceiling.

"I adjure you by that blood, the same as that which poured out upon the cross. Speak your name; say it plainly. I, the servant of God, ask you, what is your name?"

The Voice was filled with rancor at having to reveal itself. The names poured out of Lilith in a stream of vitriol. *"I am called... Ardad Lili... Lamassu... Satrinah...Thilitho... and Zefonith."*

Vasillis scrawled the names on the floor.

Ari wrote the demon's names in a text to herself.

Lilith was on all fours, her wild red hair swaying as she panted.

Fr. Leonidas looked at the list of names scribbled on the floor. He directed his attention to Samuel. "And your male consort? What are you called, demon in Samuel's body?"

Samuel's GQ demeanor returned. He flipped his hair out of his face. "I am the 'venom of God'. I do His dirty work. It was I who tempted fair Eve. Women are easier for me to persuade. Like Sarah. I couldn't convince Abraham to spare his son, Isaac. What you may not know is that I flew down the mountain to tell Sarah that Abraham had just slain her only son. She collapsed where she stood and died."

Ari searched key words in his story on the Internet. She touched Fr. Leonidas's sleeve. "Look. His name is Samael, with an 'a' instead of a 'u'. He and Lilith made many of their own demon children, until uh, God *castrated him*."

Samael said, "However, I *adapted*. Our progeny will conquer yours."

"I don't think so, Sammy. *Ιησούς Χριστός νικά*. Jesus has overcome," Fr. Leonidas said. He held the crucifix on Lilith's forehead. "I adjure thee O unclean spirit, Lilith, Ardad Lili, Lamassu, Satrinah, Thilitho, and Zefonith, by the God of Sabaoth and all the armies of the Angels of God, Adonai Elohim, God Almighty: Begone, and depart from the servant of God, Deirdre Ethane Morrigan! Tell whether you have other accomplices with you as well, and how you are and from what class, or what your leader is called."

Lilith rose to her knees. "I am of the second class of the mazziqin... a night terror. Samael is my husband."

Fr. Leonidas took the cross from Lilith's forehead and pressed it onto Samael's. "I adjure thee O unclean spirit, Samael, husband of Lilith, castrated abomination of God, by the God of Sabaoth and all the armies of the Angels of God, Adonai Elohim, God Almighty: Begone, and depart from the servant of God, Samuel!"

Samael grimaced under the pressure of the cross but did not utter a word.

"In what power and authority or where and in which place are you dwelling?" The priest asked.

Samael was silent.

"Before coming out of Samuel you must tell me to whom you are subordinate."

Lilith shook and spoke rapidly in a language no one understood.

It was similar to the speaking in tongues Ari had heard a few times, but this Voice was babel, evil, and foul. Fr. Leonidas needed help. He only had one cross that he couldn't take off Samuel's forehead. Yiayiá's prayer rope! Ari discretely pulled the prayer rope out of her pocket. Instead of vibrating, it resonated in perfect pitch. It was a pleasant tone. *If the Jesus Prayer could be sung, it would be intoned like this in Standard Pitch A440.*

Ari faced Lilith concealing the prayer rope in her hand. Diabolical gibberish poured out of her unholy mouth. Ari whispered, "*Lord Jesus Christ have mercy on me!*" and jammed the prayer rope's cross onto Lilith's forehead.

Lilith fell forward on her hands coughing, her back arching up and down.

Father Leonidas and Vasillis stood.

Ari stayed crouched in front of her, even though she was terrified of what the demon might do. She held the cross to Lilith's sweaty brow as she writhed onto her back clutching her stomach.

The prayer rope continued to sing... until Lilith turned her head and vomited out a small, round, metallic object. When her head rolled back, her eyes were normal, wet with exertion, but bright and emerald green like the Irish Sea.

Ari didn't recognize *this* woman. She kept the cross pressed against her forehead. "Who are you?"

An intelligent, likeable human voice came out of her mouth. "Quick, Ari... I have control of my body for a moment. I'm Deedee." Deedee gently pushed the cross off her forehead and sat.

Ari let her. *Was she really Deedee?*

Deedee deftly pulled off the oxblood lambskin gloves and cast them aside. She looked at her hands, now bare and beautiful, like they had just been re-attached. She spied the object in the glob of vomit in front of her. "There you are." She picked it up marveling at it.

Deedee jumped up and reached in through the Jaguar's window. She yanked the charm hanging on a chain from the rear view mirror and held it in the light. She fitted the two pieces together. Now it was a tiny doll without legs.

Ari stood and approached Deedee for a closer look. The head was a much worn smirking baby's face with two pink stones for eyes. The torso had 'Fumsup!' written in raised letters across its chest. Its arms were moveable and its thumbs in the 'thumbs up' position. It had a belly button, a simple detail that was cute on other dolls, but one which made this doll grotesque.

"Where are the legs?" Deedee closed it in her hand. She looked tenderly at Samuel. "The exorcism isn't working because his name isn't Samuel, it's *Andrew*. He's my husband."

CHAPTER 67

The Clash

Tuesday Evening | November 17th

Deedee tentatively put her hand on Andrew's shoulder, but drew it back quickly when he looked up at her. The eyes were not her husband's.

He glared at her. "I want my wife back."

"*I am* your wife." Deedee turned to the priest. "Father, I don't know how long I'll have control of my body. Lilith is still in here." She tapped her temple. "Please release Andrew from the demon! The rest of this must be in him." She held the Fumsup! doll out to the priest.

"What is his full given name?" Fr. Leonidas asked.

"Andrew Patrick Warner."

Samael gripped Deedee's forearm and dug his nails into her skin. Her whole body straightened and her eyes rolled back into her head.

"No, Deedee, don't leave." Ari grabbed her other arm.

Samael spoke not to Deedee but to the thieving spirit inside her. "Come back, darling. Join me in this." He pulled her down next to him.

Ari lost her grip on Deedee.

Deedee dipped her back into a cow pose then arched up into an angry cat.

"Hello again from the other side." Lilith was back; her Voice, her attitude, her malevolence. *"Now, Deedee, your son Justin will die. Just as I promised."*

"No, Deedee, please come back." Ari jammed the prayer rope's cross on Lilith's forehead. It intoned again in perfect pitch.

Fr. Leonidas spat on Lilith. She careened to the side.

"Geez, Father. You almost got me too," Ari said.

"You do it."

Lilith's Voice grew stronger, babel filled the garage.

"I think we're dealing with more than the bad eye here."

"Spitting is the worst insult to the devil. Do it."

Greeks. At the Annunciation Church, she fended off old Greek ladies who spat on her daughter to ward off the evil eye. They would say, «Φτου σου!» (Ftou sou!) and pretend to spit on Dorothea when they gave her a compliment. It was gross.

"Fine." Ari spat on Lilith. She immediately shut up. The demon cringed like she'd had holy water thrown on her. *Those old Greek ladies were right after all.*

Fr. Leonidas held the crucifix on Andrew's forehead and said, "I adjure thee O unclean spirit, Samael, by the God of Sabaoth and all the armies of the Angels of God, Adonai Elohim, God

Almighty: Begone, and depart from the servant of God, Andrew Patrick Warner!"

Samael's smirk straightened out into a serious line on his face. His body shuddered and he clenched his fists. He lunged at Fr. Leonidas.

The priest spat in Samael's face. The demon careened backward, gnashing his teeth.

Fr. Leonidas held the cross firmly on his brow. "Even you, a demon prince, are bowing now before the name of Jesus Christ, He for whom *every knee* bends in heaven and on earth, and in the *underworld*."

Samael laughed a gurgling, thick sound.

Fr. Leonidas pressed on. "Therefore, *listen* to the prayer and *begone*, and depart, cower before the Image fashioned and formed by the hand of God; fear the likeness of the Incarnate God, and conceal thyself no longer within the servant of God, Andrew Patrick Warner."

The beast Samael spoke from Andrew's mouth, **"Permit me to enter—"**

"In what power and authority or where and in which place are you dwelling?"

Lilith and Samael shuddered then settled on their haunches. Their voices answered in terrible unison, **"In the desert, in a cave by the Sea of Reeds."**

"Before coming out of Deirdre and Andrew, you must tell me to whom you are subordinate."

"The Ruler of the World. Lucifer, the fallen bolt of lightning, Satan." They both laughed, but there was no joy in it, only sulfurous filth from the bowels of the earth.

"Tell me when you devils emerge and what sign you make when you emerge. I adjure you by the Holy Spirit that revealed you through Peter, supreme among the apostles, in Simon Magus, and in Kynops Angkhistos, by the Apostle John the Theologian on the Island of Patmos. Answer what I have asked you, wily Devil. Humble yourself. Hades has been appointed as your seat of power; therein is your dwelling. So, there is no time to wait."

Samael hit his chest with his fist. His mouth frothed white. The legs of the Fumsup! doll charm bubbled out of his mouth and chinked onto the floor.

"That's the third piece of the charm," Ari said. "Vasillis! Take it!" she pushed it backward with her free hand.

Vasillis picked it up and rose to his feet.

Lilith grinned through her mass of disheveled red hair. She held the rest of the doll charm in her clenched fist. She lifted her hand to her mouth...

Ari grabbed her wrist. "Oh, no you don't." She struggled with the demon for a few moments.

With her last ounce of strength, Deedee forced her own hand open. She extended it to Ari as she hoarsely whispered, "Take it."

"Thank you, Deedee." Ari snatched the charm and handed it to Vasillis.

Vasillis fitted the three pieces of the charm together. He held the impish doll by its chain for a moment in the air. He moved its arms up and down and smiled. "Thumbs up to you too, little guy. You're kinda cute."

"Put it in the holy water, Vasilli." Fr. Leonidas held out the bowl.

"Hey, look at these tiny wings on his feet."

"*Now*, Vasilli. We must crush it like the serpent's head that it is."

Vasillis closed his hand around the doll. "No."

Ari winked at Fr. Leonidas. "Let me see him too." She sing sang and gently pried open Vasillis's hand. "Oh, he is cute." She grabbed the charm out of the seminarian's hand. As she did, the trance was broken. She plopped the doll in the bowl the priest held. Steam rose from the holy water like a mini diffuser.

"This'll have to cook a while to be neutralized." Fr. Leonidas set the bowl on the workbench.

"Noooo!" Lilith had taken Deedee over again. She sprang for the charm.

Ari pushed her and she fell backward.

Fr. Leonidas motioned for Ari and Vasillis to join him in front of Lilith. She was on her knees again, huffing defiantly at the priest. Samael stared at the floor.

"Let us come together to deliver these two children of our Lord." The priest shrugged his shoulders up and the sleeves of his robe hiked back, exposing his ravaged forearms. He placed his cross on Lilith's forehead and Ari pressed the prayer rope's cross on Samael's. It hummed in A440.

Lilith and Samael froze in position on their knees.

"By the God of Sabaoth, I adjure thee O unclean spirits, Lilith, Ardad Lili, Lamassu, Satrinah, Thilitho, and Zefonith, and Samael, listen to the prayer and *begone*, and depart, cower before the Image fashioned and formed by the hand of God; fear the likeness of the Incarnate God, and conceal thyself no longer within the servants of God, Deirdre Ethane Morrigan, and Andrew Patrick Warner..."

As the priest read the end of the prayer, warm cinnamon air pushed back the cerecloth of sulfur enshrouding the garage.

"... for a rod of iron, a fiery furnace, and Tartarus, the gnashing of teeth and vengeance for disobedience await thee. Fear thou, keep silent and flee. Return not, neither consort with the wickedness of the other unclean spirits, but depart into a land devoid of water, barren, uncultivated, in which man makes not his habitation."

Now the whole garage was warm and toasty, a corner bakery on a Saturday, or your mother's kitchen.

"... God alone looketh upon thee, the devil, the tempter and discloser of all evils, who didst wound all and didst purpose evils against His Image, and bindeth thee, with dark chains, unto Tartarus forever..."

A blazing star appeared behind Lilith and Samael. Sansennoi emerged in full battle regalia, a flaming sword in his right hand, and two heavy chains with fetters in his left.

Vasillis and Fr. Leonidas fell to their knees covering their heads.

"Do not fear me, gentlemen. I am Sansennoi, guardian angel of Ari and chief adversary of the demon you know as Lilith. I am here to answer your prayer and take Lilith and her mate, Samael back to the great desert by the Reed Sea. Rise and finish the prayer, Father Leonida."

Ari and Vasillis helped Fr. Leonidas to his feet. The priest intoned, "For great is the fear of God, and great is the glory of the

Father, and of the Son, and of the Holy Spirit, now and ever, and unto the ages of ages. Amen." Ari, Fr. Leonidas, and Vasillis crossed themselves.

Sansennoi loomed tall behind the demons and lifted his hands. As he raised them, Lilith and Samael's necks arched inhumanly back. Their mouths gaped and two black vapors rushed out. One materialized into the spirit of Lilith and the other into the spirit of Samael, which hovered on either side of the kneeling humans.

Lilith was a hologram of a woman with fiery hair down to her white navel where real flames began. The eyes Ari recognized.

Samael was not human at all. He was a conglomeration of four different animals: the head of a goat buck, the body of a lion, the clawed feet of an eagle, and the wings of a black condor. His brutish eyes suited the beastly head they were in now.

Sansennoi stepped in front of Lilith. He clamped her milky wrists in the fetters. He stood before Samael and secured his paws in the second set of irons. Sansennoi held both chains in one hand. The demons' shoulders were slumped in defeat.

The angel smiled warmly at Fr. Leonidas and Vasillis. "The Lord is well pleased with you."

Sansennoi then directed his gaze at Ari. "God knew your faith was lukewarm, therefore He challenged you to put another's well-being above your own. And you have. You sacrificed your life to save Laurie's on the subway tracks. That was *agápe*, unconditional love. Today you fought powerful evil despite the great danger to you and your daughter. You are living your purpose and have earned your christened name. You are now Are-*té*, a 'virtuous friend' of Laurie's and of Christ's."

She stared at her empty palms. It was difficult to form words. "I... I am unworthy."

Fr. Leonidas said, "God changed the names of others who wholeheartedly embraced His challenging purpose for them and they were transformed in the process: Abram became Abraham, Sarai became Sarah, Jacob became Israel, and Saul became St. Paul. You're no longer battling alone as Ari. You now serve God as Areté, His virtuous friend."

"Yes. It was not easy for them and it was not easy for her either. She has glorified God and learned to truly love. Well done, Areté." Sansennoi nodded approvingly at her.

Areté was overwhelmed. "I... am honored," was all she could manage to say.

Sansennoi spoke in the direction of the kitchen. "Amy and Elijah, are well. Laurie is unharmed."

Areté whispered, *"Sansennoi, is there anything you can do to help Laurie's unborn child?"*

"Laurie does not need my help."

Areté walked over to her angel and asked in a low voice, *"What about the HIV?"*

He cupped her chin. "Laurie and the child she carries is healthy in every way. The diagnosis of HIV was yet another of Lilith's many lies. She duped the emergency staff with her veil of deceit. Do not fear."

Areté hugged him. "That's wonderful!"

Sansennoi gathered up the heavy iron chains like the driver of a stage coach and slapped Lilith and Samael on the back with the brutal metal. "Straight to Hell with you two." Both demons arched their backs yowling in agony as Sansennoi drove them down on all fours. All three vanished through the concrete floor.

"That's quite a guardian angel you've got there," Fr. Leonidas said.

Deedee said, "Andrew?" Now everyone's attention was drawn back to Deedee and her estranged husband. Deedee was still on her knees beside Andrew, her head bent low to look into his face. His beautiful black hair hung forward like a rooster's comb.

Deedee lifted Andrew's chin. He looked at her, his eyes filled with shame. She held his face in both palms. They were newly-reunited prisoners of war. Deedee cried into Andrew's shoulder and said over and over, "I am so sorry, so, so sorry... I almost lost our baby girl... please forgive me."

Andrew pulled away. He spoke, in an American west coast accent, "*We* almost lost our baby. I watched you suffer. I couldn't do anything to stop it... I'm the one who should be sorry! I gave you that Fumsup! doll charm and persuaded you to follow Dr. Thom's instructions. I beg *you* to forgive me. Why wasn't I satisfied with what I had? You and Justin are enough for me—more than enough."

"Oh, Andrew, what about Justin? Where is our son?" Deedee rose to her feet and stumbled a bit rubbing her stiff knees.

"I think I left him at my mother's."

"My phone. Where's my purse? Oh my baby..."

Areté brought Deedee's purse to her. "Here it is."

Fr. Leonidas helped Andrew to his feet. "Let's give your knees a break, son."

Andrew managed a "Thank you."

Areté was by the workbench. She examined the Fumsup! doll under the lamp.

"Justin? It's me, Mommy. Are you okay? Okay, okay...tell Grandma I'll talk to her in a minute... How are you, buddy?" Deedee asked.

Areté turned the little brass doll around in the holy water with a pencil.

"Yes, Daddy's here with Mommy... yes, we're coming home as soon as we can... hopefully tomorrow. Bye, my beautiful boy." Deedee sighed, "He's okay," to Andrew. He came and hugged her shoulders as she put the phone back in her purse.

Areté put her hand on Deedee's forearm and gently asked, "Are *you* okay?"

Deedee started to cry again, then her face hardened and she swiped at the tears. "Where's the Fumsup! charm?"

Areté led Deedee over to the workbench. "Can we...?" she asked Fr. Leonidas.

He said, "Yep, it should be sanitized by now."

Deedee picked the charm out of the hot holy water. She turned the little doll around in her fingers. "Lilith was not lying to you when she said that she was, well, that *I am* a rare antiquities dealer. These Fumsup! dolls were given to soldiers by their sweethearts to protect them from death in the First World War. J.C. Vickery produced them in London in 1916. This particular charm has real pink sapphire eyes and a 15-carat yellow gold body. Only ten were made. It could bring over 10,000 £ on the British market." She quietly said, "A little poem was in the box it came with. Dr. Thom told us to recite it together and for me to swallow the torso and Andrew the legs so we could get pregnant again...

> *Behold in me*
> *The birth of luck,*
> *Two charms combined,*
> *Touchwood - Fumsup*
> *My head is made*
> *Of gold most rare*
> *My thumbs turn up*
> *To touch me there.*
> *To speed my feet*
> *They've Cupid's wings:*
> *They'll help true love*
> *'Mongst other things.*
> *Proverbial is*
> *My power to bring*
> *Good luck to you*
> *In everything.*
> *I'll bring good luck*
> *To all away –*
> *Just send me to*
> *A friend to-day."*

Deedee's eyes were cold and hard. "Let me ask you a question, Father." She thrust the doll at Fr. Leonidas. "You're a man of God. Answer for your boss. Tell me why He would let this thing hurt my family."

"Once in a while God allows the evil one to bonk us on the head to get our attention."

"Are you... are you calling what Andrew and I went through a 'bonk' on the head?" She pounded her fist on the workbench. "I almost lost my baby because of Lilith."

"I suspect it wasn't just the doll itself that endangered you. May I?" He held out his hand.

Deedee dropped the charm unceremoniously into his palm.

Fr. Leonidas pried at the back of the doll's torso with his fingernail and a tiny door opened. He turned the doll on its back and tapped its round tummy. A thin white sliver fell out. "Ah hah! See what we have here." The priest held the white piece up to the light squinting at it. "Yep, it all makes perfect sense now."

"What is that?" Andrew asked.

"Well, I reckon this is an unholy relic, most likely a chip of bone from Lilith's original body," Fr. Leonidas said. "This is what made the Fumsup! doll a 'seal,' a symbol unique to Lilith that called her to you. You were already marked by your mother, which put you at risk for possession. However, the deal wasn't sealed yet. That happened when you *willingly* swallowed this. It left your door of free will wide open to the demon."

"So it's my fault that Lilith was able to imprison me in my own mind," Deedee said.

"What was it like in there?" Areté asked.

"Horrible. I was trapped in a rib-bone cage. I could see out of my eyes, but I had no control over my physical body at all; only for a few moments. Like right here at the end."

"And at the subway station, when you pushed Laurie onto the tracks?" Areté asked.

"Yes, I took over for a few seconds there too. I know it looked like I tried to kill Laurie, but I was trying to save her by showing her how evil Lilith was."

"Even that didn't convince her."

"I paid for it because Lilith threatened to kill my son. So I laid low for a while."

"She threatened to kill all our children."

"Is Dorothea okay?"

"Yes, she's with Hector. But Laurie still needs our help." She pointed to the kitchen.

"Yes, and Amy and Elijah. Let's go check on them."

Areté put her hand on Deedee's arm. "I'll go in alone and try to explain to them that you're not the bad lady anymore."

"Right. I have a lot to make up for, don't I?"

"We all do." Areté held the screen door open. "Father, are you coming?"

"Vasillis and I need to clean up here first. Say, Areté, it looks like you've found your calling after all. You're a prayer rope warrior," Fr. Leonidas said. "It's got a nice ring to it, don't you think?"

Areté was taken aback by his insight. "How did you know I was searching for it?"

"I have my sources too, you know." Fr. Leonidas winked.

Epilogue

*Friday Morning 8:30 AM| November 21ˢᵗ |
The Entrance of the Most Holy Theotokos*

The narthex was lit by only two candles, one by the icon of Christ, and the other by the icon of the Theotokos holding the infant Christ. The Church was dark. Dorothea yawned into her Blankie. "Mamá, where is everybody?"

"I don't know, *moró mou*. But *we're* here, and that's all that should concern us. Put your dollar in the plate and light a candle." Areté had taken her daughter out of school for the day to come here. To thank another mother: the Theotokos.

Areté lit her own tall beeswax candle and placed it in the white sand next to the large icon of the Mother of God. She felt awkward, like she was approaching a stranger. *Well, I don't know you, but I want to.* As she bent to kiss the Virgin Mary's hand which held the infant Christ, she whispered, *"From one mother to another, I thank you. I'll try to follow your example."* Areté kissed the Christ child's tiny foot with the sandal slipping off. It made Him so human. "Lord Jesus Christ, Son of God, thank you for having mercy on me, and all of us this week." She crossed herself three times. Her prayer rope lightly hummed in her coat pocket.

Dorothea led her mother by the hand into the nave. It was nearly empty. Only Soula and her elderly mother ever came this early. But Areté didn't know that because she'd never gone to a weekday service in her life. Father Leonidas was in the altar. He nodded slightly and his eyes lit up when he saw them. Vasillis was at the chanter stand reading a Psalm. It was Psalm 142(3). Dorothea went to where she and Hector usually sat, to the right, in the third pew from the front.

Areté's cell phone chimed. Dorothea shot her a look. Areté took a peek at the phone as she was quickly muting it and saw it was a text from Laurie.

We're in front of your church. Can you come get us?

Areté patted Dorothea's shoulder. *"It's Laurie and her kids. Stay here, I'll be back in a second."* She quickly walked around the pews and into the narthex. She pushed open the heavy wooden door and smiled when she saw Laurie, Amy, and Elijah standing there shivering.

"Come in, it's freezing. I'm so happy to see you all!" Areté ushered them inside. She embraced Laurie warmly. "I didn't expect you."

"I had to come. After all that Father Leonidas did to save my family, I thought I owed it to him to pay my respects."

"Why don't you all light a candle?" Areté crossed herself and glanced over Laurie's shoulder at the icon of Christ. He seemed to be staring right at her, and her prayer rope resonated in perfect pitch just loud enough for her to hear. Instead of being afraid, a wave of calm washed over her accompanied by a gentle voice which whispered, *"Well done, Areté; you have shown you are trustworthy in small things; I will trust you with greater."* With tears in her eyes she answered, "I'm ready."

Idiomelon:

*Today the Theotokos, the temple that contains God,
is led into the Temple of God;
and Zacharias welcomes her.
Today the Holy of Holies is exultant,
and the chorus of Angels mystically celebrates.
Together with them let us also keep the feast today,
and with Gabriel let us cry aloud:
Rejoice, O Maiden full of grace,
the Lord is with you;
and He has great mercy.*

ACKNOWLEDGMENTS

Along the way many people lent me their insight and expertise.

Thank you, Sergeant Daniel Brow, a New Hampshire State Trooper who helped me with the character of Sergeant Randy Locke. I knocked on the door of the Headquarters in Keene, NH, and Sgt. Brow kindly showed me how a cruiser works.

Thanks to Zack Adams of Monadnock Vapor in Keene, NH.

Phil Lariviere of Penelope's Consignment Shop in Keene, NH gave me two old brass keys. He's cool like that. Thanks, Phil.

Thank you, Avenue A Writers, a group of young writers in Antrim, NH. On October 25, 2016, who helped make the dialogue of Amy, an angry teenager authentic. The coordinator of Avenue A was Jacqueline Roland. The young writers were: Oliver Ward, Rae Sturges, Odessa Vassar, Caroline Riffle, Mars Bernabeo, Sunny Badrawy, and Isabel Dreher.

In August 2017 when I saw a Harley Davidson motorcycle outside a restaurant I was leaving, I went back inside and found the owner of the bike and his wife at their table and asked them to show me their Harley. They were delighted to answer my questions about the kill switch on their fuel-injected, 2004 Electro

Glide standard with flames painted on the engine. Thanks, Dan Lord.

Thanks to my brilliant and brave beta readers: Eric Poor, Donna Straitiff, and Christofily Papadopoulos.

My warmest gratitude to fellow writer, Nancy Dunham. This novel would still be in a drawer if not for her encouragement. We cut 63,231 words. Thank you 63,231 times, Nancy.

FUBAR, my writers critique group in Keene, NH made me a better writer. How many times did I bring a chapter to the group for their honest and intelligent feedback? Thank you, David Chase, Inga Hansen, Ernest Hebert, Jack Hitchner, Norman Klein, Abigail Mather, Cara Nicholl, Sharon Phennah, Kathrine Piper, and Eric Poor.

A special thanks to FUBAR co-founder Sean McElhiney for being my "godfather of fiction." When I insisted I only wrote poetry, he told me to, "write the story, Avye."

I would like to thank my mother, Nancy for reading to me every day so I would love books as much as she does. It was her greatest gift to me along with the tandem gift of an insatiable desire for knowledge and wisdom. Thank you, Mom for believing in me and in my writing.

The Ohio State Buckeyes reference in this story is a tribute to my father, Joseph's love for the football team. Thank you, Dad for generously supporting me and my family all these years, and for instilling in me a love of words.

Επίσης, θέλω να ευχαριστήσω την πεθερά μου, Μύρτα, που με αγάπησε σαν κόρη της. Μου έμαθε να μιλάω Ελληνικά και με έκανε Ελληνίδα, σωστή σύζυγο, μητέρα και να εκτιμάω τους ανθρώπους και την Παναγία. Σε ευχαριστώ εσένα και τον παππού, «αιώνιά του η μνήμη †», που μου συμπαρασταθήκατε για είκοσι χρόνια που έμεινα στο σπίτι σας.

Thank you, Uncle Dave, for supporting me for many years both in Greece and in the US. You gave me the time to write.

To Panayiotis, I keep all the encouraging notes you leave me on the kitchen counter. Every word I dedicate to you, beloved.

To Milteva, girl, you're amazing just the way you are. Thanks for keeping your mom on her toes. Hold the bar high, my love.

To Josephine, your wise beautiful heart reminds me daily what love is. Remember the rainbow's true colors and yours.

Many movies and books about the spirit world are more Hollywood fantasy than facts. It was essential to me that the Orthodox faith parts in this story were factual and thoroughly researched. I consulted with many Orthodox priests about guardian angels, the Jesus prayer, demons, rituals, and so on. The exorcism prayers I wrote in the scenes were verified to be the same ones used for real-life Greek Orthodox exorcisms. It took me quite a bit of sleuthing to find the most experienced exorcist here in the US, as he wants to remain anonymous, but I did not want to lead anyone astray with wrong information. He assured me I had used the correct prayers and methods. My fictional exorcism is modeled carefully on actual exorcisms.

I would like to thank Rev. Fr Leo Schefe who chrismated me Orthodox, and Prezvytera Candace gave me my first prayer rope.

Rev. Fr. Eugen J. Pentiuc, PhD was my parish priest at St. George in Keene, NH for three years. His insightful sermons always had me scribbling notes. He answered my long-standing questions about Genesis 1:26-27. Thank you, Father Eugen.

Thank you, Lord Jesus Christ, for having mercy on me.

ABOUT THE AUTHORESS

Avye Andonellis, started life in Ohio, then after University followed her soul mate to his beautiful island in Greece. Ever curious, Avye writes to figure out things like "why would a parent ever hurt their own child?" (*The Marionettist* is a result of this question) and "what's the real meaning of Genesis 1:27?" (*Created Equal* grew from this query.) A lifelong bibliophile, she enjoys the classics like Jane Austen, William Shakespeare, Pearl S. Buck, John Steinbeck, and Dr. Seuss along with modern memoirs. Avye is the νοικοκυρά (noikokyrá, the lady of the house), a Divine Liturgy chanter, poet, and cat & dog trainer. Yes, cats can be trained, kinda.

Keep in touch with Avye via the web:

Website: www.AvyeAndonellis.com
Twitter: Avye@AvyeAndonellis.com
Instagram: www.instagram.com/avye_andonellis
Facebook: Avye Andonellis

www.ingramcontent.com/pod-product-compliance
Lightning Source LLC
Chambersburg PA
CBHW020900080526
44589CB00011B/369